HOW TO THINK ABOUT SOCIAL PROBLEMS

HOW TO THINK ABOUT SOCIAL PROBLEMS

A Primer for Citizens

William M. Hastings

MONMOUTH COLLEGE
MONMOUTH, ILLINOIS

NEW YORK · OXFORD UNIVERSITY PRESS · 1979

Copyright © 1979 by Oxford University Press, Inc.

Library of Congress Cataloging in Publication Data

Hastings, William M.
  How to think about social problems.

  Includes bibliographical references.
  1. Social problems. 2. Sociology. 3. United
States—Social conditions. I. Title.
HN16.H38   309.1'73   78-1874
ISBN 0-19-502420-6

Printed in the United States of America

Preface

My goal in writing this book has been to create an introduction to the study of social problems that contained everything but a summary of the social problems themselves. If I have been successful, *How to Think About Social Problems* should be a valuable companion to any treatment of specific social problem issues and areas, whether it be in popular newspapers and newsmagazines or the more scholarly social science literature. When read alone, I hope this book will help you not only to analyze current social problems but also to "discover" the social problems of the future. It is an embarrassment to academic social scientists that we have been most conspicuous in interpreting social problems discovered and popularized by other sources. To correct this lapse, even the beginning student of social problems should be encouraged to evaluate the depth and seriousness of potential social problems as well as those of contemporary concern.

How to Think About Social Problems provides an overview of the fundamentals necessary for the study of social problems. It draws upon psychology, economics, and related disciplines, in addition to more traditional sociological research. Although these various areas are mutually complementary, they do not lend themselves to a single gestalt or simple hierarchical structure. As a result, there is substantial flexibility in the organization of the material presented. The order of the chapters in the Table of Contents reflects an approach I personally find comfortable, but others may not. If you wish to start with the question of defining social problems and meeting common perspectives for understanding them, you may wish to begin with Chapter 6. Those who desire an early emphasis on the removal of popular misconceptions and confusions should read Chapters 2, 4, and 5. If you wish to begin with the mathematical and analytic tools for understanding social problems, start with Chapters 3, 7, 8, and 9. It is probably best to read Chapters 7, 8, and 9 together and in that order.

I have tried to avoid an emphasis on any particular theoretical perspective. This reflects my personal level of development more than a desire to create an air of professional detachment and eclecticism. However, one emphasis that does pervade this work is my belief that people are basically more reasonable than might appear at first glance, even when they are creating and enduring social problems. Social problems, then, can be understood as reflecting the limits, interactions, and conflicts in our collective rationality. In addition to encouraging a certain degree of optimism about our ability to deal with social problems, this focus highlights more precisely the role of compassion, empathy, and other nonrational factors in creating a better society.

I am indebted to Monmouth College for generously granting a sabbatical leave during which much of the preparation of the manuscript took place, and to Harris Hauge and the staff of the Monmouth College library for their patience and energy in ferreting out many of the sources cited. Acknowledgment is due also to Dean Wright, Charles Meliska, and Carolyn Kirk, among others, for valuable discussions and encouragement throughout the preparation of this work.

Monmouth, Illinois
March 1978   W. M. H.

Contents

ONE

THINK OF IT!   3

Thinking about Social Problems   4

Characteristics of Serious Thinking   7

Thinking is Not Dangerous   12

    Does Thinking Cause Social Problems?   12

    Does Thinking Complicate Life?   15

    Does Thinking Conflict with Feeling?   17

A Little Social Problems Test   19

TWO

KEEPING UP WITH THE NEWS   23

The Limits of Experience   23

The News Does Make an Impression   28

    The News Accentuates the Dramatic   32

    The News Accentuates the Political   35

    The News Accentuates the Superficial   37

    The News Accentuates the Negative   41

THREE

CREATING AND USING STATISTICS   48

Dealing with Large Numbers   49

CONTENTS

Dealing with Small Numbers   51
    Social Problems with Compounding   52
    Problems with Percentages   54
Sampling   56
The Limitations of Statistics   61

FOUR

WHY OFFICIAL STATISTICS ARE MISLEADING   68

The Importance of Informal Groups   69
Privacy and Personal Protection   76
The Creation of Official Records   79
Technology and the Informal   84
    The Case of Intelligence Tests   85
    The Case of Computers   88

FIVE

PITFALLS AND PARADOXES IN UNDERSTANDING SOCIAL PROBLEMS   92

Salience   93
    The Salience of Change   94
    Terrorism—The Mutt and Jeff Routine   98
Why Don't They Learn   99
    Problems with Punishment   100
    Problems with Reward   101
Looking for Bargains   107
    Lack of Responsibility   109
    The Case of Plea Bargaining   113

SIX

APPROACHES TO UNDERSTANDING SOCIAL PROBLEMS   118

Defining a Social Problem   119
Mistreatment of the Ugly   123
Approaches to Social Problems   128
    Deviant Behavior   129
    Value Conflict   134
    Social Disorganization   139
    Labeling   143

SEVEN
DECISIONS, DECISIONS   151
Accepting the Decision   152
Weighing the Good Against the Bad   153
Decision Making with Uncertainty   160
    Minimax   161
    Expected Value   164
Psychological Value—Utility   165

EIGHT
MISTAKES IN SOCIAL DECISION MAKING   175
Accentuation of the Negative   176
The Leap into the Infinite   183
Little Things Still Mean a Lot   186
Stereotyping   190
Values and Value Clarification   192

NINE
INDIVIDUAL INTELLIGENCE AND
SOCIAL INTELLIGENCE   198
Determining National Goals   200
    Cost-Benefit Analysis   200
    Social Indicators   202
    Subjective Measures of National Goals   204
Structural Abuses in American Society   206
    The Majority Abusing a Minority   206
    A Minority Abusing the Majority   209
    Everyone Abusing Everyone Else—Social Traps   213
Toward Solutions   217
    Restructuring   218
    Love   219

REFERENCES   223
NAME INDEX   243
SUBJECT INDEX   248

HOW TO THINK ABOUT SOCIAL PROBLEMS

ONE

Think of It!

THE PURPOSE OF THIS BOOK

There are some skills, like running and reading Spanish, that tend to improve automatically with practice and exposure. We would all live in a vastly different world if understanding social problems was one of these skills. We could watch the evening news, read the newspapers, discuss current problems over lunch, argue about them at the corner bar, and gradually grow wiser and wiser.

Alas, it isn't so. Thinking about social problems is one of those skills that just as often results in the practice of bad habits as the development of good ones. Many people get stuck on a plateau of ignorance or naiveté concerning social problems that mere practice cannot overcome. This book attempts to guide the reader in the study of social problems so that steady progress can be made. It is a sort of how-to-do-it book on thinking about social problems. Like how-to-do-it books on other subjects, such as gardening, buying stock, writing poetry, or being the life of the party, this one will frequently warn you against any easy solutions. There will be no "five easy steps" or "seven sure-fire methods" that guarantee success.

The goal will be the steady development of a clearer understanding of exactly why and how societies create and maintain serious problems. Although there will be plenty of facts presented, they will be used only to help you get in the habit of thinking with them and about them. That is what makes this a how-to-do-it book and not an anthology of records or a compendium of statistics. Next year the statistics will be somewhat different; the insights they can provide will remain.

In keeping with this goal, the material is not organized around problem areas, with overpopulation treated in one section, crime in another, sexism in a third, and so on. Rather, the organization is created by the theories, concepts, techniques, and common difficulties involved in studying any social problem. For example, crime statistics will be treated in the same section as employment and population statistics. The chapter dealing with social traps will consider the pollution and overpopulation traps together. In this way, the focus will remain on what you are doing to understand a problem and not on the particular problem you are thinking about at the moment.

Like other how-to-do-it books, this one will begin with a little "pep talk." In the rest of this chapter, I will argue that this book can be helpful to you. I will warn you against some of the common fears people experience when they begin thinking about social problems. I will argue that serious thought about social problems is neither dangerous nor wasteful. It may even be enjoyable.

THINKING ABOUT SOCIAL PROBLEMS

Any good how-to-do-it book will be full of general rules of thumb. I expect this book will be no exception. However, it will also give many rules about what *not* to do. A book on tennis will remind you *not* to take your eye off the ball, *not* to overrun the ball, *not* to drop your shoulder, and so on. You are reminded of these dangers not because you are considered especially incompetent, but because experience teaches that these are precisely the mistakes a beginner will make. In the same way, the rules I will be presenting are not aimed at insulting your intelligence, but rather at directing your energies away from common mistakes.

An added complication regarding social problems is that others might have deliberately confused you in the past. When practicing tennis, you probably developed your bad habits all by yourself. In thinking about social problems, many people might have encouraged particular misunderstandings. The resulting bad habits became all the more entrenched. The warnings against common mistakes become all the more necessary.

Beginners often make the mistake of thinking that there is so much to learn that they will never become skillful. Obviously, knowing everything there is to know about anything, especially social problems, is impossible. But it is not impossible to begin to develop a firm understanding of America's social problems. It is not even very difficult. We are just beginning to develop a scientific understanding of human sexuality; nonetheless, sex manuals can be quite helpful. In the same vein, sociology, psychology, economics, and the other social sciences we rely on to understand social problems have only begun to reveal their potentials. But there is already much we can learn from them about social problems. It's true that we are all mostly ignorant, but we need not be thoroughly foolish.

To some extent, thinking about social problems is different from other skills you have acquired. One difficulty in developing an understanding of social problems is that you are never sure how much of the skill you have already attained. You probably know when you need a manual on chess, tennis, or wrestling. When everyone in town beats you at a game, it is time to get some instruction. Understanding social problems does not provide such valuable feedback. You cannot "beat" people at social problems and thereby demonstrate your ability.

Of course, you can always go to the nearest bar and explain exactly what is wrong with the country. You can thoroughly expound your theories on unemployment, alcoholism, pollution, and racism. Unfortunately, the response you get will depend more on which bar you chose than the wisdom of your theories. It is often the person with the most flattering theory, the largest following, or the biggest mouth that triumphs in these informal debates. Although such arguments can create pleasant amusement, they do not provide valuable feedback on how much you really know about social problems.

A related difficulty is that we have all spent our lives enmeshed in social problems. Many people are totally without experience in chess, tennis, or wrestling, but who has not been touched by family problems, crime, or racial strife? It is very tempting to conclude that because you have been intimately influenced by social problems, you must have learned a lot about them. Unfortunately, it is often the things we are closest to that we know the least about.

Throughout human history, man has lived surrounded by light,

5

but it has only been in recent times, as history is measured, that we have discovered what light is made of. We need an expert to tell us the composition of our blood and the structure of our cells. Even though we are composed of subatomic particles, we do not have any awareness of the charge on an electron or the weight of a proton. Some things are too small to perceive clearly. In the same vein, social problems are too *big* to see clearly, even though we spend our lives enduring them and complaining about them. They are too much a part of our lives to understand objectively without effort.

I'VE BEEN THINKING

To see where thinking about social problems might lead us, it would help to analyze what thinking is all about. Like many seemingly innocent, common words, *thinking* hides a multitude of meanings. Table 1.1 gives some of the common uses of the verb *to think*, along with some examples. (Take a moment to look over the definitions.)

TABLE 1.1   MEANINGS OF *TO THINK*

DEFINITION	EXAMPLE
1. To feel, have a hunch (as opposed to knowing)	I'm not sure, but I think it's an elm tree.
2. To predict, foretell the future	I think it will rain. I think New York will win the game.
3. To have an idea, a thought	I think it would be nice to invite them. He is always thinking about sex.
4. To daydream, free-associate	Seeing the gym got me thinking about our old high school basketball team.
5. To use an intellectual rule	I think it's an example of, "out of sight, out of mind."
6. To deliberately aim mental operations at achieving a goal (serious thinking)	Don't bother him while he is thinking. She thought of an answer to problem 4.

Which definition might we mean when we say we are thinking about social problems?

In reviewing the various meanings of *thinking*, you probably recognized that thinking in one sense is not correct, while thinking in the other senses is wrong. They are all useful mental activities. Whether you are a social scientist dealing with a social problem or a physical scientist working on a problem in chemistry or physics, you would find occasion to use all these kinds of thinking.

The ultimate goal of much thought is to develop the correct rules to use in understanding reality (definition 5). However, many people skip too quickly to the formation of rules and leave out the other important kinds of thought. It is especially tempting to ignore the two most difficult kinds of thought—predicting the future (definition 2) and deliberately focusing the operations of the mind on a problem (definition 6). Skipping from a hunch to a general rule is like opening some cans and immediately serving dinner without bothering to measure, mix, and cook the meal.

Those who confuse a hunch with a rule can be easily discovered because the rules they use today contradict the ones they used yesterday. One day it is, "Birds of a feather flock together." The next day it is, "Opposites attract." If "Haste makes waste" doesn't work, try, "He who hesitates is lost." If your candidate wins, then, "Honesty is the best policy," but if he loses, then, "Nice guys finish last." Good quarterbacks are somehow always easier to find *after* the game is over. Either attempting to foretell the future with the rule (definition 2) or deliberately integrating it with other rules, hypotheses, or facts in order to achieve further understanding (definition 6) would eliminate such contradictions. As soon as you place your clichés together, you recognize that they are mutually contradictory. As soon as you attempt to predict the future, you realize that you have no clear-cut rule to use. For these reasons, serious thinking leans heavily on definitions 2 and 6.

CHARACTERISTICS OF SERIOUS THINKING

Perhaps the easiest way to understand the difference between serious thinking and just having "thoughts" float into your mind is to consider what goes into definition 6. Have you been deliberately using your mental abilities to achieve a goal of understanding social problems? This is a simpler question to answer than it might appear. There are two characteristics of serious thinking that make it easy to detect.

SERIOUS THINKING HAS A GOAL This separates serious thinking from daydreaming or merely letting your mind wander (definition 4). Serious thinking is thinking on a particular problem. Daydreaming can be quite helpful, especially when there is a trained expert to guide your thoughts and help you interpret them, as in psychoanalysis. In serious thinking, it is the object of your thoughts—the problem—and not yourself that is the focus of your efforts. Thus, in trying to understand social problems, you almost always will have a specific goal in mind. Your goal might be simply to decide if a statement about society is true or false. Perhaps it is a statement like these:

> If we reduce unemployment, inflation will increase.
> The average city dweller commits more crime than the average rural dweller.
> For the health of the nation, we must stamp out drug addiction.
> Women belong at home, taking care of the children.
> The population explosion is not a serious problem.

Or maybe your goal is broader than the above examples; you might be trying to understand crime, racism, or poverty in general. Or it might be more specific, such as deciding which of two candidates to vote for. In any case, there is always a goal to any serious thinking, including thinking about social problems.*

One of the frustrating things about thinking about social problems is that it is not always obvious when you have reached your goal. In some problems, called "Eureka" problems or insight problems, when the correct answer comes to you, it "hits you over the head." An example of an insight problem would be, "Where did I leave my car?" When someone tells you the correct answer, you probably remember and see that it is, indeed, the solution you were looking for. Another example of an insight problem would be, "What has four legs, is blue, weighs 300 pounds, and whistles?"** Many problems are not insight problems. For example:

---

* Sometimes the answer to a problem—the illumination—comes when we least expect it, when our minds are turned to something entirely different. Thinking, according to definition 6, then refers to the necessary preparation that precedes the illumination. There is still a goal that can be specified, even if we are not thinking about it when the answer comes. (Footnotes marked by (*) are given at the bottom of the page and refer to material that expands upon something presented in the text. The numbered footnotes refer to reference sources given in the back of the book.)

** Answer: two 150-pound bluejays.

What is the telephone number of the White House?

How many forcible rapes were committed in 1976 in the United States?

What percentage of the deaths in America are due to automobile accidents? *

When confronted with questions like these, it is not at all obvious when you have found the correct answer.

In general, social problems are not insight problems. Someone can tell you the correct answer, and you will go right on past it. For many social problems, all the plausible answers can be easily enumerated. You can make a short list of the alternatives and stare at it all day. The correct answer will not "hit you over the head." When you go to vote in an election, the best candidate is always given on the ballot (ignoring the possibility of write-in candidates). The trick is to know which one is the best and which are false alarms. Multiple-choice questions can be a lot harder than fill-in-the-blanks.

This is why most books on creativity and problem solving are not very helpful in dealing with social problems. These how-to-solve-problems books are aimed at helping you overcome blocks in solving insight problems. The techniques they describe, such as synectics and brainstorming, help you over the block in your thinking so that the correct answer will emerge. With social problems, bringing the correct answer to mind is often the easiest part. What is needed is not a list of possible solutions so much as a means of deciding which answer on the list is *the* best one. Technically, this is known as decision making rather than problem solving. (For this reason, Chapters 7 and 8 include a discussion of decision making as applied to social problems.)

SERIOUS THINKING REQUIRES AIDS TO THOUGHT Few people possess such powers of visualization, memorization, and calculation that they can do serious thinking without at least a pencil and paper. Serious thinking usually involves making categories, comparing items, drawing up lists, and making outlines. If you are at all visually oriented, you will draw graphs, diagrams, flow charts, etc. Very often you will want reference sources, articles, books, and notes to guide you. If numbers are involved, you will probably want a desk calculator. All this sounds terribly ambitious, not to mention tiring, but there

---

*Answers: The White House telephone number is (202) 456-1414; the official FBI figures list 56,730 forcible rapes for 1976 (many experts feel the actual total is substantially larger); out of nearly 2,000,000 deaths annually, about 40,000 to 60,000 are motor vehicle deaths for about 2 to 3 percent of the total.[1]

is a very simple reason why these aids to thought are necessary: *Human information processing is very limited.*

Here are three multiplication problems. What are the answers? (Please do not write anything down; solve them in your head.)

$$\begin{array}{r} 7 \\ \times\,7 \\ \hline ? \end{array}$$

$$\begin{array}{r} 47 \\ \times\,9 \\ \hline ? \end{array}$$

$$\begin{array}{r} 963 \\ \times\,78 \\ \hline ? \end{array}$$

If you are like most people, you could immediately give the answer to the first problem; the second one took a while, and the third was terrible. The answer to the first one was already known; all that was necessary was to pull the answer out of memory, a process that takes a fraction of a second. The answers to the second and third problems were not immediately known. What was known was the rules for generating the answers. These rules of multiplication are simple and fool-proof. Why, then, is the third problem so difficult?

The third multiplication asks you to do two things at the same time. You must apply the rules of multiplication (thinking by definition 5) at the same time as you hold in your mind the results you got from previously applying the rules (thinking by definition 3). If you could use a pencil and paper you would not lose $963 \times 8 = 7704$ while working on $963 \times 7 = ?$ The general principle that emerges is that as long as all the important ideas or information are not safely stored in memory or on a piece of paper, you will lose them as you develop more ideas or information. If you cannot do even a simple multiplication problem without aids to thought, it is unlikely you can critically evaluate a politician's speech or separate fact from fiction about poverty statistics without them.

IS SERIOUS THINKING PAINFUL?

This description of serious thinking might begin to sound like an awful lot of miserable work. It isn't really as bad as it may appear. If you reflect for a moment, you will probably recall many instances of serious thinking you have engaged in. Should you buy a car? If so, which one? Should you move? Should you break up with your boy-friend or girlfriend? Should you quit your job? Which college should you go to? Can you afford the vacation you would like to take? Questions like these often give rise to serious thought. When comparing cars, you probably did not trust your memory, but instead made notes on the options, advantages, and disadvantages of each serious contender. When choosing schools, you probably compared their costs, programs, and disadvantages with their literature spread out in front of you. When planning a vacation, you got out the maps and considered the cost of the trip, how long it would take, and what you could do or see on each possible route.

One of the reasons people get discouraged by serious thinking is that thinking like this is often done with great fear that making the wrong choice would prove disastrous. If you can relax and do the thinking leisurely and not get worked up about making the wrong choice, thinking can be quite pleasant. There are some people who are constantly shopping for cars, not because they are likely to buy one but because it is fun to "look around." Others plan vacations they are never going to take as a kind of hobby. Thinking can be quite enjoyable as long as you don't take it *too* seriously. This is why there is a thriving industry devoted to making puzzles. If you like jigsaw puzzles, you should enjoy putting the pieces together on racism or drug addiction. (It must be admitted that it does sometimes seem that one of the pieces is lost.)

Perhaps the description of serious thinking also reminded you of a student doing his or her homework, studiously jotting down notes on a desk piled high with reference books. These school experiences have also contributed to the feeling that serious thinking is not just unpleasant but downright painful. What if the assignment is late? What if the answer is wrong? What if I flunk?

Getting into the habit of thinking about social problems need not be so threatening. Imagine yourself as a happy student voluntarily doing the homework for a fun course. Carrying the metaphor one step further, perhaps our social problems will be solved more effectively when we are collectively doing our homework as citizens. This book is aimed at helping you do your homework as a citizen more effectively and more enjoyably.

Ideally, social problems should be approached from the view-point that they are serious enough to deserve serious thinking but not so serious that you absolutely have to find the right answer. It is the feeling that you are a bad person if you don't get the answer right away that encourages leaping prematurely from a hunch to declaring a general rule that supposedly solves the problem. Like any mature player at any game, someone who has formed the habit of thinking seriously about the problems of society enjoys winning but also enjoys just playing the game.

THINKING IS NOT DANGEROUS

Even when it is recognized that serious thinking is not a particularly dreadful experience, there still can be lingering fears that it will lead to other problems. The image of the serious thinker is not an entirely positive one to many persons, especially young Americans. On one level, the intellectual or scientist is admired, but on a deeper level the egghead, bookworm, highbrow, or pedant is considered somewhat unsavory, if not downright dangerous. These unnecessary fears often discourage serious thought about many aspects of life beyond social problems. In this section, we will consider three particular fears about the dangers of serious thinking and hopefully relieve any lingering discomfort you may have about thinking about social problems.

DOES THINKING CAUSE SOCIAL PROBLEMS?

A common misunderstanding about thinking is that it is responsible for many of our social problems. In this conception, thinking becomes confused with massive technology, doctors Frankenstein and Strangelove, mad scientists, and ivory-tower philosophers combining to pollute, obfuscate, and destroy. After confusing serious thought with intellectuals gone mad and machines gone wild, the temptation is to choose the simple life unburdened by thought. The danger in such an approach is that rather than enjoying a simple life, you might end up with the greater burden of being simpleminded.

Of course, it must be recognized that modern technology has not created the heaven on earth that some naïve dreamers anticipated. The automobile, rather than bringing only freedom, has brought pollution and congestion as well. The computer threatens to destroy privacy as it destroys ignorance. As soon as we conquer some long-dreaded scourge, it seems that a dozen new maladies, created by science, technology, and urbanized, mass society arise to plague us. The temptation is to blame these new evils on scientists and objective thinking in general. Our present technology then becomes equated with all possible technology, and technology is then equated with rational thought. The erroneous conclusion is that serious thinking does not solve social problems. It creates them. Such a position sounds like this:

> The whole, feeling human being in us is now dominated by *intellect*, that mental faculty which through the centuries has grown far beyond its healthy limits. It is that faculty which demands that we *think, think, think* at the expense of everything else human within us. By not allowing feelings to "contaminate" an "objective" view, intellect has helped to create a dehumanized world view.[2]

A little reflection should help dispel the illusion that our present social problems are the result of our objective, rational intellect taking over our lives. Can we really believe that the average student, housewife, or businessman is obsessed with a passion to be overly intellectual, objective, and thoughtful? Did we plunge into the Vietnam War by being overly intellectual? Are our cities blighted because we thought too much before we designed and built them? Is crime on the rise because we have been too objective in dealing with it?

Serious thinking in regard to social problems is conspicuous only by its absence. It may, indeed, be the case that science gone haywire is an integral part of some of the more difficult social problems confronting us. (This will be considered further in Chapter 6). But it is silly to focus the blame on scientific and objective thought. There is nothing inherent in science that demands we build 5,000-pound gas guzzlers rather than efficient mass transportation. It is not integral to technology to favor supersonic noisemakers over better railroads. If we spend more on dog food than on sociological research on crime prevention, do not blame the intellect. These kinds of decisions are made by lawyers, businessmen, industrialists, politicians, and most important of all, the average citizen—almost everyone but the scientists who are blamed. Organized science is, in fact, one of the weakest power blocs in our society. Any sizable labor union has more power in national decision making than the Geological Society of America or the American Sociological Association. Most scientists, engineers, and technologists, like accountants and stenographers, are salaried employees, worried about keeping their jobs, who have very little input in the decision making of our society.*

It is certainly true that, if scientists were well organized and used all the political pressure available to them, they would constitute a powerful influence on public policy. But this is equally true of housewives, truck drivers, farmers, and numerous other groups that are rarely accused of excessive objectivity and being overly thoughtful. Scientists and scholars are easy targets because they are small in number, politically weak, and often appear strange and mysterious to the average person.[3]

The problem is not that we have thought too much, but that our thinking has been lopsided. Our understanding of physical nature has leaped ahead of our understanding of human nature. The solution is to overcome our reluctance to be rational about ourselves in the same manner as our ancestors overcame their reluctance to be rational about trees and volcanoes. It is not by accident that we have records of solar eclipses going back thousands of years and have only recently gotten around to collecting decent statistics on poverty and crime. Perhaps we had to be convinced that thinking actually works by applying it in the physical sciences before we were willing to try it on ourselves. Perhaps we first had to test our tools of serious thought on simple things like stars and frogs before we could apply them to the infinitely tougher task of understanding human society.

Or maybe thinking about society has been delayed because powerful interest groups are threatened by the serious study of society. It is only rarely, as in the celebrated case of Galileo and the Copernican theory, that a physical science discovery threatens a powerful interest group. With social science findings, it is a rare case that does *not* embarrass or challenge some firmly held political, economic, or religious position. Or maybe, in the final analysis, we are simply personally frightened by what we might discover about ourselves. In any case, objective thinking about the problems of society has not failed; it has never been given a fair trial. It would be better to give it a try than to attempt to reverse the gains in the physical sciences. The answer to lopsided thinking is broader thinking, not broader ignorance.

---

* Before President Carter, a nuclear engineer, the only recent President of the United States who was at all connected with science was Herbert Hoover, who was a mining engineer. It is doubtful that most of our social problems can be traced to his administration.

DOES THINKING COMPLICATE LIFE?

A related criticism of thinking in general and science in particular is that somehow they make life overly complex and difficult. This argument claims that, by increasing confusion and inefficiency, science actually generates more ignorance than enlightenment. The usual complaint goes something like this:

> The reason our ignorance increases along with our collected knowledge is that we need so much knowledge in order to exist in an increasingly complicated world. Since our knowledge does not increase as rapidly as our need for it, the result is what we can call increasing ignorance.[4]

Or as a university president recently grumbled:

> We live in a society so sophisticated technologically that it depends on a vast and complex range of highly developed skills. . . . Knowledge has become so technologically complex and fragmented by specialization that our values are threatened with disintegration, and our communications are sinking to an ever lower common denominator.[5]

Meanwhile, another authority is reminding us that our brains are becoming overloaded:

> The brain of a man living in the 20th century has daily to store and deal with a quantity of information that a previous generation would have taken a lifetime to consume.[6]

These cries of distress for the modern world are misleading for two reasons.

First, the complexities of modern life, such as they are, are not the result of science, or thinking, or an increase in information. For example, many people commute an hour or more each way to and from work, which adds a fair amount of complexity to their lives. Such situations result from a complex combination of racial and ethnic residential patterns and prejudices, tax regulations, patterns of building and highway construction, a yearning for the "wide open spaces," and a variety of other psychological, socioeconomic, and political factors. It is not simply due to the automobile, although the automobile is the handiest thing to blame. If the same combination of factors existed without the automobile, the commuter would be *walking* an hour or more to work.

In the same way, the development of the airplane, the computer, and the electronics industry has added many complications to our lives, but these complications are not inherent in the inventions themselves so much as their misuse due to lopsided thinking. Most of the real areas of increasing complexity—taxes, insurance, the constant filling out of innumerable forms, and the endless proliferation of laws, rules, and regulations governing countless details of our lives—are the action of lawyers, bureaucrats and politicians, and not active social scientists.* These complications are often the result of the desire for increased power, prestige, or financial gain on the part of various groups in our society. They are not due to an excess of serious thinking about the common welfare. Once again, it is easier to blame intellectuals out of control than the people, like ourselves, who actually are in control. (We will return to the question of forms, rules, and regulations in Chapter 4.)

Second, even though some things are more complex, life in general is much simpler today than it was years ago, and this is due mostly to the advancement of science and technology. It is the essence of science to simplify. Complex science, like a weak weight lifter or a slow race horse, is a poor specimen of its breed. It is only in the beginning stages in the development of scientific understanding that knowledge appears complex. Economics, sociology, and psychology appear complex precisely because our thinking is poorly developed in these areas. In other areas, such as astronomy, where science is truly advanced, scientific knowledge is beautifully simple. We can now determine the position of any planet at any time with a handful of equations and a few parameter values. Before our present understanding of the solar system, this would have required endless pages of complex tables. When the processes are clearly understood, prediction becomes simple. If society seems terribly complex to us, it is because we have yet to develop adequate theories for understanding it.

One of the reasons science is seen as a nuisance to many students is that they are forced to use it when they don't want to. Some misguided teachers feel it is their duty to make their unfortunate students memorize the answers to all sorts of questions they never felt like asking. The students eventually come to fear a new scientific discovery, frightened that it will be on the next test. Please do not blame science for this fear. This is poor education, not good science. There is nothing inherent in serious thinking that demands we memorize the answers to questions we never thought to ask.

---

* Throughout this discussion, I have been using *technology* in the limited sense of physical technology. Technology can also be construed in a broader sense which includes forms, laws, and social structures. In this sense, technology has little to do with serious thinking as presently considered.

Another aspect of this fallacy is the belief that we must spend more and more time in school in order to learn all the "new information." If there is new information (assuming the phrase is meaningful at all), it would mean that we can spend *less* time in learning because understanding is always easier and faster the more information we have. What is really happening is that we are learning more and more in school that our grandparents either learned at home or never learned at all. Today, for instance, high school students take driver education. This does not mean that technology has made life more complex, with all the "new information." Rather, it means that there has been a shift in responsibility from the home to the school. In the past, children learned to ride a horse at home or they never learned at all. Horseback riding was usually not taught in the schools.* This does *not* mean that riding a horse is easier than driving a car. It certainly is not; ask anyone who is skilled at both.

There are some people who enjoy feeling sorry for themselves, no matter how easy they have it. It gives them solace to think they have it so much rougher than their carefree ancestors. Bergan Evans describes the situation well:

> One element in the complexity-of-modern-life theory is self-flattery. We love to think that we bear upon our shoulders a load that would have ruptured Atlas. "It is doubtful," says a modern writer, "if any Roman emperor needed the executive ability required to run General Electric"—a statement which, however flattering to our executives, is in actuality more doubtful than the doubt it poses. Of course a Roman emperor couldn't operate a comptometer or even a typewriter, but most modern executives can't either. He probably could operate an abacus, though, and it is doubtful if many executives of General Electric could do that. All that any executive can do is to make decisions and accept the responsibility for them, and the Praetorian Guard was somewhat stricter than the average Board of Directors when it came to the Annual Report. Very few Roman emperors retired on a persion after making a serious mistake.[7]

DOES THINKING CONFLICT WITH FEELING?

Another reason people fear serious thinking is that the image of the thinker is often that of an anemic bookworm without energy, emo-

---

* Horseback riding is being taught in schools today, with a number of colleges granting credit for it.

tion, passion, or soul—as if one had to choose between thinking and feeling, reason and the emotions. In line with this fallacy, we have created the fantasy of monsters such as King Kong, Godzilla, and their kin who are fierce, impassioned, spontaneous, free, and stupid. Meanwhile, we have cultivated the complementary image of bloodless science fiction creatures—robots, cyborgs, androids—who are terribly calculating, cold, logical, dangerous, and inhuman. (Somehow even King Kong seems more human than a walking computer.) This modern American mythology nourishes an artificial dichotomy between reason and the emotions. A noted example of this dichotomy in modern science fiction is the character of Mr. Spock, science officer of the starship *Enterprise*, who is both perfectly logical and completely devoid of emotions.* To modern Americans, it is hard to imagine a creature who is completely logical *and* full of passion, although this is, in fact, a much more plausible combination.

It is reason and the emotions that are the true complements, for without values, goals, and even passions, there is nothing to think *about*. Serious thinking is what you do to achieve your goals, attain your desires, realize your passions, and find your soul. Thinking, then, is not the enemy of feelings; it is their guide. This is why a rational person often appears more predictable than a madman or a fool. For example, if a house were set afire, you would predict that the people inside would leave it. This prediction would work for any normal, rational person but might fail for those who are in a drunken stupor, blind or crippled, or suffering from pathological masochism. Thus, the rational person might appear to be less spontaneous, but when the house is burning down, we do not envy the unpredictable. The rational person is spontaneous when it is best to be so; he or she is predictable when that is called for. This conception of the rational person is very similar to Carl Roger's description of the "fully functioning person" who "not only experiences, but utilizes, the most absolute freedom when he spontaneously, freely, and voluntarily chooses and wills *that which is also absolutely determined.*" [8] Freedom, spontaneity, rationality, and predictability are all the product of the same understanding. This is not just a philosophical maxim; it is another reason why it pays to think seriously about social problems.

---

*In fairness to Mr. Spock, this is only approximately correct. Every few years, according to the story, he feels a tremendous romantic urge and degenerates into a sort of Vulcan rut.

THE PLAN OF THE BOOK
AND A LITTLE TEST

This book is written not in a straight line, but in spirals, as thought proceeds. Hopefully, the perspective you will develop will be like that of a hawk that slowly spirals higher and higher in ever-widening cricles. Upon occasion, the hawk swoops down to earth to grab a particularly choice morsel, and then is off again to the broader perspective. To someone on the ground, the hawk might appear to be only flying in circles, but this is an illusion of the limited perspective. In reading this book, when you find yourself returning to a familiar topic, you should notice that it emerges with a broader field of view or a clearer perspective.

Before you take off, however, please stay on the ground long enough to take this little test. It may help you later on. These are all noninsight questions about social problems. Although some of them are rather difficult, they are not trick questions. The answers will be given in the next chapter.

A LITTLE SOCIAL PROBLEMS TEST

TRUE-FALSE   (Write T if the statement is basically true and F if it is false.)

1. The percentage of college professors that are women is greater today than it was 30 or 40 years ago.
2. The syphilis rate in the United States is rapidly increasing.
3. At least 20 percent of the persons on welfare are able-bodied men who either cannot find a job or will not work.
4. In spite of uncertainties such as the weather, food production in the United States has substantially less year-to-year variation than does industrial production.
5. At least 75 to 80 percent of the homicides in the United States are solved.
6. Homicide is at an all-time high in the United States.
7. The average number of hours worked per week in American manufacturing industries has remained about the same over the last generation.
8. At least half of the inmates in local jails are serving time for minor (nonfelony) offenses.

MULTIPLE CHOICE (Mark the best answer.)

9. The average (median) felony trial lasts
   a. A couple of minutes.
   b. A couple of hours.
   c. A couple of days.
   d. A couple of weeks.

10. The average (median) income per family is highest if the family head is descended from immigrants of what nationality?
   a. German
   b. Polish
   c. English
   d. Irish

11. The nation with the longest life expectancy is
   a. Iceland
   b. The United States
   c. France
   d. Japan

12. The population of mental hospitals in the United States is
   a. decreasing
   b. roughly constant
   c. increasing slightly
   d. increasing rapidly

13. Which disease kills the most Americans annually?
   a. acute bronchitis
   b. meningitis
   c. asthma
   d. syphilis

14. Which year saw the highest murder rate in the United States?
   a. 1930
   b. 1945
   c. 1955
   d. 1969

15. According to the 1970 census of the United States, approximately _____ percent of the population lives in cities of 100,000 persons or more.
   a. 27
   b. 47
   c. 61
   d. 74

16. For each staff member in an American mental hospital, there is (are) about _____ patient(s).
    a. 1
    b. 5
    c. 9
    d. 12 or more

17. Which city has the lowest average (median) income (city only, not the surrounding suburbs)?
    a. New York
    b. Boston
    c. Washington, D.C.
    d. Houston

18. Americans of which ethnic background have the highest level of educational attainment?
    a. English
    b. German
    c. Cuban
    d. Russian

SUMMARY

This is a how-to-do-it book on thinking about social problems. Its goal is to facilitate the development of a lifelong habit of reflection and analysis about the problems of society. This kind of serious thinking is challenging, problem oriented, and easily distinguished from merely having thoughts about society drift into your mind. Although serious thinking is enjoyable, it is not yet widely practiced by the average citizen.

Many people are discouraged from serious thinking about social problems because of several unfounded fears about the nature of scientific analysis. First, although the misuse of technology has contributed to some problems, it is not true that science and technology are basic causes of social problems. Scientists are easy targets for blame, but other social groups are the ones responsible for the present course of society and the development of lingering problems. Second, neither are science and technology responsible for complicating modern life; when properly applied, they simplify daily life. Third, serious thinking does not lead to a flattening of the emotions and a lack of feeling about society. Thought and passion are complements. It is the combination of passionate concern and scientific analysis that will eventually actualize our potential to solve social problems.

TWO

Keeping Up with
the News

The logical place to begin our analysis of how to think about social problems would be to consider the opinions, information, and impressions that form the foundation of our thought. If there are serious distortions or inaccuracies in our information about social problems, the most powerful analysis will be unable to generate correct conclusions. In this chapter, we will consider the sources of some of these faulty impressions. Problems in using personal experience as well as common folk wisdom will be considered, but the major concentration will be on the mass media as sources of misinformation. I will discuss several of the major misconceptions generated by the television news and newspapers, and in the process all the answers to the test in Chapter 1 will be presented.

THE LIMITS OF EXPERIENCE

Some people have a simpleminded faith in their own powers of observation and limited personal experience. They use the old adage—

Seeing is believing. They forget that this one also has its opposite—*The hand is quicker than the eye.* In fact, most personal experience is a very poor guide to what is happening in our society. Even the "experts" with the most exciting adventures in dealing with social problems would be unwise to trust their personal experience.

Consider the example of a white policeman who lives in an all-white neighborhood, has only white friends, sends his children to an all-white school, and goes to an all-white church. He might well decide that "all blacks are troublemakers" if he fails to appreciate the limits of his experience. When he meets blacks only in his official position as policeman, it should not surprise him that most of them are in trouble. His experience is simply one-sided. He is in the same position physicians were in years ago regarding masturbation. After observing patients in mental hospitals masturbating, they often concluded that masturbation led to all sorts of mental problems. After all, no famous physician, successful businessman, or United States Senator had been caught masturbating!

Psychiatrists, social workers, and other experts on dealing with the misery caused by social problems must constantly remind themselves of the bias in their personal experience. Social workers have many clients who smoke marijuana, get in trouble with the law, and can't find a job. It is very tempting to conclude that somehow the use of marijuana is intimately connected with the other difficulties. Psychiatrists have many neurotic patients with a history of homosexuality. They are tempted to believe that homosexuality must have something to do with being neurotic. They need to remind themselves that happy homosexuals are reluctant to spend $50 to $100 an hour to tell a psychiatrist how happy they are. Merely dealing with the problems can give a very biased view of the nature of the problems. One must deal with the successes also. Because the experts frequently have very one-sided experiences, they can hold some of the most ridiculous notions about social problems.

Even when your experience is not particularly biased, you are probably not going to learn a great deal about social problems by relying on your personal powers of observation and recollection. Most people have very inefficient abilities in processing even simple information.[1] In order to clarify this point, try taking the following little test of your memory.

A SHORT MEMORY TEST

1. Which words are more common?
    Those that begin with *S*
    Those that begin with *D*

2. Which words are more common?
    Those that begin with *K*
    Those that have *K* as the third letter

3. Here are some questions about United States currency:
    a. What is the basic color of the face of a $1 bill? (The face is the side with the portrait on it.)
    b. What is the basic color of the face of a $5 bill?
    c. What color is the back of a $5 bill?
    d. What color is the serial number on the $10 bill?

4. What is your social security number?

5. Which light is on top of the traffic signal, red or green?

6. Are there any letters missing from the telephone dial? If so, which ones?
    (If you are wondering how your answers compare with others, try giving this test to some friends.)

Very little that *could* be remembered actually is remembered. Even if you clearly attend to something, such as your social security number, unless you make an effort to remember, you are likely to forget. Some people even have trouble remembering that the red light is on top of the traffic signal, although they have stared at it thousands of times.

If you do not clearly attend to the information presented, there is even less chance you will remember it. Many people never recognize that the letters *Q* and *Z* are missing from the telephone dial. Maybe you have not noticed that United States currency is printed with black ink on the face, with the treasury seal and serial numbers in green, and the backs are printed all in green. (That is how money got to be called *greenbacks*.) Being repeatedly exposed to something is no guarantee it will be remembered.

Since most things are forgotten, those bits of information we do remember carry a great deal of weight in influencing our final decisions. If there is a bias regarding which information we can recall, we are liable to make serious errors in our decision making. For example, most people correctly recall that more words begin with S than with D because there is little systematic bias in their recollection. But they often decide that more words start with K than have K as the third letter, even though in the average text twice as many words have K in the third position than the first.[2] Here, there is a bias in information processing. We can recall first letters more readily, which is why it is easier to figure out a word in a crossword puzzle if we know the first letter than if we know the third. Because we can think of more examples of one category, we erroneously conclude it must be more common. When we use such biased information, we cannot help but get a biased conclusion.* The most powerful calculations cannot make the correct decision if the information is distorted. Computer technicians have a catchy way of putting it: G.I.G.O.—Garbage In, Garbage Out.

FOLK WISDOM

Inadequate personal experience is not the only common source of misinformation about social problems. Another wellspring of confusion is the popular folk wisdom of our society. For example, when Americans think of Iceland, they think of a small, backward, primitive country. But in many respects, Iceland is one of the most progressive nations in the world. On many indicators of the quality of life, such as life expectancy, literacy, and infant mortality, Iceland is more advanced than the United States, France, Japan, the Soviet Union, and most other industrialized nations.[3]

Many Americans also hold inaccurate stereotypes about American cities. Washington, D.C., is "poverty stricken," New York is "broke," Southern cities are "poor," and so on. In fact, in terms of average (median) family income, Boston is poorer than Washington, D.C., New York, Houston, and most other major cities, but poverty somehow is not a part of the image of New England cities.[4] It is also commonly believed that we have become a nation of big cities, although only about 27 percent of the population live in cities as large as

---

* If we know the precise extent and direction of the bias, it is sometimes possible to correct for it. Usually this is not known.

100,000 in population.[5] Actually, about as many Americans live in rural areas as live in cities of 100,000 or more.[6] Somehow this just does not fit our common image of America, the "industrialized giant."

Misleading stereotypes like these are not due to biased personal experience or biased recollection; it is doubtful that many Americans have much personal experience—biased or unbiased—about Iceland. These confusions are due to the general stereotypes that are a part of the folk wisdom of our culture. One of the most popular aspects of our folklore is the ethnic stereotype. First, we classify people according to some grouping—race, religion, nationality, etc. Then we specify characteristics and evaluations that we associate with each group. These characteristics are often misleading and sometimes completely wrong. For example, Americans of Russian extraction are better educated than those of most other ethnic groups, including the German, English, Irish, Italian, and Cuban.[7] They also earn more in terms of average (median) family income than other major ethnic groups. Americans of Polish extraction are second only to the Russians in income.[8] In spite of all the "Polish jokes" and other aspects of our misleading folklore, the Poles are doing quite well in America.*

People who seriously think about social problems usually realize that both the conventional wisdom and their personal experience are poor guides to understanding society. Recognizing this ignorance, they try to broaden their understanding of society and social problems by watching the evening news on television or reading newspapers and news magazines. In the current jargon, they are attempting to become "informed citizens." This attempt to do one's homework as a citizen is certainly praiseworthy, but it has its own considerable dangers. The tragedy is that people turn to the news in a sincere effort to overcome their personal bias, and often end up getting a worse bias from the news. All of the difficulties I have briefly described regarding stereotypes and the inadequacies of personal experience also apply to most of the information presented on the news, and in many cases, one's own personal experience is a much better guide than the impressions created

---

*The misconception of Polish-American poverty and lack of education might also be related to a bias in personal information processing concerning the category "Poles." The Poles who emigrated to America were usually either poor Catholics escaping poverty or poor and affluent Jews escaping persecution. The Jews had a head start over the Catholics in terms of education and social resources. When we meet a Polish-American Catholic, we file the experience away as a meeting with a "Pole," but when we meet a Polish-American Jew, he or she is often categorized as a "Jew." Thus, those "Poles" we recollect having met might be poorer and less educated than the Poles we actually did meet.

by the news. It is worthwhile to consider the imperfections of the news in some detail because they give rise to some major distortions that stand in the way of thinking clearly about social problems.

THE NEWS DOES MAKE AN IMPRESSION

At first glance, it might appear that the news goes in one ear and out the other without making any lasting impression. This is not completely correct. Much of the material on the news might be totally forgotten, but an important residue seeps down into the great mass of undigested ideas and recollections that we eventually use in our thinking. This occurs because the news uses various devices to help the material presented overcome our usual tendency to ignore and forget information. First, the television news and newspapers use pictures of dead bodies, crying children, mob scenes, funerals, and other attention grabbers. Second, they surround themselves with an air of authority that gives the impression that what they are presenting is really important. Third, they intersperse news items with pieces on Hollywood stars, sports figures, and other magnets for our attention. Last and perhaps most important of all, the news has an effect due to constant repetition. If a constant bias does exist in the news media, our "informed citizen" will be presented with that bias day after day, year after year. The effect of any one presentation might be minimal, but the cumulative effect is substantial.

Even in the course of one day, the person who listens to a popular music station on the radio may hear the same newscast a dozen times. Maybe the news contained a story about the latest political accusation—perhaps something like this: *Candidate Smith alleged today that his rival, Candidate Jones, might have been receiving campaign contributions of a possibly illegal nature.* If you repeatedly heard this accusation, you would probably not recall the specifics unless you paid very close attention. However, later on you might vaguely recall something like, "Jones is associated with crooked dealings." In recalling the information, you reduced it to a vague impression. You might forget the qualifications and weasel words—*alleged, might,* and *possibly*—and the fact that the charge came from Jones' rival, Smith, who is hardly an unbiased source. As a result, the residual vague impression you recall can actually be more powerful than the original impression when the item was first presented and more of the facts were known.[9] In order for the news to leave an impression, it need not be a clear one. Sometimes vague impressions are the most dangerous.

It was the practice until recently for newspapers to label blacks, but not whites, by race when they were associated with a crime. Reading the newspaper, you would come across headlines like these: NEGRO ACCUSED OF RAPE; NEGRO COOK MURDERS WIFE; and FARMER SHOOTS NEIGHBOR IN FEUD (that one was done by a white person). Happily, this practice has generally stopped as far as racial characteristics are concerned, but the vague impressions created by the news probably still remain in many minds.

Associating crimes with certain kinds of persons in the news still occurs with regard to other personal characteristics, such as "mental patient." How many times have you seen headlines like these: EX-MENTAL PATIENT COMMITS SUICIDE or POLICE HUNT MENTAL PATIENT IN AX MURDER? Have you ever seen headlines like these: EX-MENTAL PATIENT WINS GRAND PRIZE IN BAKING CONTEST or EX-MENTAL PATIENT ELECTED HEAD OF PTA? When a woman who was once labeled "manic depressive" puts her head in the oven, she is an "ex-mental patient," but when she pulls a prize-winning cake out of the oven, she magically becomes a "homemaker and mother of four." Because of such prejudicial impressions, many people firmly believe that those who have been hospitalized for mental disorders are a truly dangerous lot who spend their time staring glassy-eyed while sharpening their axes.

The fact of the matter is that there have been many studies of crime rates for those who have been mental patients compared to those who have never been officially labeled "mentally ill." Some studies have observed that the mental patients have somewhat lower crime rates; others have found that they have somewhat higher crime rates, and still others have found no difference.[10] The most plausible conclusion to be drawn is that there may be some slight difference between mental patients and others depending on the particular crime in question, but overall there is no substantial difference between the two groups.

Understanding whether mental patients are really dangerous or not is one of those areas where personal experience is often a better guide than the impressions left by the news. Most people know several persons who have needed psychiatric or psychological help in one form or another. You can make a list of all such persons, excluding all those mental patients you heard about on the news. (Remember not to be confused by the euphemisms we habitually employ to describe mental disorders. Someone else's aunt might "go crazy," but your aunt probably had a "nervous breakdown." Someone you don't like had to be "locked up" because he was a "drunken bum," but your friend went to a "rest home" for a "drinking problem.") Ignoring all the polite expressions, if you can put together a list of people you personally have known who have had mental disorders, you will see that these ex-mental patients do not fit into any simple category and, on the whole, are not particularly dangerous.

Sometimes the news can create a social problem out of thin air. This was the case with the famous "Seattle windshield pitting epidemic" of 1954.[11] In late March and early April of that year, the Seattle newspapers carried accounts of damage to automobile windshields in several towns north of Seattle. At the same time, residents of the area were concerned about the possible harmful effects of the Pacific H bomb tests conducted earlier in the year. By April 14, reports of pitted windshields in Seattle itself were publicized in the news. Then the dam burst.

In the two-day period beginning April 14, more than 3,000 autos were reported damaged by mysterious windshield pitting. Many persons reported their windshields somehow became pitted in a matter of minutes; others discovered strange metallic-looking particles on theirs. On the evening of April 15 the situation was out of hand, and the mayor of Seattle made an emergency appeal to the governor and the President of the United States for assistance. What mysterious process was at work?

There was certainly nothing happening that was at all mysterious *physically*. The scientific commission assigned by the governor to study the situation concluded that what was observed on the windshields was nothing more than ordinary road damage. The mysterious process that was actually at work was the social phenomenon known as a *collective delusion*. After the first reports of windshield damage— presumably the work of vandals—were publicized in the news, people stopped looking through their windshields long enough to look *at* them. Of course, many noticed pits, cracks, holes, and strange spots they had never noticed before, and with thoughts of H bombs floating in their minds, the delusion of a mysterious force destroying windshields was born. An interview study conducted several days later revealed that half of the residents believed that some strange physical agent was at work, and three-fourths of them first heard about the pitting from the mass media. In this case, the news helped people see something they had never noticed before, but it also resulted in a completely wrong interpretation.

Sometimes the impressions created by the news can be a matter of life and death. For example, the effects of highly publicized suicides in increasing the rate of suicide were studied by David Phillips.[12] For the twenty-year period 1947–1967, Phillips observed a significant increase in the number of suicides during the month following the publicity of some noted person's suicide. Using various statistical procedures, Phillips controlled for possible artifacts, such as the season of the year and changes in the overall suicide trend. The analyses all indicated that the rise in suicides was most likely due to the suggestion implanted in the minds of potential suicides by the publicity accompanying the prominent figure's suicide. This interpretation was strengthened by the fact that the more highly publicized the suicide, the greater the rise in the number of suicides following the publicity. Furthermore, the rise in suicides was greatest in the geographical region where the publicity was greatest. Nor were these increases numerically trivial. Probably the most highly publicized suicide in America during this period was that of the film actress Marilyn Monroe, reported on August 6, 1962. Phillips estimated that in the United States alone, the subsequent two months saw an increase of 303 suicides over the base rate. In a later study, Phillips observed that an increase in traffic deaths also occurred after highly publicized suicides, suggesting that some auto deaths were actually suicides precipitated by the publicity.[13]

A similar investigation was conducted by Leonard Berkowitz and Jacqueline Macaulay at the University of Wisconsin on the effects of mass publicity on violent crimes, such as aggravated assault and robbery.[14] Berkowitz and Macaulay focused on crimes following two highly publicized murders—the assassination of President John F. Kennedy in November, 1963, and Richard Speck's murder of eight student nurses in Chicago in July, 1966. As in the Phillips study, they statistically controlled for such artifacts as the seasonal and yearly trends in violent crime. The analyses indicated that following the murders and the subsequent flood of publicity, there was a significant increase in violent crime in America. Moreover, negligent manslaughter did *not* show this pattern, suggesting that the rise in violent crime was due to an increase in aggression and not a general rise in crime.* Berkowitz and Macaulay suggest that the effects of highly publicized crimes can last for some months and that "the persistence of the high crime rate in the year or two after the President's assassination and then again in the period following the Speck murders could well be due to the phenomenon of crime breeding crime."[15] That is, publicized murders cause more murders, which cause more publicity, which causes more murders, and so on. Such a vicious circle might have had a lot to do with the increase in violent crime during the Vietnam War in the United States.

Whether you call it suggestion, imitation, or contagion, it certainly does seem that the news leaves a very real impression. Let us look at some of the specific kinds of impressions created by the news that might confuse our understanding of social problems.

THE NEWS ACCENTUATES THE DRAMATIC

A fundamental problem with the news is that it is NEWS. The news is dramatic, exciting, strange, unexpected, thrilling, and shocking. In a sense, the news presents precisely those things that rarely happen. As a result, getting your understanding of society from the news is like getting it from a soap opera, a murder mystery, or a Broadway musical. You are likely to get the impression that nobody ever sleeps, relaxes, reads, listens to music, or daydreams. Life is actually much more boring, staid, and dull than the news suggests. When a change in a few percentage points in the ratings can mean a decrease of several million dollars in advertising revenues, it is understandable that the television news avoids the commonplace, which would cause the viewer to change the station.

Even the typical murder is, in its own way, rather boring. About 12 percent of the murders consist of husbands killing wives or vice versa, and another 10 to 12 percent involve the killing of some other relative. About half of the murders are due to quarrels between friends or acquaintances. Only about 25 percent of the murders are "felony" homicides in which the killing accompanies rape, robbery,

---

* Negligent manslaughter is a killing, such as a drunken driver recklessly running over a pedestrian, in which there is no intent to kill but there is criminal negligence. Presumably, negligent manslaughter is not a direct result of aggressive impulses and so can be used as a kind of statistical control.

mugging, and the like.[16] Since murder is usually a crime of passion, the killer typically makes little serious effort to escape, and often calls the police himself to report the crime. This is why at least 75 to 80 percent of the murders are solved.*[17] When those accused of murder come to trial, as is the case with most trials, the trial usually will last only a few minutes, because it will be merely a formal procedure to accept the prearranged guilty plea.[18]

Because the news focuses on the dramatic and the exciting, it presents quite a different picture. The murder trials shown on the news often involve famous, rich, or powerful victims or defendants, or else the murder itself is particularly bizarre or spectacular. Even if the defendant is poor, the notoriety of the case usually ensures that the defendant will be more or less vigorously represented by able, or at least ambitious, lawyers. Merely selecting the jury might take longer than scores of the more common trials, at which the accused waives such rights and simply pleads guilty. These well-publicized trials can last for many weeks, and each day the television viewer or newspaper reader is reminded of the subtle and complex machinations of the American criminal justice system when the prosecution and the defense are blessed with great resources.

The parade of expert witnesses, the elaborate psychiatric defenses, the constant charges and countercharges as the jury is marched in and out of the jury box, the casuistic manipulation of legal minutiae, followed by the seemingly endless appeals—all this is what the average person is likely to think of when he or she imagines a criminal trial in America. It is no wonder that people often believe that criminals are "getting away with murder." Those who believe that no one goes to prison in America today should note that recently the number of prisoners in state and federal prisons reached an all-time high.[19] (Local jails are also pretty full, but not with those convicted of minor offenses. Many of those in local jails have been convicted of serious crimes, and a large number, about 40 percent, are awaiting trial and have not been convicted of anything. Only a minority have been convicted of minor crimes.[20])

As was the case in deciding how many words start with *K* or have *K* in the third position, faulty remembering of exactly what murder is all about will lead to faulty decision making. If your impres-

---

Solved means that the crime was cleared from the police books by determining the presumably guilty party.

sions are biased, your decisions will be wrong. Those who get their understanding of murder from the news are likely to try to protect themselves from being involved in murder by putting extra locks on the doors, avoiding members of dangerous groups, voting for the "law and order" candidate, and fighting to "untie the hands" of the police. On the other hand, an objective consideration of the nature of murder in our culture would suggest different actions—getting rid of that old gun in the dresser drawer, going to a marriage counselor, choosing one's friends more judiciously, and avoiding arguments while drinking.

Another misconception fostered by the overemphasis on the dramatic in the news is the accentuation of airplane crashes and other catastrophic accidents. Because major airline crashes, when they do occur, often involve scores of fatalities, they are given prominent coverage in the national news. Meanwhile, 100 auto crashes with only one or two fatalities each are ignored. The result is that many people feel that airplane travel is more hazardous than automobile travel. Flying on scheduled airlines is actually much safer than driving an automobile in terms of fatalities per passenger-mile.[21]

Yet another example involves the weather and farm production. In a country as large and varied as the United States, it is to be expected that each year one or more crops will be threatened by adverse weather. When that happens, the television news focuses on whatever section of the country has too little rain (or too much), shows us heart-rending pictures of farmers holding handfuls of dust (or mud), and tells us that unless the rain starts (or stops), the farmers will be ruined. We are led to believe that once again, America is faced with national catastrophe. In fact, the United States grows so many varied crops requiring varied weather conditions, in so many different regions at so many different times, that even though some crops may be disappointing, the total farm production is quite stable. Thus, variation in agricultural production over the years is substantially less than variation in industrial production.[22]

Whenever there is a big storm in the news, the news producers like to tie in other stories to the "weather angle." The result is a headline like this: ELEVEN INCHES OF SNOW BLANKET CITY—FOUR DIE OF HEART ATTACKS. This too is misleading, for there is no simple relationship between such storms and the death rate, and often the number of deaths in a city goes down after a big storm.[23] Maybe four died of heart attacks shoveling snow, but eight might have died if there were no snow, and they had all gone to work as planned.

The logic of the news dictates that you will not see a headline like this: BEAUTIFUL WEATHER CONTINUES—EIGHT DIE OF HEART ATTACKS.

THE NEWS ACCENTUATES THE POLITICAL

That area of the world known as Ulster or Northern Ireland is about 3,500 miles from the United States and has a population of about 1.5 million. Beginning in the late 1960s, there has been a resurgence of the bloody political feuding that has periodically erupted in Ireland throughout modern history. Over an eight-year period, this political hostility has resulted in the killing of about 1,780 persons, an average of about 223 killings per year.[24]

That area of the world known as Detroit is in the heart of the United States and also has a population of about 1.5 million. In 1974 alone there were 714 murders in Detroit, and in the three-year period 1974–1976, homicides rose to over 2,000—about three times the rate of slaughter in Northern Ireland.[25] Nor is Detroit unique in having a higher murder rate than Northern Ireland's political slaughter. In reality, most major American cities, including New York, Chicago, Los Angeles, Philadelphia, and Cleveland, have higher murder rates.[26] Yet the news has constantly bombarded us with stories about the violence in Northern Ireland. There are incessant stories about the fear, the hatred, the deleterious effects on the economy and the social health of the nation, the terrible influence on the minds of the children. These stories might well be true, but they could just as easily be told about many places closer to home than Armagh or Londonderry. The important difference between the killings in Ireland and those in America is that the killings in Ireland are political while those in the United States are the standard nonpolitical murders.

On a recent weekend in the greater Chicago area, there were 42 shootings, 6 stabbings, and a total of 16 persons killed.[27] If the victims had all been killed in one stroke by a terrorist's bomb or in a guerrilla attack thousands of miles away, the national news would have carried stories on the "massacre" for days. However, there was little news coverage of the Chicago killings because they were not the single act of a violent political gang; rather, they were the diffuse actions of a violent society. A young man was shot to death in a barroom quarrel; another was murdered in an alley arguing over money; yet another was stabbed

35

to death after a quarrel at a birthday party. And so on. Typical American murders.

It is understandable that journalists, who are often well-traveled experts on international politics, find the actions of political gangs more interesting than sordid domestic quarrels, even if they are not as deadly. But this bias helps create the false impression that political violence or terrorism is a much greater threat than it actually is. The bias is further confounded by the fact that the journalists give greater coverage to events that are more accessible to them. If 60 people are killed in a relatively free country, such as Ireland, Israel, or Australia, it will make a bigger splash on the news than if 6,000 are killed in China or Burundi.*

Consider the problem of bombing in the United States. FBI records reveal that in 1976 there were 1,570 bombing "incidents" and 1,257 actual bombings, including both explosive and incendiary devices. These resulted in only 50 deaths, 212 injuries, and about $11,000,000 in property damage.[29] In comparison with other killings and destruction in the United States, bombing is a minor problem. For the years 1972 to 1976, for example, an average of only 38 persons per year were killed by bombs. This is less than the number of persons killed by their husbands or wives in America in an average *week*.[30]

Furthermore, in the bombings for which the FBI can estimate a motive, less than 5 percent are attributable to political or "anti-establishment" motives, while about 66 to 75 percent are attributable to personal animosity or malicious destruction.[31] In terms of property damage, arson is far more destructive than any other form of bombing in America. Of course, the actual extent of arson is exceedingly difficult to determine. When terrorists destroy a building, they are more than willing to take the blame, and may even declare responsibility for bombings they had nothing to do with in order to get some "free" publicity. But professional arsonists—or "torches," as they are called—rarely leave any trace of their incendiary activities. It has been estimated that the United States suffers $1 to $2 billion in property damage every year due to arson.[32] New York City alone loses several hundred buildings a month due to fire, and most of these are thought to be the work of arsonists.[33]

Due to the influence of biased reporting in the news, when

* In fact, in 1972 an estimated 100,000 Hutus were slaughtered in Burundi with very little news coverage.[28]

many people think of bombing, they think of terrorist gangs trying to overthrow the establishment. The real problem of bombing in America is the problem of organized crime, irate husbands, angry neighbors, businessmen looking for insurance money, pyromaniacs looking for thrills, and the usual variety of cruel crackpots. It has little to do directly with terrorism or politics, but you are not likely to realize this if you gain your "information" on social problems from the news.

To put the matter of bombing in further perspective, consider that accidental choking on food and other objects placed in the mouth kills approximately 3,000 persons every year in the United States— more than the total killed in more highly publicized accidental shootings.[34] Death by accidental choking, being neither especially dramatic nor political, and occurring singly rather than in large groups, is given little exposure in the news. Truly informed citizens who wish to apply their energies to reducing the number of needless deaths in our society would be wise to focus on neglected areas like choking rather than on more popular causes for outrage like terrorism. One program likely to be helpful would be a public awareness campaign aimed at getting people to take smaller bites of food.* Another would be a program to make better-fitting dentures more readily available so that people would enjoy chewing their food rather than swallowing it whole. (Many elderly people with bad teeth or poorly fitting dentures find chewing so painful thay simply do not bother to do it.) These are sensible programs from the perspective of making life in America longer and happier. However, keeping in mind the emphasis in the news, how would you like to be a political candidate running on a platform of better dentures for the elderly, campaigning against an opponent who is running "against" terrorist bombing?

THE NEWS ACCENTUATES THE SUPERFICIAL

Do you remember the old world history textbooks popular some years ago? They were filled with stories about kings, generals, emperors, and conquerors. Reading one of those texts would lead you to believe that the history of the human race was one long series of excit-

---

*Physicians who have studied the problem of choking reported on the size of pieces of food found in the victims' throats: "The average size approximates that of a pack of cigarettes—the largest piece encountered at autopsy was over eighteen cm. [seven inches] long."[35]

ing battles and blockades, thrilling wars and conquests, spectacular crownings and dethronings. You could read for hours and hardly catch more than a hint that throughout history people were really interested in finding fresher meat and sweeter wine, having a more forgiving spouse and more respectful children, or stopping a nagging toothache or leaky roof. The news is a lot like those old history books; it gives the fluff, the lace, the whipped cream, and neglects the substance of human existence. To put it another way, the news focuses on *public* events and *public* persons, while disregarding the important private events that in their total impact create and solve social problems.[36]

It is a kind of annual ritual in America to ask people to name the living man they most admire. Table 2.1 contains all those mentioned in lists of the top-ten most admired living men throughout the early 1970s.[37] (The number in parentheses gives the number of times each made the top-ten list.) If you take a minute to look over Table 2.1, you will probably be struck by the great diversity of opinions and attitudes found among the most admired men. Selecting two or three of them at random, it would be difficult to say what attitudes or positions they hold in common that makes them so admired.

As Russell Baker has pointed out, these "most admired" lists do not actually enumerate those with some particularly valuable talent. Rather, they reflect a man's ability to get his name in the newspaper or on the television screen.[38] These men are admired because they are *news*. Predictably, 15 of the 19 men are political figures, and 2, Billy Graham and Pope Paul, are religious figures, both of whom have had some association with politics. Bob Hope is an entertainer who also has

TABLE 2.1 MOST ADMIRED MEN IN AMERICA, 1970–1973

Rev. Billy Graham (4)	Pres. Harry Truman (2)
Sen. Edward Kennedy (4)	Willy Brandt (1)
Pres. Richard Nixon (4)	Pres. Gerald Ford (1)
Pope Paul VI (4)	Sen. Barry Goldwater (1)
Vice-Pres. Spiro Agnew (3)	Bob Hope (1)
Gov. George Wallace (3)	Sen. Henry Jackson (1)
Sen. Hubert Humphrey (2)	Sen. George McGovern (1)
Pres. Lyndon Johnson (2)	Sen. Edmund Muskie (1)
Sec. Henry Kissinger (2)	Gov. Ronald Reagan (1)
Ralph Nader (2)	

been at least vaguely connected with political issues. Only one man on the list, Ralph Nader, is known for his work in dealing with social problems outside of political office. The omissions from the "most admired" list are even more striking. There are no noted scientists, writers, or educators among the most admired. Nor are there any famous inventors, philosophers, medical researchers, or historians. Perhaps we would have more such men if they were given more recognition.

Surveys of the most admired living women reveal the same pattern. The lists are top-heavy with political figures like Queen Elizabeth II, Mamie Eisenhower, Jacqueline Onassis, Rose Kennedy, Coretta King, and the wife of whoever happens to be President when the survey is taken.[39] Once again, it is difficult to find what attitudes, values, or opinions these women have in common. In fact, it is difficult to imagine some of them even holding a strong public position on an important social issue. Many of these most admired women are not admired in their own right at all, but are basking in the reflected glory of their male relatives. They would seem strangely out of place on a list with Susan B. Anthony, Jane Addams, Dorothy Day, Margaret Sanger, and other independent and courageous women who actively fought social problems in America.

By concentrating on the political and superficial, the news turns some names into household words, but in the process it does not necessarily shed any light on social problems. For example, several men on the "most admired" list gained fame (and votes) by attacking "welfare cheats"—the infamous army of shirks who live on the labors of the "hard-working American taxpayer." Sociologists have known for many years that there are very few able-bodied men on welfare. Most welfare recipients are women and children; many are aged or blind or disabled. One recent study estimated that less than 1 percent of those on welfare are able-bodied adult men.[40]

Of course, it is not only politicians that one meets in the news. Occasionally a famous love affair or scandal will temporarily propel someone into the limelight. Television and the newspapers have also made many sports figures famous throughout the country. Americans can easily recognize the names of comedians, singers, actors, and those entertainers whose talents are so nebulous that they are known only as "personalities." But how many important living scientists, historians, or inventors can we name? Might they not have something to do with solving social problems?

In a recent survey by the National Institute of Student Opinion, 15,000 young Americans answered the question: "Is there a man or woman *living today* whom you consider your personal hero?" The biggest vote getter was wild-haired television actress Farrah Fawcett-Majors, who edged out gymnast Nadia Comaneci, decathlon winner Bruce Jenner, skater Dorothy Hammill, Farrah's husband Lee Majors, the "six million dollar man," and other popular heroes.[41] In another poll of students' heroes, the most popular turned out to be football star O. J. Simpson, with rock star Elton John, astronaut Neil Armstrong, and movie star John Wayne being the runners-up.[42] In yet another survey, teenage girls listed the women they most admired. The winner this time was tennis star Billie Jean King. The runners-up were about evenly divided between political figures such as Golda Meir, Rose Kennedy, and Coretta King and entertainers Mary Tyler Moore, Barbra Streisand, Marlo Thomas, and the like.[43]

The emphasis of the news media on transitory "stars" to the neglect of those involved in social problems is not a new phenomenon. Many years ago, a survey was conducted to see which supposedly famous people Americans could recognize. The two persons most well-known were John Barrymore and Joan Crawford. Aimee McPherson was better known than Albert Einstein. Texas Guinan (a nightclub hostess) was more familiar than Mahatma Gandhi, and Mae West was better known than Joseph Stalin. Some people even thought the Mayo brothers were a circus act![44]

Not only does the news emphasize the wrong people, it also concentrates on the big public events, turning our attention from the soft, slow, private developments that ultimately create the causes and cures of social problems. In 1848, the big news was the toppling of thrones all over Europe, but in the same year Marx wrote the *Communist Manifesto*, which was one of those long-fused time bombs that ultimately influence our lives more than the temporary ups and downs of kings and queens. Journalist George Will has pointed out that the big "news" in 1932 was the election of Franklin D. Roosevelt as President. The news ignored the discovery of the neutron at Cambridge University in the same year, but it was this advance in nuclear science that paved the way for the atomic bomb and probably did more than the New Deal to alter the nature of political affairs. Similarly, the news in 1953 was concerned with President Eisenhower and the armistice in Korea. The discovery of the structure of DNA in 1953 was not news, even though it heralded the beginning of our understanding and manipulation of genetics and the growth of a host of profound challenges to our social structure.[45] The growth of television and the automobile industry, the expansion of education, the proliferation of birth control technology, industrialization, and the migration of the poor from the countryside to urban areas are among the true revolutions that drastically alter the fabric of our society. We must learn to understand them and foresee their impact even if they are rarely news.

THE NEWS ACCENTUATES THE NEGATIVE

The news does seem to be mostly bad. Airplane crashes, political scandals, bombings, tragic homicides, bankruptcies, and other horrors are surprising, dramatic, shocking, and are standard topics for political oratory. To put it simply, they are news. And they are *bad* news. Those who derive their understanding of society from the news, therefore, frequently develop an extremely pessimistic attitude about life in America. Perhaps the most unfortunate suggestion presented in the news is that our social problems are getting worse and worse, and there is nothing we can do about them.

Certainly, over the years some things have not improved. In spite of all the talk about increased leisure, the average number of hours worked in the manufacturing industries has remained approximately constant over the last several decades.[46] Some things have even deteriorated. For instance, the percentage of women on college and university faculties and professional staffs is lower now than it was 30 or 40 years ago.[47] However, in general, the social health and quality of life in the United States are better now than they were at any time in our nation's history. Racial prejudice, sexual discrimination, poverty, violent crime, lack of medical care, narcotic addiction, housing conditions, and injustice have all been a lot worse than they are now.

The area of mental health presents a good example of progress in combating social problems. Of course, a large number of people still suffer from various psychoses, emotional upheavals, and problems in living. But the suffering and the dislocation to their lives caused by these problems have been greatly reduced in recent years. Through the use of tranquilizers and other forms of chemotherapy, greater flexibility and availability of psychotherapy, more sophisticated social service support, and other advances, the population of the mental hospitals in the United States has been steadily declining over the last generation.

In 1955, when the widespread use of psychopharmaceutical drugs began, there were over 500,000 patients in government mental hospitals; by 1970 there were about 340,000—a decrease of almost 40 percent.[48] With the decline in mental hospital residents, there is now about one staff member for every patient.[49] This does not mean that we have solved the problem of mental illness. It does mean that thousands of troubled people have been spared the deleterious effects of a prolonged stay in a mental hospital. That is something we can take pride in, even if it is not news.

Or consider the problem of the "skyrocketing" rate of venereal disease, the so-called V.D. epidemic. If by "V.D." we mean the total of both syphilis and gonorrhea, then there has, indeed, been an increase in the number of V.D. cases in the 1970s. This increase is due to a growth in the less harmful venereal disease, gonorrhea. The rate of syphilis, the truly dangerous venereal disease, has varied substantially over the last generation, but the general trend has definitely been *downward*. By the 1970s, the number of reported cases was a fraction of what it was during the peak of the syphilis "epidemic" of the 1940s.[50] By 1974, only about 300 deaths in the United States were attributed to syphilis, lower than the toll of such diseases as acute bronchitis, meningitis, and even asthma, the deadliest of the four.*[51] Furthermore, the improvement as revealed in the official statistics is probably an underestimation because present means of detection are better than those of the past.

In addition to improved medical technology, winning the fight against syphilis is due to a number of those slow, soft developments that ultimately alter the nature of social problems. Among the important changes are the expansion of V.D. and planned parenthood clinics, improved methods of "casefinding" those who have been exposed to venereal disease, the development of public awareness through advertising appeals, and relaxing state laws to allow the treatment of teenagers without their parents' consent. Somehow the failure to deal with gonorrhea appears more newsworthy than the success in curbing syphilis.

The incidence of murder presents another example of the overly depressing picture of American society presented in the news. Unfor-

---

* One must be cautious in interpreting the deaths due to syphilis because, unlike most diseases, syphilis is so slow-acting that the death rate in one year reflects the rate of contraction of the disease many years previously. Therefore, we can expect that the number of deaths due to syphilis will continue to decline.

tunately, there is little solid information on the overall number of murders in America during the 19th and early 20th centuries. It was not until 1930 that the International Association of Chiefs of Police in conjunction with the FBI began collecting nationwide crime statistics in what became known as the *Uniform Crime Reports*. Because participation in this record keeping is voluntary, the statistics have always been imperfect. The *Uniform Crime Reports* are now fairly complete, but even as late as 1974 the FBI received reports covering only 84 percent of the rural population.[52] Therefore, caution must be exercised in interpreting even the best crime statistics we have. However, these statistics do indicate that throughout most of the period from 1930 to 1970, the murder rate in the United States was actually *decreasing*![53] It was only in the mid-1960s and early 1970s that homicides substantially increased. In the period 1974 to 1976 the trend was again reversed, and the murder rate actually declined by about 10 percent.[54] It is most probable that the incidence of homicide today is only a fraction of what it was in the "good old days" of the wild West, frontier justice, and lynch mobs.[55]

One of the major reasons for the overly pessimistic slant to the news is that the mass media lean heavily on the reports of government agencies, public officials, and other experts. I have already pointed out that the experts, due to their one-sided experience in dealing with problems and ignoring successes, frequently have a very poor understanding of the extent of social problems. In addition, many experts have a personal motivation to exaggerate the extent of the problem they are supposed to solve. In order to justify their position, power, and annual requests for budget increases, those empowered to fight social problems tend to overestimate the need for their services. As a result, the sources of the most depressing stories regarding social problems are precisely those authorities whose job it is to solve the problem they now tell us is out of hand. Howard Becker, a prominent theoretician on social problems, describes the awkward predicament of those who have to enforce the rules:

> In justifying the existence of his position, the rule enforcer faces a double problem. On the one hand, he must demonstrate to others that the problem still exists: the rules he is supposed to enforce have some point, because infractions occur. On the other hand, he must show that his attempts at enforcement are effective and worthwhile, that the evil he is supposed to deal with is in fact being dealt with adequately. Therefore, enforcement organizations, particularly when they are

seeking funds, typically oscillate between two kinds of claims. First, they say that by reason of their efforts the problem they deal with is approaching solution. But, in the same breath, they say the problem is perhaps worse than ever (though through no fault of their own) and requires renewed and increased effort to keep it under control. Enforcement officials can be more vehement than anyone else in their insistence that the problem they are supposed to deal with is still with us, in fact is more with us than ever before. In making these claims, enforcement officials provide good reason for continuing the existence of the position they occupy.[56]

In order to resolve this dilemma, social-problem solvers not only present an overly pessimistic view of life in America, they also can create thorough confusion about the nature of the problem they are supposed to be dealing with. Criminologists Kurt Weis and Michael Milakovich present an interesting example from the area of law enforcement:

> In other words, police should be pleased most with the *simultaneous decrease and increase in crime*, seemingly a logical impossibility. These mutually exclusive alternatives are reconciled only if one considers the political feasibility of a "decreasing rate of increase." This tactical maneuver was first announced by ex-Attorney General John N. Mitchell, who proclaimed a decrease of increase as a reliable index of victory in the war on crime. The notion is currently being parroted by federal and state officials who are enthusiastic about a measure which allows them to claim victory in their fight against crime but does not threaten the continued existence of bureaucracies formed to distribute federal anticrime funds.[57]

What would be the effect on the average citizen if the mass media presented more of the good news? Harvey Hornstein, Stephen Holloway, and their colleagues at Columbia University attempted to answer this question. In a number of studies, Hornstein and Holloway had students listen to an apparently ordinary radio broadcast which included a news bulletin. Actually, the students heard a tape recording of false news items.[58] Sometimes the news reported a great kindness—a clergyman donated a kidney to save a man's life—other times a great cruelty, such as a senseless murder. One important finding was that the students showed a more positive view of human nature when questioned after hearing the good news. For example, a higher percentage of persons were considered "basically honest." Furthermore, after hearing the good news, the students played more cooperatively with their partners when playing a game for money.[59] In another study, a group of middle-aged women were much more likely to find an accused man guilty of murder in a mock trial situation if they had just heard bad news rather than good news.[60]

As we might expect, knowing the nature of human information processing, when interviewed after the experiment, the people did not think the news had any effect on them. In fact, most of them did not recall hearing any news at all! The effects of any one "real" newscast are likely to be short-lived.[61] But the cumulative impact of years of bad news might have a substantial effect on our conception of life in America. As Hornstein and Holloway conclude:

> It requires only a small stretch of the imagination to see what might be happening *outside* the laboratory when people hear bad news. They are likely to become more competitive and less cooperative. Therefore, competition, cooperation, and feelings of "we" and "they" are partly the result of the information about human beings that we gather from the news.[62]

Concerning the particular matter of solving social problems, constant exposure to bad news is likely to create the illusion that our problems are getting worse and worse, and there is nothing we can do about it. In addition to being simply false, a steady diet of bad news, therefore, can also create a dangerous, self-fulfilling prophecy. If most people become convinced that our social problems will inevitably get worse, they will stop trying to solve them. As a result, social problems will indeed get worse.

THE SOCIAL PROBLEMS TEST REVISITED

In the course of this chapter, all the answers to the test presented in the first chapter were given. In case you missed any, here is the complete scoring.

1. The percentage of college professors that are women is greater today than it was 30 or 40 years ago. *False; it is less.*
2. The syphilis rate in the United States is rapidly increasing. *False; it is decreasing.*
3. At least 20 percent of the persons on welfare are able-bodied men who either cannot find a job or will not work. *False; hardly any of those on welfare are able-bodied men.*
4. In spite of uncertainties such as the weather, food production in the

United States has substantially less year-to-year variation than does industrial production. *True.*

5. At least 75 to 80 percent of the homicides in the United States are solved. *True.*

6. Homicide is at an all-time high in America. *False; it probably was a lot higher in the bad old days.*

7. The average number of hours worked per week in American manufacturing industries has remained about the same over the last generation. *True.*

8. At least half of the inmates in local jails are serving time for minor (nonfelony) offenses. *False; the majority either haven't been convicted yet or are serving time for serious offenses.*

9. The average (median) nonfelony trial lasts a *couple of minutes.*

10. The average (median) income per family is highest if the family head is descended from immigrants from *Poland.*

11. The nation with the longest life expectancy is *Iceland.*

12. The population of the mental hospitals in the United States is *decreasing.*

13. *Asthma* kills more Americans than any other of the diseases listed.

14. The year with the highest murder rate is *1930.*

15. About *27 percent* of the population of the United States lives in cities of 100,000 or more.

16. For every staff member in an American mental hospital there is about *1* patient.

17. *Boston* has the lowest average (median) family income of the four cities.

18. Americans of *Russian* background have the highest level of education.

SUMMARY

Due to the limits of human observation and recollection, the distillation of folk wisdom and personal experience from which many people conjure up their solutions to social problems is actually a very poor guide. This is equally true for "experts" because of their one-sided experience in constantly dealing with problems and ignoring successes. In order to avoid the limitations of personal experience, many people turn to the information provided in the news in the honest hope that it will provide a sufficient background for understanding social problems. Due to several important biases in the news, this hope is usually unrealistic.

The news is a kind of entertainment, and those who produce it feel a need to maintain high television ratings or newspaper circulation.

As a result, the news focuses on the sudden, the dramatic, and shocking, and in the process presents information as one-sided as any personal experience. The news also accentuates political happenings even though much activity related to social problems occurs on a nonpolitical level. In attempting to be entertaining, the news concentrates on the shenanigans of sports figures, Hollywood stars, and popular political personalities and neglects the efforts of less glamorous individuals who are actively combating social problems. Lastly, the news accentuates the negative in human affairs, showing more interest in catastrophes than in the slow improvement in social conditions. Reliance on the reports of professional problem solvers also leads to an exaggeration of the negative in the news because these professionals have a personal interest in maintaining public fear of the problem.

The cumulative effect of exposure to these biases is the creation of an overly pessimistic attitude toward social problems and a concentration on certain minor but dramatic problems while ignoring the major causes and solutions of important social problems.

THREE

Creating and Using Statistics

In order to avoid the biases referred to in the last chapter, social scientists use statistics. But they too have their dangers. Statistics are merely numbers that condense information. Their purpose is to communicate what is to be communicated in as few symbols as possible. If you had 30 hits in 100 times at bat in the baseball season, it is a lot simpler to say you are batting .300 than to explain each of the 100 times at bat. If you drove 400 miles on 20 gallons of gas, it is easy to say you averaged 20 miles per gallon; you do not have to describe each mile in detail. In cases like these, you are condensing information, and in the process, the statistics *must* leave something out. If you wish to describe reality in its absolute complexity, its full existential uniqueness, you will not use statistics.

In order to interpret social problem statistics correctly, you have to cultivate an awareness of what the statistics are leaving out as well as a knowledge of what they are leaving in. Human nature being what it is, when we create statistics we have a tendency to leave out the undesirable information and highlight the desirable facts to create a misleading impression. This approach uses statistics the way a drunk uses a lamppost—for support and not illumination. After being fooled a number of times by such misleading statistics, it is tempting to mistrust all statistics. But to think all statistics are meaningless is equally as foolish as accepting each one uncritically. Whether we like it or not, we *need* statistics to overcome personal bias. Our goal in thinking seriously about social problems is to use statistics wisely; we cannot do without them.

All communication leaves something out; it is the advantage of statistics that what is left out is to some extent known. This is true because statistics employ rules; they are not created by whim. When someone reports a "typical" case, we really do not know what he thinks is typical. When someone reports the median case, we know the rules he used to arrive at his example. The advantage to statistics, therefore, is that we do not have to trust the communicator completely. To some extent, we can understand what he is *not* saying and evaluate its importance.

DEALING WITH NUMBERS

LARGE NUMBERS

The simplest condensation of information is the total or sum of a series of numbers. We usually have no problem in interpreting totals in our daily lives when we meet them in the form of grocery bills or restaurant checks. However, when we are handed the bills for attacking social problems, the totals become so staggering that they can overwhelm more than enlighten. When you read that a fully equipped Trident missile submarine costs about $1 billion,[1] or that the total annual cost of social welfare programs is $331 billion,[2] or that between 1945 and 1970 the United States spent $1 trillion on the military,[3] you are apt to read right past these figures without any real appreciation of the amounts involved.* Numbers such as billions and trillions all tend to blur together into the area of the unimaginable and uninterpretable.

One way to get a grip on large numbers is to convert them into per capita figures and consider what they cost *you*. If you have a calcu-

---

*In case you have forgotten: A million = 1,000,000 = 10^6
A billion = 1,000,000,000 = 10^9
A trillion = 1,000,000,000,000 = 10^{12}

lator handy when you read the news (which is not a bad habit to develop), you can simply divide the total expenditures for the United States by its population—about 215,000,000 in 1977. Without a calculator a rough, but generally satisfactory, measure of per capita costs can be obtained by dividing the total cost by 200 million—simply divide the total in half and then move the decimal point eight places to the left. In the case of the Trident submarine:

$$\frac{\$1 \text{ billion}}{\text{Population of the United States}} = \frac{\$1,000,000,000}{200,000,000} = \$5$$

In other words, adding another fully equipped, missile-carrying submarine to our arsenal will cost you about $5. This is a very rough estimate which does not take into account the imprecision of the calculations, inflation, cost overruns, and the fact that you are not exactly average. The goal is not to develop a mathematically exact figure but to get a feel for how much $1 billion is personally.

A social expenditure of $1 for every person in the United States totals a little more than $200 million. This amount can be called a *capita*, and is a handy figure to use as a basic unit in measuring social costs. Remember, the capita is a dollar for everyone in the country and totals a little more than $200 million. A hundred capitas, about $20 billion, is roughly the amount Americans spend on alcoholic beverages each year ($22.9 billion in 1974).[4]

A trillion dollars, or 5,000 capitas, is about as large a sum as you are likely to meet in the context of social problems. One way to think of $1 trillion is to remember that it is approximately the total personal disposable income in the United States per year. (In 1975 the estimated per capita disposable income was $5,040.)[5] In short, $1 trillion, or 5,000 capitas, is roughly all Americans have to spend each year.

When the expenditures are not allocated to individuals, it can be misleading to think in terms of per capita amounts. In counting such things as automobiles, television sets, or burglaries, it is more appropriate to think in terms of households and not individuals. For example, in 1974 there were about 105,000,000 automobiles registered in the United States.[6] Since automobiles are used by households rather than individuals, it would be helpful to think in terms of automobiles per household. In 1974 there were about 70,000,000 households in the United States.[7] So there were roughly 1.5 automobiles per household.

To change cost per capita into cost per household, simply multiply by 3. If a social program costs $2 billion, it costs $10 per capita or about $30 per household. As you might expect, most households are actually families; that is, they contain two or more relatives living together. But a household is not quite the same thing as a family; many households contain only a single person. You might want to note that there are about 55 million families in the United States.[8]

In confronting large numbers concerning social problems, it would help to memorize the following figures. They are not meant to be exact.[9] They have been rounded off to make them easier to remember and calculate with.

Total population of the United States = 200,000,000
Total number of households   = 70,000,000
Total number of families   = 55,000,000
Total number of births per year   =   3,000,000
Total number of deaths per year   =   2,000,000
Total number of marriages per year   =   2,000,000

SMALL NUMBERS

The problem with small numbers is just the opposite of the problem with large ones. Large numbers tend to be overwhelming; small numbers tend to be ignored. Some of the little numbers regarding social problems do mean a lot and cannot be ignored. The most important small numbers relevant to social problems are percentages.

PERCENTAGES Just as total costs can be converted to per capita cost, some numbers become more meaningful when they are converted into fractions of other numbers. A percentage is simply a fraction which is expressed in terms of hundredths. In 1975, for instance, there were 11.4 million people in the United States receiving Aid to Families with Dependent Children.[10] Because 11.4 million is hard to conceptualize, it is more revealing to say that roughly 5 percent of the population was receiving public assistance for families with dependent children.

Percentage change from one period to another is a common use of percentages in the study of social problems. It is less impressive to say that there were 56,730 forcible rapes reported in 1976 than to point out that from 1967 to 1976 the number of reported forcible rapes increased 105 percent.[11]* Percentage change over time can become very tricky when it is *compounded*—that is, when the percentage increase for

*If a number more than doubles during the time period, the percentage change will be more than 100 percent. But as athletes are fond of pointing out, you cannot *give* more than 100 percent. It is obviously meaningless to claim to be behind someone 1,000 percent.

51

one period becomes part of the number from which the next percentage increase is taken. The most common example of compounding is earning interest on previous interest payments in a savings account.

To see how important small compounded percentages can be, we can consider the most famous business deal in the history of the United States—the buying of Manhattan Island. According to the old story, in 1626 Peter Minuit purchased Manhattan Island from the Indians for a bundle of trinkets and cloth worth an estimated $24.[12] This has been cited as a great bargain showing the shrewdness of the early Europeans in dealing with the Indians. However, we should not be too hasty in coming to a conclusion, for this is a situation involving compounded interest. One way to evaluate what the $24 would be worth today is to assume it could have been invested at, say, 7 percent interest compounded annually. The formula for annual compound interest is:

$$A = P\,(1+i)^n$$

where A is the present value of the original principal P invested at interest rate i (expressed as a decimal) compounded annually over n years. For example, after 100 years, the original $24 would be worth $24\,(1.07)^{100}$, or over $20,000. In 1976, 350 years later, the $24 would have compounded to roughly $450 *billion!* Even ignoring the hazardous state of New York City's finances, it seems that Peter Minuit did not get such a great deal after all.

SOCIAL PROBLEMS WITH COMPOUNDING The effects of compounding small rates of increase are important in understanding a number of social problems. The population explosion provides a striking example. On the surface, the population increase hardly appears to be an explosion. In the early 1970s the world's population was creeping up at the rate of only about 2 percent a year.[13] If you ignore compounding, this increase might appear to be moderate and well-controlled.

To help you interpret compounded increases, here is a rough rule of thumb: If you divide the percentage increase into 70, it gives the approximate number of years for the original amount to double. For example, the $24 paid for Manhattan Island invested at 7 percent would double every $70 \div 7 = 10$ years. From 1626 to 1976 it doubled about 35 times. The earth's population, increasing at 2 percent a year, would take about $70 \div 2 = 35$ years to double. The world population in

1975 was estimated at about 4 billion, so if the 2 percent annual increase were to continue, 35 years later, in 2010, it would be about 8 billion. In the year 2080, a little more than a century later, it would have doubled three times, to reach the staggering total of 32 billion! Now, that is a population explosion.

Education is another social problem area which is intimately related to compounding, although in a less obvious way. That education is of vast importance in gaining financial success is an article of faith for most Americans, and on the whole, those with more education do earn more money. Nevertheless, there is substantial doubt among sociologists that increasing education is actually an effective way to increase earnings.[14]

Determining the value of education is basically a question of compounding, because continuing one's education demands giving up money early in life in order to get more money later on. Money in hand is always worth more than the same amount in the future, because it can be invested and compounded all the time you are waiting for the future money to start rolling in. Therefore, the future earning must be substantially greater than the initial loss in order to offset the loss in interest. As economists put it, the future earning must be *discounted* for the time it takes to get it. Whether college or graduate study actually "pays" will then depend on both the initial cost of going to school and the rate of interest available for investing the savings made by working rather than going to school.[15]

For the sake of an example, let us assume that four years of college cost $25,000 in tuition, fees, and income lost by not working.[16] We will further assume that the $25,000 can be invested at 7 percent compounded annually. After only 30 years, that original investment of $25,000 would grow to $191,000. The person who went to college would have to gain more than that to make college a good investment. Of course, whether college or graduate school is a sound investment for any particular person depends in part on that person's access to good jobs after graduation. It might be that, due to discrimination and other considerations, higher education is a good investment for white men but a poor one for women and members of minorities.[17]

It is often difficult to convince a young person yearning for a new car, a good stereo, and a fancy apartment to invest the money saved early in life. And if that money is not invested, no interest will be compounded, and the advantage of working over going to school might well be lost. This suggests the ironic conclusion that a young person who is present-oriented and short-sighted should go to college, and one who is future-oriented might do better to forget about higher education, get a job, and start saving.

Determining the value of education also points out another basic principle of statistics: *Correlation does not imply causation.* A correlation between two characteristics or factors only means that they tend to change together. For example, height and weight are correlated because a tall person also tends to be a heavy one. To say that education and income are positively correlated is merely to say that those with more education tend to have more income. It does not mean that the increase in education is the *cause* of the greater income.

What often happens when two characteristics are correlated is that some third factor which is not being considered is the actual cause of changes in the other two. Every social scientist has a favorite example of a correlation that obviously is not due to one factor causing the other. My favorite is the one cited by Rudolf Flesch in *The Art of Clear Thinking.*[18] Flesch points out that in Stockholm there has been a very high correlation over the years between the number of babies born and the number of stork nests.* Keep that correlation in mind the next time you hear someone confuse correlation with causation.

In the case of education, there are a number of possible third factors that might explain why someone has both more schooling and a higher income. The family income is one such factor. If you have a rich father, he might pay for your continued education and also help you find a good job when you finally do leave school. In such a case, the increase in income is not due to education at all, and without a rich father, more education is not likely to increase later earnings. It is likely that such third factors as parents' income, occupation, and connections, race, innate intelligence, ethnic group, geographical region, and similar factors account for at least some of the correlation between income and education.[19]

PROBLEMS WITH PERCENTAGES Although percentages are handy statistics, they do have their limitations. Stating one number as a fraction or percentage of another says nothing about the absolute value of either number. This can be quite misleading when the absolute values

---

* It is not difficult to think of third factors that are likely suspects as the true cause of the correlation between storks and birth. Perhaps an increase in the total prosperity of the community is causing more births and, at the same time, luring more storks to larger nesting sites on the roofs of the prosperous houses.

are small. For example, from 1972 to 1974 the number of women candidates for the United States Senate increased by 50 percent.[20] This might suggest a great increase in women's participation in politics until it is recognized that in 1972 there were only two women running for the United States Senate. The 50 percent increase was an increase of only one candidate and was of no significance. When the initial number, called the *base*, is relatively small, even a small increase in the absolute amount will create a deceptively large percentage increase.

The size of the base can also create problems in comparing percentage increases across different groups. For instance, from 1973 to 1974 the average (median) earnings of women increased 6.9 percent, while those of men increased only 5.8 percent. These data might suggest that women were drawing closer to men in income, but in fact, just the opposite was happening. Due to their larger base salary, the men were actually increasing their lead over the women. Women's earnings increased from $6,335 to $6,772, but the men's increased from $11,186 to $11,835.[21] In spite of the greater percentage increase, the women fell $212 further behind the men in annual earnings. Many social problem statistics, such as those that relate changes in income or education to race or sex, have substantial differences in their base figures, and extreme care must be taken in interpreting these percentage change statistics.

A similar problem can arise with percentages when there is a natural limit, or *ceiling*, on the size a number can reach. As the number approaches its natural limit, percentage increase *must* get smaller and smaller. For example, one writer on social problems reported that from 1920 to 1960 the average (median) level of schooling for blacks jumped from 5.4 to 10.8 years, a 100 percent increase. During the same 40-year period, the average schooling for whites increased "only" 45 percent, from 8.5 to 12.3 years.* It was concluded that, "Significantly, the *rate* at which Negroes are increasing their educational level is greater than that of whites."[22] Actually, these data are not very significant. In order for the whites to have increased their years of schooling 100 percent, they would need an average of 17 years of schooling in 1960. Over half of the white population would have to have gone to graduate school! This was clearly impossible. Because of a ceiling on education, the figures for whites could not have increased as much as those for blacks.

---

*It should be noted that perhaps due to different definitions of "schooling," these figures are somewhat different from other common estimates.

When there is a choice in what base to use, you can be sure that people will choose the most flattering one. An incumbent politician running for reelection will probably cite the economic indicators as a percentage of the figures from the latest recession year to make them appear all the better. The opponent will doubtless choose the base figures from a boom year to make things seem all the worse. A technique used by manufacturers and retailers is to describe their profits in terms of percent of sales, which makes them appear smaller than if they had used percent of invested capital or costs. As a general rule, profits should be reported as a percentage of investment.[23]

When the base is chosen completely arbitrarily in order to make a figure more "meaningful," just about anything goes. If your pet program would cost about $5 billion, you can point out that it will cost less than 40 percent of what the nation spends on tobacco every year. Meanwhile, opponents of your program can report that this "extravagant waste of the taxpayers' money" will cost more than twice the total annual expenditures for the nation's judicial system.[24] Both percentages are correct simply because we spend a lot more to support our craving for nicotine than our craving for justice. It is best to ignore such comparisons and convert to capitas. By using the same capita scale for all expenditures, you will be able to compare the costs of programs without bias. Five billion dollars is 25 capitas regardless of what the nation spends on tobacco, alcohol, chewing gum, dog food, or other popular statistical smoke screens.

SAMPLING

Many people are unduly bothered by social science sampling or polling. Whenever an opinion poll predicts incorrectly, these people enjoy a perverse satisfaction, as if their free will and personal dignity had been vindicated. Actually, if your goal is to be unpredictable, the best way to make your decision would be by flipping a coin at the last possible moment. No poll taker would be able to predict your decision. Of course, you will not have saved your free will; you will have lost it in order to appear unpredictable.

The fact is that opinion polls can predict your opinion fairly well by determining that of your friends and neighbors. They can predict the opinion of the nation as a whole by asking a small but representative sample of its citizens. On the average in recent national elections, the Gallup Poll has successfully predicted the final vote within about one and a half percentage points.[25] That is a pretty fair batting average.

You should not be deceived by the vast size of the population of the United States and other populations pollsters must deal with. In reality, it makes little difference in practical procedures whether the population being sampled is 1 million or 200 million. For most statistical purposes, it is satisfactory to assume the population is infinitely large and then ignore its actual size.

Nor is the size of the sample all that important. Obviously, poll takers have to sample more than a few individuals if they wish to generalize to the total population. But samples of hundreds of thousands or millions are a waste of time. Perhaps the most famous failure of a political opinion poll was the *Literary Digest*'s prediction that Alfred E. Landon would defeat Franklin D. Roosevelt in the 1936 presidential election. Roosevelt proceeded to win by a landslide, and the *Literary Digest* and political polling, in general, were acutely embarrassed. The *Literary Digest*'s erroneous prediction was based on analysis of more than 2 *million* questionnaires.[26] Clearly, their problem was not too small a sample. The Gallup Poll and the Roper Poll, using much smaller samples, correctly predicted a Roosevelt victory.

Most national opinion polls found in the news, such as the typical Harris Poll or Gallup Poll, use a sample of about 1,200 to 1,600 persons.[27] In estimating simple dichotomized responses (whether someone agrees or disagrees with a statement, is for or against a proposal, will vote Republican or Democratic, etc.), a representative sample of 1,200 to 1,600 will generally give results accurate to within two or three percentage points of the total national average. Pollster Louis Harris has stated, "The sampling is painstakingly pursued, so that by 1973, we can say confidently that any national sample we construct will be accurate to within 3 percentage points on a sample of 1,500 or over in 95 out of 100 cases."[28] This degree of accuracy is sufficient for most purposes, and unless many thousands more respondents are added, it will not be substantially improved. Many people find it difficult to believe that a survey of less than one thousandth of 1 percent of a population can tell us very much about the population as a whole, but statistically that is precisely the way it is.

The real problem with sampling is achieving a representative sample, one that fairly reflects the average person. In the *Literary Digest* poll, for example, the sample was drawn from lists of telephone and automobile owners. In those days, the people with telephones and automobiles were more well-to-do (and more Republican) than a representative sample of the American voter. The ideal technique in any scientific survey is random sampling, in which all members of the population under study have an equal chance of being surveyed. Unfortunately, there is no list of all persons in the United States to draw a random sample from. Instead of a completely random sample, present-day pollsters use a system of certain key geographical districts. When put together, these districts represent the nation as a whole in terms of population density (e.g., rural versus urban), geographical region (e.g., North versus South), racial composition (e.g., black versus white), and other important considerations. When feasible, random sampling is used in selecting representative districts and individuals within each district.

Even if the sample is representative in theory, numerous possibilities for bias remain. Questions might be worded with a certain slant that influences the response. By means of unconscious gestures or intonations, the interviewer might suggest a certain answer. The sex, age, race, or appearance of the interviewer can also affect the response. The interviewer might be tempted to skip a house with a large growling dog outside or one with a surly band of young men sharpening their switchblades on the front steps. As a result, those who keep watchdogs or belong to street gangs might be underrepresented in the survey. Contemporary professional poll takers have done a pretty good job of minimizing such biases, but occasional mistakes can still happen.

It should also be remembered that an adequate sample for surveying the nation as a whole might be entirely inadequate for making finer analyses. A representative sample of 2,000 Americans would be of little value in comparing rural Jews with rural Catholics. If certain specific comparisons between groups are desired, the sample would have to contain a disproportionate number of members of those groups.

AVERAGES

Whether a sample is surveyed or the total population is observed, the basic goal of many studies is to determine the average or, as statisticians like to put it, the *central tendency* of the population. There are three common measures of central tendency found in studies of social problems.

The *mean*. The mean is simply the total of a set of scores divided by the number of scores that went into the total. Bowling average, earned run average in baseball, and average yards per carry in football are familiar examples of means. When someone simply reports the "average" without explanation, it is usually the mean that is being used.

Both the advantage and the disadvantage of the mean is that it is influenced by every score in the total. An increase or decrease in any one score will always change the mean. As a result, the mean can be quite deceptive when one score is markedly different from the rest. If a city block has 19 families which earn $1,000 a year and one that makes $1 million, the mean income per family on that block is $50,950. When there are a few extreme scores, the mean should not be used as a measure of central tendency.

It also should be remembered that the mean attempts to describe *all* the scores in general; it does not attempt to describe any *one* in particular. If half the people in a certain district have a Ph.D. and the other half never finished grade school, on the mean they have a 12th grade education. In cases like these, we have the paradox that no one is "average." The situation is like the man who has one foot sizzling in a bucket of hot water and the other freezing in a bucket of ice water—on the average, he is quite comfortable.

The *median*. In order to avoid the problem of a few extreme scores overly influencing the average, statisticians sometimes prefer to use the median or middlemost score as the measure of central tendency. They simply rank-order the scores from smallest to largest and then find the score that divides the list exactly in half; that is the median score.* Since half the scores are above the median and half are below, it does provide a handy measure of the central tendency of the total distribution. If the whole distribution moves up or down, the median will change accordingly, but if only a few extreme scores shift at one end, the median is not affected.

However, the median, like the mean, may be a poor measure of any one in particular. In the case of the population where half had a Ph.D. and the other half never finished grade school, the median would agree with the mean that the average person had a 12th grade education.

*If there is an even number of scores, they would take the distance halfway between the two middle scores as the median.

The *mode*. When you wish to make sure that at least some people do fall on the average, use the mode as the measure of central tendency. The mode is simply the most common score. If more people use brand X than any other brand, brand X is the mode.

To see how these different measures of average compare, look at the distribution of scores below that might represent the number of children per family in an apartment building:

0
0
0
1
1
2
3
3
4
4
5
6
8

These 13 numbers have been listed from smallest to largest to make the median easy to find. The 7th or middle score is 3, so the median number of children per family is 3. The mean of these numbers is $37 \div 13 = 2.9$,* which agrees rather well with the median. However, the mode of the scores is 0, which does not seem to represent the distribution very well. As this example shows, one problem with the mode is that in attempting to find a score that represents at least some people, you might find a score that represents *most* people rather poorly. The mode is still a very useful average for some kinds of data that cannot be added together or ranked from smallest to largest. We can say that the average person in the United States is white because we are using the mode as the definition of average. It would make little sense to add together the skin colors of the people in America and conclude that the average American is slightly brownish pink.

---

* Sometimes, in order to create a false impression of precision, a mean or similar statistic will be reported to a number of decimal places. This is fine if the sample is quite large, but with a small sample like the one above, it would be mathematically correct but statistically fraudulent to report the mean as 2.846154.

THE LIMITATIONS OF STATISTICS

As we have seen, mathematical tricks can be played with statistics. However, in dealing with common statistics regarding social problems, the greater danger is that, while you are worried about the mathematics, the basic *idea* behind the statistics will be completely fooling you. One limitation of social problem statistics is so important that the entire next chapter will be devoted to it. Several more limited difficulties can be briefly mentioned here.

MISPLACED PRECISION

Here is an important rule to bear in mind concerning social problem statistics: *It is better to have a rough measure of what you are really interested in than a precise measure of something unimportant.* If you forget this rule, you are likely to make the error of misplaced precision. Those who fall into this error expend great time and effort in the creation of mountains of precise figures that have little to do with anything important. The news will dutifully report these figures with the usual air of solemnity, and many people will become convinced that the statistics are of the utmost importance.

A famous recent example of misplaced precision was the "body counts" issued regularly during the Vietnam War. Corpses are handy things to count, but as we eventually discovered, they are easier to produce than victories. The body counts may have been inflated by overzealous arithmetic on the part of the military, yet they suffered from the more serious error of misplaced precision. Body counts simply do not measure an enemy's capacity or will to resist. America won the body counts, but it did not win the war.

THE CASE OF UNEMPLOYMENT Americans are fascinated by economic indicators. Monthly, quarterly, and annual reports on unemployment, housing starts, the balance of payments, and the Gross National Product are as common as murders and football scores on the evening news. To borrow Hobart Rowen's phrase, we have become a nation of "economic hypochondriacs."[29] Unfortunately, most economic indicators are examples of misplaced precision as far as social problems are concerned.

Let us consider the case of unemployment statistics, the economic index which probably causes the most worry. In early 1977 there were approximately 90 million people employed in the United States.[30] Since there were about 215 million persons in the country, 125 million were *not* employed. But it would be misleading to report an unemployment rate of 58 percent (125 million ÷ 215 million) because most of the 125 million unemployed were children and others we would not expect to be working. To make the unemployment figures meaningful, they must be taken as a percentage of those who should be working and not the total population. But this only highlights the problem: How do we determine who "ought" to be working?

The government defines the official civilian labor force as those who either are working or who are looking for a job as determined by government polls of the population. Using the official labor force as the base, the unemployment rate in 1977 fluctuated around 7.5 percent. A major problem in this definition of the labor force is that many of those who neither had a job nor were actively looking for one had simply given up the frustrating search. Many others felt it was wrong for them to look for a job, although they might earnestly wish to have one. These would include the disabled, many housewives, older citizens who are "supposed" to be retired, and the young who are "supposed" to be in school. Many of them would eagerly join the labor force if they thought a decent job would be available. At the same time, the number of those considered employed is inflated by counting those working part time, those working a few days at a temporary job, those who are on strike, and those who are idle due to bad weather or illness. In other words, many of the employed are earning little or no money.[31]

Other difficulties with the official unemployment figures have the opposite effect of exaggerating the "unemployment problem." A man who quits one job and lives off his wife's $25,000-a-year salary while leisurely looking for another is officially unemployed. So also is a teenager who lives at home, spends his time at the beach, and claims to be looking for work. So also is a prostitute who earns $30,000 a year while supposedly an unemployed waitress. So also is a New Yorker who spends his winter playing golf in Florida while collecting unemployment insurance. As economist Milton Friedman has argued:

> Anecdotes are not proof, but they illustrate the principle that changes in social arrangements that have made unemployment more attractive have also tended to increase the number of persons who so record themselves.[32]

Many of those officially listed as unemployed are suffering no great economic hardship.

Those who emphasize the problem of unemployment point to the fact that many of the unemployed are not fairly represented in the official records.[33] Those who wish to minimize the unemployment problem point out that many of those who are officially unemployed are living quite comfortably. Both are right. The unemployment figures, while of great interest to professional economists, are not measures of economic hardship or poverty.

Nothing makes this point more clearly than the presence of millions of "working poor" in the United States. In 1974 the heads of the *majority* of families living in poverty worked at least part of the year, and about one-fifth of poor families were headed by someone who worked *year-round, full-time*.[34] We have been told so often about the poor on welfare that we tend to forget that poverty can also be associated with work. Many of those who are supporting a family while earning the federal minimum wage are living in poverty, and some workers do not even earn the minimum wage. In summary, as a measure of social problems, the unemployment figures, like the body counts of the Vietnam War, are examples of misplaced precision.

WHO IS GETTING WHAT FROM WHOM?

One of the most common kinds of social problem statistics is the report on how much something costs. Earlier in this chapter, we considered ways to interpret the enormous costs of social programs. Even when the cost of a program becomes meaningful, however, there are still important questions to be answered. A good habit to get into when listening to a news report on the budget for some social program is to ask yourself: *Exactly who is getting what from whom?*

Those who are responsible for naming social programs have an understandable tendency to describe them in the most favorable light. Like the names for perfumes, the titles of social programs are more often alluring than descriptive. A program that makes you poorer is likely to be called an *antipoverty* program. One that will increase your taxes and give the money to someone else will probably be called a *job creation* program. Your job in hearing about the program is to determine exactly *who* is getting *what* jobs, and *who* is paying how much for them. Analyzing the three *w*'s of *who* is giving, *who* is receiving, and *what* is being accomplished can help you decide if the popular label placed on the program is really accurate.

At the beginning of this chapter, I mentioned a news report that $331 billion is spent annually on social welfare programs. When the word "welfare" is mentioned, the association with "public aid" for the poor immediately comes to mind. But who is actually getting that money? A sum of $331 billion is $1,655 capitas. That is an awful lot of money! If the poorest 25 percent in the United States received that amount every year from the other 75 percent, they would be receiving more than $6,000 apiece. Obviously, a poor family of four is not receiving an income of $25,000 a year from the government. The phrase "social welfare" in this context actually refers to *all* programs that are supposed to encourage the social health of the nation. This includes social security, which costs the poor relatively more than the affluent because it is a tax on the lower part of one's earned income. It also includes aid to higher education, which goes more to the well-to-do because the poor drop out of school earlier. The phrase "social welfare" has powerful associations, but it is too broad to be meaningful. It tells us nothing about the three *w*'s.

Even in the case of smaller, more specific programs, it is often difficult to determine who the people are that are gaining the real benefit from the program. The food stamp program, for example, is often considered an aid to the poor, which it is. But it aids the farmers and food manufacturers by encouraging the poor to buy more food, especially more expensive, processed foods. The fact that the food stamp program is administered by the Department of Agriculture suggests that farmers have more than a passing interest in this "welfare" measure.

And, of course, the administrators, bureaucrats, and lawyers involved in social programs cannot be forgotten. To take an extreme case, a small township near Chicago spent $4,105 for "general assistance" in a recent year. An investigation by a local newspaper revealed the following breakdown in costs for that "assistance" program:

$2,500—administrator's salary
   720—office rent (which also went to the administrator, who used his home as an office)
   585—secretary's salary
   200—phone expenses
   100—food for the needy[35]

When asked how it could possibly cost $4,005 to distribute $100 in assistance, the administrator explained, "A lot of people make false claims for relief, and they have to be investigated."[36] The taxpayers certainly would not want to be taken advantage of by the poor!

Along the same lines, it has been estimated that if all the money spent on various agencies and assistance programs for "Indian affairs" were simply handed to the Indians, every man, woman, and child would receive more than $8,000 annually.[37] Rather than being among the most impoverished citizens in the United States, the Indians would be among the most affluent if only they received all the money spent in their name. In general, all of the poor would be much better off if they received all the "antipoverty" funds spent supposedly in their behalf.[38]

PARADOXICAL STATISTICS

Sometimes a measure of how *bad* a social problem is will show an *increase* when times get *better*. These contradictory or paradoxical statistics are quite common and, if they are not interpreted with caution, can give a completely inaccurate impression.

Unemployment figures furnish an excellent example of a paradoxical statistic due to the fact that someone must be looking for a job in order to be officially unemployed. A housewife might really want a job but feel too discouraged to actually search for one. When she perceives an improvement in the economy, she will be encouraged to dust off her résumé and start looking. As a result of her increased prospects for a job, there has been an *increase* in the number of unemployed. In the same vein, it has been argued that as more young women enter the labor force, they must begin with the lower-paying jobs. Therefore, a *reduction* in sexual discrimination in hiring can result in an *increase* in the income gap between women and men as the women move into the lower-paying jobs.[39]

Crime statistics also can act paradoxically because there is a volunteer effect. Many crimes must be reported to the police by the victims in order to be officially recognized as crimes. When the victims have little faith in the police, they may simply fail to report the crime. As a result, when faith in the police increases, the official number of crimes will also increase. Along the same lines, if the police employ more efficient methods of record keeping, the result can be an apparent crime wave.[40] Doubtless, it was with such thoughts in mind that one mayor recently proclaimed, "There has been an increase in reported rapes every year I've been mayor—and I'm proud of it."[41]

Sometimes the relationship between an improvement in society and an increase in the official incidence of a social problem is quite indirect. For example, sociologist Phillips Cutright has shown that the increase in illegitimate births in the United States in the last several decades was due in large part to better nutrition and health care for young women.[42] Poor health can result in a reduction in fertility and an increase in the number of miscarriages. Without any change in premarital sexual habits or the use of birth control, healthier women will have more illegitimate children. Therefore, the rise in out-of-wedlock births might actually reflect more on the increased health of the nation than on any changes in our sexual habits.

This concludes our overview of the potentials and limitations of statistics in understanding social problems. In the next chapter, we will see what is really wrong with common social problem statistics.

SUMMARY

In order to escape dangerous biases in information processing, social scientists rely on statistics. These numbers, which condense information into manageable size, are too often misunderstood or ignored. The tremendous cost of social programs and other large numbers are usually more meaningful when considered in per capita terms or as a percentage of some other figure. Percentages are valuable, but tricky, statistics because of such problems as choosing an appropriate base and interpreting percentage change. Due to the rapid accumulation of their effects, compounded percentages relating to the value of education, the population explosion, and other problems are especially deceptive.

Three different averages—the mean, median, and mode—are valuable in different situations as measures of the overall average. Even though the average or other statistic is based on a sample or poll, it still can be important. In spite of appearances, a sample of a fraction of 1 percent of the population can be quite valuable.

There are dangers as well in the use of statistics. It is easy to get so wrapped up in the numbers that you lose sight of the thing that is supposed to be measured. The result is a precise figure that measures nothing important. Unemployment, Gross National Product, and other economic indicators are not direct measures of happiness, poverty, or well-being. The label placed on a statistic can also be misleading. To say an amount is *for* a purpose, like reducing poverty, does not prove that the amount really *goes* to that purpose. Lastly, some statistics, such as unemployment figures and the incidence of reported crime, are paradoxical in that they may appear to get worse when social conditions actually improve. In general, when interpreted with caution, social science statistics are invaluable aids to understanding social problems.

FOUR

Why Official Statistics
Are Misleading

It would seem that statistics are the one thing we have enough of. By the time you have reached middle age, you will have filled out enough questionnaires, surveys, inquiries, polls, and forms to create an ocean of information. Every time you do anything the least bit unusual—sell a car, buy a gun, get married, obtain a passport, go to school, or get a job—you are hit with another wave. And when you finally go to your reward, by a kind of statistical inertia, your mortal remains will continue to contribute to the death certificates, coroner's reports, and estate and inheritance records.

It might seem that understanding social problems merely involves putting all these data together in some meaningful order, and that the only real danger would be drowning in the sea of useless information before finding the pertinent facts. Unfortunately, this is not so. Much information for the study of social problems has yet to be collected. Due to several interrelated social processes, the important material for understanding social problems is often precisely the information that is lacking. In this chapter, we will examine these processes to see why official records are misleading. We must begin with a review of some sociological theory.

THE IMPORTANCE OF INFORMAL RELATIONS

It was the pioneer American sociologist Charles Horton Cooley who first pointed out the important distinction between primary and secondary groups.[1] A secondary group has formal rules, explicit roles, and specified authority relations; it is typically a large social enterprise. Examples of secondary groups would include the United States Army, the Catholic Church, and any large business company. In these structures, there is an explicit set of rules governing the interaction among members. Even if you have never previously met the person with whom you are dealing—a common experience in secondary groups— you still know which of you is the boss. Uniforms, insignia, titles, and other devices make it possible for complete strangers to "know their place." Thus, the junior executive defers to the vice president, the monk to the bishop, and the major to the general.

Primary groups, on the other hand, are small, personal groups characterized by sustained, intimate, face-to-face relations. There is no need for titles or uniforms because the individuals know each other personally. The family is the fundamental primary group. It is through the family that individuals achieve the basic socialization that allows them later to associate successfully in larger secondary groups. Other primary groups, including the peer group, the adolescent clique, and the "neighborhood," are also instrumental in creating a fully socialized member of society.

Sometimes two people may belong to common secondary and primary groups simultaneously and must change from formal to informal relations depending on the situation. The boss may have a love affair with his secretary. At dinner she may call him "Johnny." In bed it may be "Tiger" or "Lambkins." But in the office, it is still "Mr. Snodgrass."* As you can imagine, making such swings in social relationships is not always easy, and the subsequent conflicts between formal and informal can compromise the normal functioning of either group. To protect itself from such compromises, the secondary group frequently creates norms or regulations forbidding the intrusion of informal relations into the structure of the secondary group. Many cor-

---

* Roger Brown reports an interesting example of the shift from formal to informal address. French mountain climbers who are not close friends will address each other by the formal *vous* when they begin their ascent. But when they reach a critical altitude, they shift to the more intimate *tu*, as if in recognition that their lives are now intimately joined together.[2]

porations have nepotism rules forbidding executives from hiring their relatives. Colleges may forbid professors from dating their students. Corporations often warn management about becoming too friendly with the workers. And in the army, an officer is not supposed to fraternize with the enlisted men. In general, there is friction between official authority structures and intimate, friendly relations.

FORMAL REALITY VERSUS INFORMAL REALITY

The possibility of conflict between the formal and the informal provides a clue as to why official records are misleading. Official records concentrate on the formal structure of secondary groups and tend to ignore primary groups. It is the secondary groups that provide the explicit regulations, and relationships that are easily converted into statistical information. It is the secondary groups that communicate by means of letters, memoranda, invoices, order forms, and other official papers. Primary groups do not usually keep records because their members know what has happened without having to create a file on it. It is also possible that members of primary groups do not actually know what they are doing; their relationships may be unconscious.*

Thus, official statistics focus on secondary, formal actions which omit a great deal of social reality. These omissions are extremely important because primary groups are not only primary in the sense that they precede the formation of secondary groups. They are also primary in the more important sense that they are *fundamental*. They provide the foundation for secondary groups. Behind the skeleton of formal relations, there are always informal relations giving life to society. No matter how many secondary groups you belong to, you still need the intimate, friendly, trusting relationships that define primary groups. A person needs to let her hair down, relax, be spontaneous, and interact with others on a personal basis. Primary groups do contain authority or status hierarchies, just as parents have authority over their children,

---

* Numerous television game shows are based on this fact. A husband and wife may be asked separately such questions as, "Who is the boss in the family?" or, "Who is in charge of disciplining the children?" The frequent disagreements that result provide for the embarrassment of the couple and the enjoyment of the audience. Such disagreements are not possible in large secondary organizations because official records explicitly state who is the boss. Of course, the official records could be misleading, but at least there is an official answer that will be the same for everyone.

but authority in the primary group is overshadowed by a sense of solidarity among the members.

These primary groups do not exist alongside and apart from the secondary groups; they are *within* and *a part of* all secondary groups. In spite of frequent attempts of the secondary group to minimize the influence of such informal relations, they exert a great influence on the total operation of the larger group. As Peter Blau has observed, the emergence of important informal relations is not the accidental result of some particularly inefficient bureaucracy. It is the inherent byproduct of any large organization.

> When we examine sufficiently small segments of bureaucracies to observe their operations in detail, we discover patterns of activities and interactions that cannot be accounted for by the official structure. Whether the work group is part of the armed forces, a factory, or civilian government, it is characterized by a network of informal relations and a set of unofficial practices which have been called its "informal organization." This concept calls attention to the fact that deviations from the formal blueprint are socially organized patterns and not merely the consequence of fortuitous personality differences. . . .
>
> Regularities do not occur accidentally. That official rules bring them about is expected, but what is the source of those regularities in social conduct that do not reflect official standards? They are also the result of normative standards, but standards that have emerged in the work group itself rather than having been officially instituted by superiors or formal blueprints. In the course of social interaction at work, there arise patterned expectations and norms, which find expression in a network of social relationships and in prevailing practices.[3]

A famous example of the importance of these small, primary groups was provided by Edward Shils and Morris Janowitz's study of the Wehrmacht (German armed forces) in World War II.[4] Shils and Janowitz attempted to determine why the German Army fought on to the bitter end when realistically they should have known their cause was lost. In thinking of answers to this question, a number of hypotheses come to mind: indoctrination in Nazi Youth Camps, the Hitler propaganda machine, the traditional Prussian military mind, the rigid authoritarianism of the Wehrmacht, and fear of retaliation by ruthless Nazis. But none of these were sufficient to make the German soldiers fight on. It was the soldier's primary group that kept him going. From numerous interviews with German POW's, Shils and Janowitz concluded that as long as the soldier's primary group remained intact, he was determined to fight with them. When asked why he did not surrender, the typical German soldier would reply, "What? And let my buddies down?"

One of the most formal organizations in America is the New York Stock Exchange. The exchange is regulated by an abundance of laws and rules, and generates more than its fair share of paperwork. But in spite of all the formalities, at its heart is a personal deal between two members of the same "club." At the exchange, a bid to buy stock

> . . . is accepted with a simple nod and a word, no time here for signatures, legal forms, or even a handshake. On the floor of the exchange, a man's word must *literally* be above question. Just one attempt to wriggle out of an oral deal in which he discovers that he made an error, and the broker is professionally dead.[5]

Legislative bodies provide yet another example of the importance of primary relations. Any state legislature is explicitly defined in all aspects of its operation, from the procedures for gaining membership to the most minute details of the rules of deliberation. Nevertheless, in order to make the official structure work at all, it must be interwoven with a network of informal rules. In spite of their mutual public criticism, especially at election time, all the legislators are members of the same informal club. The informal rules of the club take precedence over the formal in two respects.

First, the informal rules are the real center of activity. Most of the important decisions are made in offices, restaurants, and the legendary smoke-filled rooms far from written records and the rules of parliamentary procedure. At a later time, the members will come together in committee or in the General Assembly to record officially the decision they have agreed on at these informal meetings.

Second, when there is an explicit conflict between the formal and informal rules, the informal usually wins. Legislators, like other workers, learn to bypass the official rules. These subterfuges range from major departures from the constitution to minor fictions, such as stopping the clock in the Assembly to maintain the illusion that the session ended on time.

The last hours of the legislative session are a particularly hectic time which leads to abandoning even the more modest attempts at decorum and public deference to the official rules. The *Chicago Tribune* created a minor stir in 1973 when it published photographs of the last moments of the Illinois General Assembly. Included were pictures of the twelve-year-old son of one of the representatives voting for seven departed legislators.[6] (Legislators, like other workers, will sometimes "cover" for a co-worker who has to leave early.) The official electronic scoreboard of the Assembly dutifully recorded the votes of the missing legislators on millions of dollars in appropriations. Reaction to the publication of the pictures was interesting. Representatives urged a ban on taking photos in the Assembly.[7] When the *informal* activities were made *formal* (by being photographed), the cry was for *formal* regulation forcing the activity to remain *informal* (hidden). Thus, the official structure is employed to protect the informal structure, which itself contradicts the formal structure.

This description of the formal and informal levels of activity that are found in any large organization should make it clear that reading official records can give a very misleading impression of the actual decision making, communication, and exercise of power that exists in our major institutions. It is like a tailor trying to understand a fabric by examining only the horizontal threads. This does not mean that the informal is generally in conflict with the formal over ultimate goals. The conflict can be merely a difference in procedure.[8]

For example, when workers ignore management's safety regulations, they are not necessarily trying to sabotage the mutual goal of efficient production. They may honestly feel that they can work more efficiently by ignoring the official rules. There are few workers who have not at one time or another decided they can fulfill the company's ultimate objectives better by skirting its rules. But because this does constitute violation of the rules, knowledge of these activities must be kept within the informal group. So even when everyone in the primary group knows what is actually happening, they cannot let the official records reveal what is going on. The official records and formal statistics will be made to coincide with the official rules. *As a result, official records sometimes bear little resemblance to what is really happening in society.*

In many cases, the authorities of the formal organization know that the official records are greatly in error. They too may "look the other way" and ignore the violations of the rules and the creation of false statistics. In the case of safety rules, the management may have created the regulations only to satisfy some third party, such as an insurance company, the general public, union officials, or the state regulatory agencies. The third party, in turn, may have forced the creation of the rules only to satisfy another, fourth party. The result is that many of our official rules and the official records they generate are thorough fictions which have little to do with social reality. The groups involved, all of whom really know better, continue the masquerade because no one is quite sure what the other really knows.* Meanwhile, statisticians continue dutifully to record the official misinformation, and the illusion is maintained that what is being recorded is an honest reflection of what is happening in our society.[9]

GOING BY THE RULES Perhaps the easiest way to see how this fiction operates is to consider the strategy of "going by the rules," which is sometimes employed in labor disputes. The strategy is similar to striking, only in striking labor refuses to work, and in going by the rules labor reduces output by obeying all the official rules precisely. In some industries, the official rules have been ignored for so long that they have lost all resemblance to the work that is actually performed. Therefore, by obeying all the rules, the workers can substantially reduce their effectiveness, still officially do their jobs and get paid, and simultaneously embarrass management by exposing the silliness of their official rules.

British workers are particularly adept at going by the rules. In 1974, when the cost of buying Britain's essential oil was soaring, the coal miners refused to work overtime, a ploy that reduced coal production by an estimated 40 percent.[10] By working a "normal" work week, it became clear to the miners, the coal companies, and the nation as a whole that overtime was actually an economic necessity. About the same time, the British locomotive engineers refused to operate engines not equipped with speedometers, employing a rule that was previously ignored, which had much the same effect as a strike.[11]

In 1975 thousands of British doctors in a dispute over wages and hours decided to hold strictly to the work schedule stipulated in their contracts, rather than providing the usual overtime work. The effect was to precipitate what one medical journal called "the greatest threat to the NHS [British National Health Service] in the 26 years of its history."[12] Whether you are a coal miner or a physician, the official work week may bear little resemblance to the job that must be done.

As a general principle, the further the rules are removed from social reality, the more powerful is the technique of following them. Because the rules of "law and order" have drifted quite far from social

---

*In traditional folklore, such as the story of "The Emperor's New Clothes," it is often a child who breaks out with the truth that everyone is avoiding.

reality, one of the most powerful job actions available to the police is simply going by the rules. For example, if a policeman were to write all the traffic tickets he could according to the law, he would be a very busy man, indeed. The police usually develop an informal quota of tickets that represents a "good day's work," and minor violations, such as going only seven miles over the official speed limit, are ignored.[13] As one policeman facetiously put it: "I've written a lot of citations this month, so now a guy would have to run me over to get a ticket."[14]

In September, 1972, a group of disgruntled Chicago policemen went on a "ticket blitz," writing several times the usual number of traffic tickets.[15] When a small number of police began writing up to ten tickets a day—certainly a modest number for one day—it tilted the delicate balance of "law and order" away from the expected, informal routine and toward the actual enforcement of the letter of the law. Naturally, it launched a torrent of protest. One alderman, whose Cadillac got a citation for being parked too near a fire hydrant, cried that they were "crucifying the people of Chicago."[16] The chief judge of the Traffic Court bravely proclaimed that they could handle the increase in cases "as long as they don't keep it up too long."[17] Cab drivers protested that they were in danger of losing their licenses, and hence their jobs, by unfair ticketing.[18]

Six of the eight police organizations quickly denounced the blitz.[19] One city newspaper editorially condemned the ticket writing as a "display of petty zealousness that did absolutely nothing either for law and order or for the image of the policeman."[20] Another newspaper attack more bluntly warned that the campaign to enforce the letter of the law was "brutal enough to turn everyone in the city into a cop-hater almost overnight."[21]

Meanwhile, the forces of informal law and order were moving into action. The Chicago Police Superintendent vowed that policemen guilty of excessive ticket writing would be punished.[22] One district Commander sentenced those suspected of being overly zealous to that cruelest of fates—walking the beat.[23] Another hit even harder by threatening the loss of permission to hold a second job.[24] A spokesman for the ticket writers could only weakly respond, "How can they punish a policeman for doing his job?"[25]

The dissident policemen quickly broke under the pressure, and the ticket-writing campaign stopped only four days after it began. Their only defense was that they were doing their job, a poor excuse when the average citizen knows that the official rules are not supposed to be strictly enforced. But all that occurred during the blitz was that a small number of policemen increased their output in one category—traffic tickets. One can only imagine what would happen if *all* the police started enforcing *all* the laws.

PRIVACY AND PERSONAL PROTECTION

Another reason why the important facts remain unrecorded is that collection of information is contrary to the cherished American value of privacy. Even if we are not engaged in any particularly embarrassing activity, we still don't like strangers listening to our conversations, reading our mail, looking over our shoulders while we work, or snooping into our personal affairs. Although all people cherish their privacy, some are in a better position than others to realize their desire. Privacy, like money, education, leisure, and other valued goals, is most easily obtained if you have wealth and power to begin with. Therefore, those whose activities are most important for understanding social problems are the ones whose activities we know the least about. By contrast, those at the bottom of the social ladder are more easily subjected to surveillance. To take the extreme case, those at the very bottom, such as prisoners in jail, may be watched twenty-four hours a day over closed-circuit television.

The differences in the amount of privacy allotted various groups can be observed clearly in the operation of the average manufacturing corporation. The blue-collar workers are expected to punch a time clock which records their work time to the nearest minute. Unless their job requires mobility, they are expected to be at their stations at all times except for specified breaks. Lower-level workers are frequently monitored on their progress in meeting various schedules, rates, quotas, and "keeping up with the line." Secretaries and lower-level white-collar workers are allowed slightly more privacy, but are still expected to be at their desks. If a secretary has an office, it typically has a glass door so that she can be observed on the job.

The boss, however, has his own private, sound-insulated office, with heavy wooden doors guarded by at least one secretary. Unlike the common laborer, the boss cannot be "seen." When dealing with a really important executive, it is not always possible to determine if he is even "in." The ultimate in privacy for the powerful was exemplified by the case of billionaire Howard Hughes. In the last years of his life, Hughes was so successful at not being seen that there was serious doubt that he even existed. Only a man of great wealth can be so important that it is uncertain whether or not he is alive.

We still know so little about the rich that some sociologists have been forced to employ the rather pathetic data-gathering technique of analyzing the Social Register or the society columns in the newspaper.[26] This frequently provides some interesting data about the lifestyles of the wealthy—where they vacation, where they live, etc.—but is obviously of quite limited value in understanding their activities regarding social problems.

PROTECTING POLITICIANS

Many of those who recognize that as a rule the rich lead sheltered lives mistakenly believe that politicians form an important exception to the rule. It is true that, with recent trends toward income disclosure and other considerations, we now know more about politicians than we did before. But many of the recent revelations have served only to remind us of how little we do know. In recent years, the public has received intimations concerning the extramarital affairs of three modern American Presidents (Warren Harding, Franklin D. Roosevelt, and John F. Kennedy). We have discovered the most egregious misconduct on the part of the FBI, CIA, and other government agencies. We have endured the amazing complex of disclosures known collectively as "Watergate," in which a number of high government officials have been found guilty of assorted felonies. The Congress has been disgraced by the "Koreagate" scandals and revelations that Congressional workers have been employed for their sexual rather than secretarial services. A recent Vice-President of the United States resigned under accusations of bribery, while his opponent for the job had to resign from the campaign upon disclosure of a long history of emotional instability. The President of the United States, leaving office under a cloud of disgrace, was granted an unprecedented special pardon from prosecution.

The fact that many of these embarrassments have been discovered only by accident reminds us further of how little we really know about the private lives of politicians. When Ted Kennedy drove off the bridge at Chappaquiddick or Wilbur Mills was discovered in an awkward situation with a strip-teaser, many people began to realize that even those presented as Presidential prospects are largely unknown persons. It was probably the publication of the Presidential tapes of Richard Nixon that was most instrumental in revealing the all-important informal level of political life.[27] From the sociological perspective, the wonder is not that the President of the United States committed misdeeds in the White House, but that he installed an automatic system for tape-recording them!

There are a number of techniques cultivated by politicians to insure their privacy. Because most political work is done behind the scenes and not in committees where official records are taken, it is often difficult to determine even where a Congressman is. The Congressman may be on vacation, but his public relations personnel and press secretaries will swamp the public with position papers, white papers, working papers, announcements, and other material prepared by his staff and presented in such a way as to create the impression that the Congressman is incessantly working on solutions to America's social problems. The Congressional Record has traditionally printed materials "presented" by members of Congress without hesitation. It is therefore possible for a Congressman, according to official records, to deliver half a dozen "speeches" to various Congressional committees while he is actually in Paris on a "fact-finding" tour of foreign affairs. In one extreme case in 1976, an entire set of hearings on $2 billion worth of allocations for health care was fabricated from presubmitted materials. The 700 pages of public "testimony" documents flowery introductions to speakers, interrogations, and witty asides, even though the hearings were a complete fiction.[28]

Politicians and other important persons have hired experts to ghost-write speeches and other official statements meant to impress the public with their grasp of the issues. It is grounds for expulsion from many colleges if a student hands in a paper written by someone else. In fact, some states have passed laws against selling term papers for others to submit as their own.[29] Yet many of the same university presidents who vociferously condemn plagiarism on the part of students have "research assistants" to help them produce the speeches and articles necessary to impress the learned community with their scholarly endeavors. And we are no longer surprised to hear that the President retired with his speech writers to draft "his" State of the Union message.

A related popular misunderstanding is that the press is determined to reveal even the slightest indiscretion on the part of important politicians. It is true that if a misdeed has already been made public, the press will delve into it at length, but usually it does not go out of its way to unearth the offense. Newspapermen are more often content to report the official announcements of press secretaries and committee minutes. The press also observes an informal rule of discretion in reporting on the pesonal lives of politicians. The general rule seems to be: Do not report a problem if it is potentially embarrassing but is not likely to affect the politician's competence. A noted instance of this rule was the treatment of Franklin D. Roosevelt's affliction with polio. It was standard practice not to photograph or record the painful awkwardness with which Roosevelt walked or got out of an automobile. The impression was maintained that the President was a thoroughly strong and robust man when, in fact, he was substantially crippled.*

Nor has it been typical for the press to report the sexual or drinking habits of politicians, even though they might make interesting stories. If such reports are thought to be needlessly embarrassing, they are avoided. As Congressman John Lindsay put it:

> It used to be that there were two areas reporters never went into. The "double B's" they called them—booze and broads. . . .
> When I was in Congress, I saw guys in incredibly important positions get up on the floor of the House so drunk they could just barely stand—and nobody said a word about it.[30]

In recent years, the press has become somewhat more aggressive in reporting on the total lives of people in important political positions, but it still has a long way to go. Public officials are still very private citizens.

THE CREATION OF OFFICIAL RECORDS

I have pointed out that official records do not reflect the essential activities of primary groups, and that they often deliberately avoid focusing on important figures. A third reason for the inadequacy of official records is that many of them are deliberately created and applied in order to avoid embarrassing powerful interest groups. It is precisely these groups whose activities would shed the most light on social problems. Official statistics, records, and reports are like arrows. They have

---

*It has been observed that the press did not carry on this tradition regarding Governor George Wallace's 1976 campaign for the Presidency.

a point, and they have a *direction*. Official statistics are *aimed* from one place to another.

One of the first things the beginning social-science student learns is that people are not always eager to fill out even the simplest anonymous questionnaire. They get positively hostile when confronted with a complex, fourteen-page statement to be sworn to, notarized, and filled out in triplicate. There has to be some power behind these statistics to keep them rolling in. Usually that power is the government.

Any statistics that claim to cover all of a specified population cannot be voluntary; they must be obtained with some force behind them. If a company has data on all employees, it is because the employees had to give the data to keep their jobs. If a school has information on all students, it is because the students had to submit it to stay in school. Statistics that are based on samples rather than measures of the total population may be voluntary. But if the information requested is at all personal or potentially embarrassing, people are not likely to volunteer sufficiently to make the figures applicable to the average person. Even if the statistics are relatively easily obtained, someone must still create them by means of interviewing, distributing questionnaires, going through archival records, and other procedures that require at least some effort.

For statistics to exist, therefore, someone must *want* them to exist; there must be some incentive to create them. That someone might be a government agency or large foundation willing to supply a grant to a social scientist. It might be a large corporation willing to pay a marketing research firm to obtain survey data on its products. It might be a university or social science professional group that is interested in the data and will "pay" a scientist to get it by offering prestige, publications, or continued employment. Or maybe a university will "pay" a student to create the statistics with course credits or a university degree. In any case, almost all data relevant to social problems are generated because some person or group with something to offer is interested in those data. The less interest powerful groups have in generating the information, the more unlikely it is that the information will be created in the first place.

A related point to remember is that it is difficult to compare statistics on various groups unless the groups have equal motivation to contribute honestly to those statistics. The official statistics might theoretically cover everyone, but be applied unequally in practice. Income tax records supply an obvious illustration. By means of regulations forcing employers to independently report wages to the Internal Revenue Service, the IRS has a good idea how much members of the working class have made even before they declare their income. By contrast, a wealthy attorney or physician has a greater chance of misstating income than the average wage earner. The next section expands on the difficulties that result when one set of statistics is generated more thoroughly or aggressively than a comparison set.

COMPARISON ACROSS OFFICIAL RECORDS

The most misleading comparisons are those that compare generically different classes of statistics. It is frequently tempting to compare the statistics from one group based on one technique with those on another group using an entirely different technique. These comparisons are usually worthless. For example, periodically the mass media carry a report about abuses in welfare, food stamp programs, Medicare, unemployment insurance, and similar social service programs. It is tempting to interpret these reported abuses as moral statements, but they are actually statistics. They are numbers generated by certain procedures. From the point of view of economic efficiency, revelation of abuse in a social service program may be valuable. But from the perspective of morally evaluating either the program or the people involved, they are uninterpretable.

Let us assume, for the sake of illustration, that we discovered that 25 percent of the recipients of a welfare program are getting more than they "should" according to the official rules. What does this mean? In order to interpret it, we would like to know how this rate of overpayment compares to the rate for other government programs, such as income tax, farm subsidies, and military procurement. But these programs are not usually investigated in such a way as to allow comparison across programs. If we did have different rates of overpayment for two different programs, what would this indicate? It might mean that one program is more closely supervised or is enforced with more severe punishments. Or it could indicate that one set of regulations is easier to understand or more competently administered than the other. Or it might mean that the people who benefit from one program are less skillful in following directions, or are more larcenous or more desperate. It requires a great deal of effort to decide among these alternatives, and the effort is rarely given.

To take a specific example, several years ago the New York State Controller, Arthur Levitt, issued a report on the efficiency of New York City workers.[31] The report observed that inspectors for the Buildings Department spent "considerably less than the full day performing their assigned work." It was estimated that at least one third of the inspectors' time was wasted. Drivers for the Municipal Service Administration were observed to work the functional equivalent of a half day for each "workday." At the Bureau of Water Register, clerical employees left before the end of the "workday" and showed a "general low level of performance while in the office." Some field workers actually worked only about half a day.

The efficiency of the Social Services Department is especially interesting because this department was the one responsible for checking up on welfare recipients. Here too the State Controller's report found a low level of performance, with some employees leaving early, others not working while in the office, and some wasting up to two-thirds of their time.[32] Regarding the job performance of those who keep track of the welfare recipients, the New York Times observed:

> Two New York City welfare caseworkers played chess from noon to 2 P.M.—then went out together for half an hour, brought back sandwiches and ate until 3 P.M., when one of them left for the day. The other did no work the rest of the afternoon.
>
> Another caseworker went out at noon, returned at 2 P.M. with shopping bags full of packages and was joined by her sister and nephew, with whom she left about 3 P.M. Her time card showed that somebody had punched her out at 5:02.[33]

The story does not end here. After the New York Times denounced city workers for loafing on the job, an organization of municipal employees turned the tables by sneaking a photographer into the Times' newsroom. The workers subsequently published photos of the newspaper's employees themselves loafing on the job.[34]

It is fashionable in some circles to complain about "welfare shirkers." In other circles, it is stylish to denounce the affluent for making money by sitting on their securities. Could it be that all of us, rich and poor alike, are really not as dedicated to hard work as our official statements might proclaim, and that where the next scandal appears is determined mostly by who is aiming the statistics and where? *Do not take one set of statistics and compare them to another set unless they have been obtained under comparable conditions.*

OFFICIAL RECORDS AS MORAL STATEMENTS

In most cultures there are numerous norms, rules, and laws that are not seriously enforced. They exist to provide a statement of the moral ideal. Sometimes they serve to keep some small but powerful interest group happy. Often they are valuable in keeping a minority group "in its place," or as a means of forcing an activity out of the public view.[35] In cases like these, the official regulations and the records they generate, such as tax records, crime rates, number of licenses issued, etc., are not valid social indicators, and it would be foolish for a student of social problems to take them seriously. At the same time, the government and the sociological research it funds or inspires does not often focus on the fact that the institutions actually are engaged in a moralistic ritual. The official statistics must be aimed elsewhere. The statistics usually get aimed at various groups without a great deal of social power—the young, minority groups, and members of the "lower classes." In Ralph Nader's phrase, American society tends to "study down" and not "study up."[36]

Many statistics generated by the police are a kind of moral exercise. In his book *American Social Order*, University of California sociologist Jack Douglas has shown how the official statistics on crime and delinquency have developed out of traditional police work.[37] Historically, the job of the police has been to maintain public order, keep the streets safe, keep "troublemakers" in line, and maintain a "rational" society. One of the earliest instances of police action, and hence police records, is the search for and removal of vagrants, drifters, the unemployed, and other members of the "dangerous classes." In keeping with this tradition, any respectable urban police force will have a vice squad and a narcotics squad. It is unlikely to have a "tax evasion" squad or a "medical malpractice" squad. Furthermore, because of their concern with *public* order, the police are more concerned with things that happen in the streets, where the poor perform more of their activities, than what happens behind closed doors. To the typical patrolman, pollution is what a drunk does on the sidewalk, not what a steel company does to a river. To some extent, government regulatory agencies have filled the gaps in police work, but the historic inertia is still a powerful factor in both official records and public attitudes.

Considerations like these have led Douglas to conclude:

In fact, when we do systematically investigate the nature of these official statistics, we find that they are not simply unreliable, but rather, *give a completely false idea of the nature of deviance in our society, so that only false (official) theories will be "statistically verified" by them.* [38]

TECHNOLOGY AND THE INFORMAL

A commonly accepted opinion is that much of the previous discussion is rapidly becoming outmoded due to the development of technology and the modern industrial state. The argument is that privacy and the informal are being replaced with efficiency, objectivity, formality, and a legalistic, mechanistic approach to social activity. [39]

In some areas a slow movement toward a more formalized, rational approach to social organization has developed, most notably in the growth of bureaucracies. And certainly technological innovations such as wiretapping have created threats to personal privacy. Nonetheless, the informal is alive and well and existing within the most rationally organized bureaucracy. Remember, the formal and legalistic dimension of social activity can exist side by side with the private and informal dimension. These two dimensions may conflict or they may complement each other; one does not replace the other. [40] The situation across all of society is analogous to the little slice of history known as the *Paris Peace Talks.* From the late 1960s to early in 1973, the various factions involved in the Vietnam War met in Paris for official peace talks. After scores of sessions and extended debate, the only thing they agreed upon was the shape of the table at which they were to argue. [41] Meanwhile, the unofficial, informal, and more important talks between Henry Kissinger and Le Duc Tho took place in private at various scattered locations. To follow the official talks as a means of understanding the negotiations was not inherently wrong, but it gave only half the picture. The official may have reflected what was going on indirectly as a kind of mirror. But things got done, as they usually do, on the informal level.

The desire for formalization and technological control often creates a dynamic interplay or dialectic between the formal and the informal. One group will attempt to impose formal, official restrictions on a second group, and the second responds by creating new informal rules, procedures, and communications that circumvent the formal procedures. The first group then responds with new rules and more sophisticated record keeping which in turn are circumvented, and so on.

This battle—or game—can be seen in any number of social problem areas.[42]

For example, consumers have fought for and obtained explicit pricing of merchandise. In this way, they can make a purchase without having to haggle with the salesperson or visit a number of shops before deciding on their purchase. The stores have responded by offering so many special sales, promotions, and other gimmicks that the *regular* price listed above *OUR* price on the label has become virtually meaningless. A recent study of car sales observed that only about 2 percent of all American cars are actually sold at their "list" price, and that the average discount off the list price was about $500.[43] In spite of the clearly marked prices, the consumer returns to haggling with the salesperson.

The formalization of political activity provides another example. Periodically, a corrupt political machine is swept out of office by outraged voters. The newly elected officials pledge complete reform. But after a few years have gone by, more often than not, a new political machine arises from the ashes of the old. The new machine employs private, informal techniques for controlling vice, allocating jobs, and granting contracts. As Robert Merton has pointed out, political machines have arisen so often to circumvent the official procedures that they must have something to offer besides corruption.[44]

THE CASE OF INTELLIGENCE TESTS

The way in which a technological advance becomes incorporated into the existing social structure so as to maintain privacy is nicely illustrated by the use of tests of intellectual abilities. Theoretically, intelligence is the basic quality that separates man from the lower animals. It is the ability to manipulate symbols, combine ideas, remember past experience, and productively use what is remembered in adapting to a changing environment.

Early in this century, psychologists began to develop various tests aimed at measuring this important ability.[45] These tests are formal, technologically sophisticated, and in many cases can be scored and analyzed by a computer—perhaps the ultimate criterion for objectivity. The creation of objective measures of such a crucial psychological characteristic as intelligence is a technological achievement that one might think would have had a profound effect on American social problems. For example, using modern intelligence tests, candidates for political office can publicly report their IQ's, allowing voters to choose the brightest person for the job. The President might brag that the average IQ of his appointments is 5 points higher than that of his predecessor's appointments. Management could objectively demonstrate that they are more intelligent than labor, rather than merely assuming it is the case. Republicans could scientifically demonstrate whether or not they are smarter than Democrats. And so on.

Of course, none of this has actually happened. It is not that there has been a lack of research on intelligence. There is, in fact, an enormous literature revolving around intelligence tests. Yet this research literature has had very little effect on the way things are done in American society. Intelligence test scores are weighty arrows that are most comfortably aimed downward. As a result, the only people who are systematically administered intelligence tests are youngsters, students, mental hospital residents, and applicants for low-level jobs—all relatively powerless positions in American society. In keeping with the populations studied, psychologists have focused on such questions as the relationship between race and IQ, sex and IQ, social class and IQ, and heredity and IQ.[46] Topics such as these are germane to certain interesting psychological theories, but are only of minor interest in furthering our knowledge of social problems. What is needed is the application of intelligence tests to those whose intelligence really matters in creating and solving social problems. As long as those in powerful positions can maintain their privacy and aim the possibility of being called "stupid" somewhere else, the development of a technology for measuring intelligence is unlikely to precipitate major changes in American society.

One of the major formal applications of tests like intelligence tests is the use of tests in academic screening. In order to gain admission to colleges and universities, students must "pass" examinations like the Scholastic Aptitude Test or the Graduate Record Examination. Strictly speaking, these are not intelligence tests, but rather tests of intellectual or academic accomplishment. Like the more general intelligence tests, they provide a fine example of the use of official records.

Entrance to the university community for the prospective student is typically dependent on high school grades and entrance test scores. These data are objective, formal, and allow numerical comparison across competing students. They can be fed into a computer programmed to put all the data together and select the best student according to a scientifically determined formula. In many universities this is, in effect, the way the freshman class is selected. (Sometimes special consideration may be given to a candidate with exceptional talents, such as the ability to propel a football with power and accuracy.) Thus, the weakest members of the university community are subjected to a precise, formal, competitive evaluation which is aimed at objectively determining the best applicants. It is illuminating to compare this approach with the method of selecting the important members of the university community, such as the Board of Trustees, who officially control the university.

Selection of trustees is usually completely informal. Typically, they are simply appointed by some person or group in positions of power after informal, secret deliberation. In state schools, they may be appointed by the Governor and confirmed by the State. In church-related schools, they may be appointed by the church. In many private institutions, the Board of Trustees is self-perpetuating, new members being selected by the Board itself.[47]

Because of the privacy of the selection process, it is a matter of considerable conjecture exactly what a trustee has to offer a school that led to his or her selection. It may be prestige, money, academic ability, links with other important institutions, or an appropriate combination of these factors. It is unthinkable to ask an important industrialist being considered for the Board of Trustees to submit to objective intelligence testing. The result is that we have at least some idea if the students are failing because they are not intellectually prepared. We do not know if the school itself is failing because its administration is intellectually unprepared.

The failure to employ objective intelligence test scores to classify and evaluate is not due to a total disdain for objective classification in American society. We have at least one very important formal classification system—age. Your age, like your IQ, is a number, but unlike IQ, age is used extensively to allocate your rights and privileges. To some extent, all societies divide people into categories on the basis of their age. But most societies employ only a few divisions, such as the simple dichotomy between child and adult. Moreover, these age levels are often based on physical rather than chronological measurement. (For instance, a woman may be considered an adult after her first menstruation.)

In contemporary America, however, there is an elaborate system of age classification making such fine distinctions as young adult versus late adolescent and high school versus junior high. Most of these levels are based soley on the chronological measure of years since birth, which often is not highly correlated with physical, emotional, or intellectual maturity. As Philippe Ariès has demonstrated in his noted study of the family, *Centuries of Childhood*, this obsession with age stratification is a recent development in Western culture which was unknown in the medieval period.[48]

You must have achieved a minimum age before you can get married, drive a car, receive social security, run for Congress, or be President. You must have a minimum age in order to get a job and a maximum age before you are forced to retire from the job. When asked to justify this system, many people would respond that age is a measure of intelligence and maturity, and therefore can legitimately be used to classify people. But psychologists have developed intelligence tests in order to provide a *direct*, objective measure of intelligence so that we do not have to rely on rough measures such as chronological age.* The failure to employ the technology of psychological measurement to replace age as a means of classification demonstrates clearly how technological advancement, in itself, does not alter informal patterns of social organization unless it is desired by those in positions of power.[49]

COMPUTERS

Computers are probably the most infamous technological device reputed to be reshaping society by destroying privacy and the personal life. Indeed, the computer could drastically alter the storage, analysis, and transmission of all kinds of information on all levels of society, and in the process greatly reshape American life.[50] But like other, more primitive devices for gathering and manipulating information, the com-

---

*It is of interest that intelligence is often *defined* in terms of age. This is why intelligence is also called IQ, which is short for "Intelligence Quotient." Intelligence is defined as the quotient of mental age divided by chronological age times 100. For instance, a six-year-old child who has the mental ability of the average nine-year-old has an IQ of 150 ($9/6 \times 100 = 150$). The IQ loses this interpretation, but not the name, when applied to adults. It is not particularly informative to say that a thirty-five-year-old has the mental abilities of the average seventy-five-year-old.

puter must be aimed, and development of the computer has not caused society to change its aim. For this reason, the computer has done little of what it could be doing to alter the fabric of society.

The computer could be used to store all real estate holdings in an official, centralized location. If you wanted to buy a house, a quick, inexpensive memory search could take the place of the present expensive system of title search and title insurance. Similarly, the manipulation of stocks and bonds could be almost totally computerized. Instead of the present "Big Board," we would have thousands of little television screens reporting all transactions taking place at the centralized electronic exchange. Such procedures would make use of all the trends that many now fear are taking over our lives—efficiency, computerization, centralization, bureaucratization—and in the process put a number of professions out of work. There has been very little movement in this direction.

The computer could also challenge educational and clinical psychologists and psychiatrists whose job it is to administer and analyze psychological tests. By now, a large body of evidence has accumulated showing that in many situations computer-like, actuarial analysis of personality test results is a better predictor than personal, clinical analysis.[51] But so far, diagnostic psychologists, like title searchers and stock brokers, have successfully protected themselves from substantial computer inroads in their domains.

Educators have been perhaps the most successful professional group in avoiding modern technology. Most college teachers still use the basic lecture and discussion method of instruction developed not only before the advent of the computer but even before Gutenberg's invention of modern printing in the fifteenth century. J. F. Gibbons and his associates at Stanford University summarize the failure of technology to change education:

> In the early 1920's, shortly after radio broadcasting was proved to be economically feasible, Robert Hutchins is said to have predicted that this new technology would undoubtedly have a dramatic impact on education. Subsequent events have shown that his assessment of the educational potential of radio was probably correct but, for a variety of reasons, the potential did not materialize. In the early 1950's instructional television was introduced with a similar fanfare. However, with a few notable exceptions, its potential also failed to materialize. It seems that more recent innovations such as computer-aided instruction

and satellite-based educational delivery may come to a similar fate. Why is it that these technological aids to education seldom seem to live up to their potential?[52]

The electronics and computer industries may have revolutionized techniques of scientific data analysis and the storage and retrieval of gas bills, tax records, criminals' fingerprints, and the like. But in cases like these, the computer is only making more efficient society's traditional record keeping and data analysis. It has not markedly altered the nature of the records kept, who they are kept on, and what they are kept for. In the years to come, we will probably see slow computer inroads into the work of the major professions, but so far, professional groups have been quite successful in keeping their traditional, personal, informal way of doing things.

SOCIAL PROBLEMS AND THE INADEQUACY OF OFFICIAL RECORDS

Knowledge of the power and ubiquity of the informal and private dimension of social affairs has important implications for the study of social problems. Most directly, it reminds us not to take the reports of official statistics too seriously. These statistics do provide important information regarding social problems, but they are necessarily incomplete. To truly understand social problems, we must go beyond the official records and investigate the private activities of informal groups. This means that the student of social problems must be a kind of detective and journalist as well as a traditional scientist and statistician. The student must cultivate an appreciation of unobtrusive, informal, and indirect measurement of societal activity.

The method of participant observation is an especially helpful counterbalance to the use of official statistics. In this method, the researcher becomes an intimate member of the informal group he or she is investigating. By gaining the trust of the members of the primary group, the investigator frequently can gain important insights into the decision making, communication, and motivation of the members which are not reflected in the official records. Participant observation of the criminal subculture, police, groups of industrial workers, bureaucrats, and professionals should continue to complement other records in providing a more complete picture of the problems of American society. We will meet such informal reports often in the remaining chapters.

Too great a concentration on the official records also has the disadvantage of encouraging an overly pessimistic attitude regarding social problems. Social problems appear mysterious and unknowable. When the informal activity that contributes to the problem becomes more thoroughly understood, the problem often becomes less mysterious and much more understandable. People are seen to be rational creatures after all. An awareness of the informal dimension of social action, therefore, provides a further justification for optimism in understanding and combating social problems.

SUMMARY

In spite of an abundance of information available on many aspects of our lives, we are often lacking precisely the information we most need for understanding social problems. One reason for this situation is the prevalence of informal activities, personal power, and private information across all levels of society. The ubiquitous informal dimension does not generate official records and statistics that reveal its contributions to social problems and solutions. Those with positions of power in society are often precisely the ones whose activities are most unknown. Politicians, in particular, are capable of shielding themselves from public scrutiny.

Another aspect of the situation is that those in positions of power are capable of aiming the direction of official records and statistics. In order to maintain their cherished privacy, they aim them away from themselves. The result is that we have better data on those who are socially weak. Police records and intelligence test data exemplify this process. The development of technology and bureaucracy has done a little to change the situation, but they neither replace the informal level nor drastically change the way statistics are aimed. The introduction of the computer demonstrates how technology does not replace traditional, informal activities. In order to avoid an overemphasis on official records, sociologists have developed participant observation and other means to understand the informal, hidden level of social reality.

FIVE

Pitfalls and Paradoxes in Understanding Social Problems

In attempting to understand social problems, there are some things that just don't seem to make sense. In reading the daily newspaper, for example, you often run across perplexing statements like these:

> *We do not want to destroy any people. It is precisely because we have been advocating coexistence that we have shed so much blood.*
>
> A Palestinian leader explaining his policies.[1]

> *We must increase our spending for defense in order to carry out the nation's strategy for peace.*
>
> President Richard M. Nixon explaining his policies.[2]

> *For the very weakness of the Soviet position may make the Russians all the more reluctant to sign a strategic arms limitation agreement.*
>
> From an analysis of Soviet foreign policy.[3]

If we quit making appeals, people will begin to wonder if something is wrong with our operation.

> An official of Boys Town explaining why they continue to appeal for funds although they possess assets estimated at over $200 million. [4]

If there weren't these disruptions, it would mean these meetings are not significant.

> An official at a scientific conference commenting on the throwing of tomatoes at a United States Senator. [5]

Statements like these are usually ignored, misread, or dismissed as additional proof of the crazy world we live in. However, paradoxes, contradictions, and apparent nonsense can provide very important information in thinking about any problem, especially a social problem. They should not be disregarded; they are signals to start thinking.

In this chapter, we will consider a few of the more common paradoxes and pitfalls confronting the student of social problems. We will focus on three interconnected areas: (*a*) paradoxes regarding the salience of social norms and related phenomena, (*b*) problems in attempting to apply rewards and punishments to social activities, and (*c*) confusions about social bargaining and negotiations. These three areas are certainly not the only sources of paradox and confusion, but they have been responsible for more than their fair share. In addition, there has been a substantial amount of theory and research devoted to illuminating these areas, so that social scientists are now beginning to unravel the nature of the puzzles.

Once again, our goal will be to find method in apparent madness, and the moral of this chapter can be stated very simply: *Whenever "common sense" starts to fail you, it is time to reexamine your assumptions.*

MANIPULATING SALIENCE

Salience is simply the quality of being thought of. If something is salient for you, that means you often think of it; it is frequently on your mind. For example, for the average American teenager, cars, sex, and school are more salient than, say, snowshoes, fireplugs, and canaries. For the average banker, money is more salient than telephone poles.

SALIENCE VERSUS EVALUATION

First, we must distinguish salience from evaluation or attitude. Your evaluation of something is just how much you like it or dislike it, whether you think it is pleasant and good or unpleasant and bad. If you think something is good, you are said to have a positive attitude toward it. Salience and attitude are independent concepts. A thought can be nonsalient and pleasant, salient and unpleasant, or any other possible combination. When a thought is both salient and pleasant, it might be called an enjoyable fantasy. When it is both salient and unpleasant, it is called a worry.

In order to measure your evaluation of something, you are simply asked whether you like it or how much you like it. This does not measure salience, because the very act of asking the question puts the thought in your mind. For example, if an interviewer asked you, "Do you like elephants?" he has made elephants salient for you. In order to determine how salient elephants are for you, in general, the interviewer must ask an open-ended question, such as "What's on your mind?" If you answer, "I hate elephants," he has discovered both your evaluation and your salience for elephants. (A common method is to begin an interview with open-ended questions and then slowly to make the questions more and more specific. This is often called a *funnel* interview because it is open at one end and restricted at the other.)

A general problem in human decision making is that our thinking is too often confined by what is salient for us. It is one of the functions of statistics to broaden what is salient. Without such broadening, we are likely to overly limit our thoughts to ones that come readily to mind. In Chapter 2, we met this problem regarding the news, which is constantly making unimportant things salient and neglecting the important things. We met it again in Chapter 4 when we saw that the official records are often more salient than crucial informal activity. We will deal with the problem of salience again when we consider decision making regarding social problems in Chapter 7. Now we will turn to some specific confusions concerning salience.

THE SALIENCE OF CHANGE

On the whole, the human mind is constructed to consider changing input and ignore continuous, unchanging stimulation. As advertisers know well, movement, fluctuation, and sudden shifts in our experience attract attention. This phenomenon can be observed in even our simplest sensory experience. Stare at any clearly defined figure for any length of time, and you will feel a strong tendency to look away. If you maintain your focus, you will find the figure tends to shimmer and glow, its edges become blurred, and your perception becomes strangely distorted.* On a somewhat more complex level, the same thing happens to the meaning of words. If you repeat the same word over and over for several minutes, the word begins to lose its meaning. For example, after repeating "table" many times, it becomes difficult to find the word "table" in a list of words.[7] The constant focusing of attention or the repetition of words can be employed to create altered states of consciousness, and are common techniques for inducing hypnosis and meditation. All of this indicates that there is a great deal of truth in the old maxim that the fish would be the last one to discover water.

In the same manner, the completely accepted and universally followed rules, habits, and roles in society are the last ones we become aware of. It is the shifting, fluctuating rules and roles that are salient.** If you were to ask the average American to mention some of the important norms of our society—the rules and laws of expected or proper behavior—you would receive answers like these:

> Do not smoke marijuana.
> Do not steal from the place where you work.
> Do not cheat on your income tax.
> Do not insult or belittle members of your family.
> Do not get drunk.
> Do not commit adultery.

These are the norms parents instill in their children, textbooks inculcate in school children, and ministers urge on their congregations. They are examples of the salient norms of our culture, and they are precisely the norms that are presently under attack. Some of them have

---

*This is not really a good test because all the time you have been staring, your eyes have been making rapid, unconscious movements which ensure at least some fluctuation in your visual input. By means of special equipment, an image can be presented in a psychological laboratory in such a way as to circumvent these unconscious eye movements. When this is done, an amazing thing happens—the image disappears.[6]

**Another aspect of this phenomenon is that we are most aware of exercising a skill when it is not yet learned very well. After we have mastered it, it is no longer salient, and our minds are freed to think about something else. Someone who has to think of swimming, typing, or driving a car in order to do it correctly is still a beginner. Similarly, it is only when you are just learning a role or to follow a rule that you are conscious of doing it.

been under attack for ages. It is not an accident that the only common weed that is dried and smoked, marijuana, is also the only common weed that it is unlawful to possess.

In general, those norms that are salient are the ones that are disobeyed, under attack, and represent conflicts among different groups in society.[8] Perhaps the foremost example of a list of norms in Western culture is the Ten Commandments, which is also a nice summary of the actions that many ancient Hebrews condemned and many others practiced. Viewed in this light, it can be seen that published norms are inherently conflictual, and the most salient norms are likely to be the most conflictual of all.

To appreciate this relationship more fully, imagine what a list of well-obeyed norms would look like. It would contain items like these:

> Do not rape a sheep.
> Do not eat grasshoppers.
> Do not rub yourself with Jimson weed.
> Do not give away your clothes.
> When you are a guest at a marriage, do not have sex with the bride.

Each of the actions condemned above could be performed—in fact, often have been performed—in other cultures. The reason these norms are not salient in our culture is that they are successful; they are rarely broken.

The important implication of this discussion for understanding social problems is that the average citizen greatly underestimates the power of social norms. Most norms are operating so well that we obey them without being aware of the norm that is operating. On the other hand, the norms that come readily to mind are apparently not working well. This creates the mistaken impression that "law and order" is breaking down and anarchy is taking over society. In reality, society may be much more stable, orderly, continuous, and smoothly functioning and social problems much less severe than would appear at first glance. Furthermore, it is possible that many social problem activities represent not only the violation of salient norms but also obedience to the nonsalient norms of our culture. (We will consider this point further in the next chapter.)

DISSOCIATION OF PERSONAL INTEREST FROM NORMS

When a norm is salient—that is, when it is a source of conflict in society—the groups or individuals responsible for the norm frequently attempt to dissociate themselves from it. The norm itself remains salient, but the forces that maintain and enforce it are not. The impression is generated that the norm exists due to the operation of some vague, abstract, unreachable, and unknowable source. The norm is perceived as mysterious when it is actually the work of fairly simple and understandable social processes.

An example with which many of us are familiar occurs when a policeman gives a traffic ticket for a modest violation of the law. The policeman could point out that it is his *personal* decision to apply a traffic law against you because he needs to make his quota or he simply doesn't like you. He is much more likely to invoke the norm as an absolute and declare he has no choice but to give you a ticket. "I'm sorry, but you broke the *law.*" In this way, personal animosities and endless hassles are avoided by making laws and other norms salient rather than the people responsible for them. The anger and frustration of those who are harmed by the norms are directed at disembodied abstractions. In sociological terminology, the *personal power* of those behind the norm is not salient.[9] If you ask people to do something as a personal favor, they might well comply. If you keep asking personal favors, soon people will begin asking you for something in return. It is easier to exercise your personal power only once—to establish a norm, create a rule, or pass a law. Then you can sit back and utter that famous expression, "Don't blame me, it's the law!" As long as the norm is salient and not the human agencies that created it, you are likely to forget that it is precisely those who are saying "Don't blame me" that are the ones to blame.

A variant on this theme is the third-party tactic in which some convenient third party, usually the government, is found to establish and enforce the norm against the first party and for the benefit of the second party.[10] For example, when a teenager (first party) wants to quit school, the parents and teachers (second party) say, "You can't quit now, it's the law." They usually fail to point out that they would be the first to complain if anyone attempted to remove the law. In the same fashion, a businessman will say, "I'm sorry, but the rates are fixed by law," forgetting to mention that his corporation engaged in strenuous, behind-the-scenes efforts to create the law that limited the rates. The result is that, once again, the source of social power is not salient.

TERRORISM—THE MUTT AND JEFF ROUTINE

A tactic similar to the third party in manipulating salience is the *Mutt and Jeff* routine, also known as the *Good Guy—Bad Guy* or *Big Brother* ploy. To use the Mutt and Jeff routine, two people work as a team, one person playing the role of the good guy, the other becoming the bad guy. A common use of the Mutt and Jeff routine is in interrogating suspected criminals and prisoners of war.[11] In a typical version of the act, one interrogator, the bad guy, acts mean and cruel; he insults, threatens, and abuses the prisoner. The good guy then appears and sends out the bad guy, who leaves with the threat, "When I come back, you're really going to get it!" The nice guy oozes respect for the prisoner, sweetly coaxes the prisoner to tell them what they want to know, and vaguely hints that he can't hold the bad guy off much longer. The prisoner often does confess, and by confessing relieves his fear of the bad guy and at the same time saves face by talking to the nice guy. "I showed them," he tells himself, "rough stuff won't work with someone like me." The fact that the two interrogators are a team working for the same goal, and may even switch roles for the next prisoner, is naturally not made salient.

Terrorism provides an illustration of the Mutt and Jeff routine in the area of social problems. Given the news media's tendency to feast on the drama of a skyjacking or political kidnaping, it is not surprising that terrorism is still very much with us. Nonetheless, sometimes people are surprised that rebels resort to terrorism because it apparently results in an increased hatred for the terrorists' cause. The key to understanding terrorism is to recognize that a well-publicized act of terrorism is likely to create all of the following perceptions simultaneously:

1. The terrorists are wicked, evil persons.
2. They should be punished severely.
3. They are dangerous, and hence to be feared.
4. They are angry and desperate about something.

For terrorism to be successful, it is necessary for people to separate the first two perceptions above from the second two. They then are determined not to give in to the terrorists, and simultaneously would like to reduce their fear of these desperadoes.

The time is ripe for the Mutt and Jeff routine to begin and for the nice guy to appear to plead the terrorists' cause. Of course, the nice guy categorically condemns the evil deeds of the terrorists, at the same time hinting that there are a lot more of those nasty people ready to do a lot worse if the nice guy is not negotiated with. The government or other agency can then negotiate with the nice guy, reduce fear of the bad guy, and still proclaim it will never give in to terrorists' demands. Because salience is separate from evaluation, the nice guy may have a favorable reputation as a spokesman for the downtrodden even though his cause was first made salient by bombing, arson, kidnaping, assault, or murder.

When the nice guy is successful, the bad guy customarily disappears. For example, the bicentennial of the American Revolution in 1976 celebrated almost every conceivable aspect of the Revolutionary War. But one facet that was rarely mentioned was that the Sons of Liberty had a nasty habit of beating up those who were loyal to the British.[12] There is no sense dwelling on *that*. After all, the nice guys won!

WHY DON'T THEY LEARN?

One of the greatest sources of paradoxes and misunderstandings in the area of social problems is the application of rewards and punishments to change behavior. When these manipulations fail to stop socially destructive activities, we get that sinking feeling that people are completely irrational, and the cry becomes, "Why don't they learn?"

It is not just a folk belief that rewards and punishments will alter your behavior; it has been demonstrated countless times in the psychological laboratory. However, there are not one, but two, general principles that emerge from the burden of the psychological research on learning. First, other things being equal, when a reward is presented in a particular situation, the behavior that occurred immediately prior to presentation of the reward tends to occur in the future in the same situation. This is called the *principle of reinforcement* because the reward reinforces or strengthens the behavior.* Similarly, a punishment reduces the strength of the behavior that occurred immediately before it was presented. The second general principle is that *other things are rarely equal*.

PROBLEMS WITH PUNISHMENT

The complications are particularly severe when applying punishment to solve social problems. Unfortunately, many people have a predisposition to use punishment rather than rewards. Punishment appears faster, simpler, and less expensive than rewards. When we look beyond the initial appearance, however, we can detect at least three major problems in making punishment work.

1. It is often difficult to punish the undesired behavior immediately, and if there is a delay in applying the punishment, it loses its effect. A classic instance is beating your dog to make it stop chasing cars. If you wait until the dog returns to beat it, you are not punishing it for chasing cars; you are punishing it for returning to you. The dog will learn to chase the car and keep right on going! And how can you beat the dog while it is chasing the car?** Many of the punishments used in attempts to decrease social problems, including fines, imprisonment, and public embarrassment, occur too long after the actual offense to have much influence on the undesired behavior.

2. The effects of punishment can be offset by the influence of imitation. When a punishment is being administered, the punisher is setting an example or providing a role model which may create exactly the opposite effect from the one intended. This can be seen most clearly in the case of aggression. If a mother spanks her daughter for hitting her little brother, she is *saying*, "Don't hit your brother," but

---

* This use of reinforcement should not be confused with the technique of Ivan Pavlov. You probably recall that Pavlov presented food to his dogs as he rang a bell. Eventually the dogs would salivate to the sound of the bell alone. This is called *classical conditioning* or *learning by association*, which is different from the *learning by doing* that we are considering. There is little interest among American social scientists in applying learning by association to reduce social problems.

** A better method would be to reward the dog with a snack when it comes back to you. That should make it shorten the chase, and eventually the dog may eliminate the chase entirely and run to you as soon as it sees a car coming. If the dog is to be punished, the punishment must be given while it is chasing the car, such as by having friends drive by and dump a bucket of water on the dog. This should at least encourage the dog to chase the car from a safe distance. Probably the best method would be a combination of both the reward and the punishment.

she is *showing* what to do when you are angry with people—beat them. The child may learn to do what the mother does and not what she says.[13] On the broader level of social problems, a punishment-oriented society may encourage by imitation revenge, personal animosities, and various sorts of aggression which would contribute substantially to social problems.

3. Punishment can directly produce feelings or behaviors which interfere with learning the appropriate response. Fear of social punishment, like other fears, can make it difficult to concentrate, focus on long-range goals, or maintain the self-respect necessary for productive behavior. An extreme illustration would be trying to teach someone to play chess by threatening his life. "Checkmate in ten moves, or I'll blow your brains out!" The anger, agitation, and anxiety aroused by the threat would ensure that the average player would lose the game.

One reason punishment can work effectively on laboratory animals is that they are locked in a box. In the general society we are not locked in place, so that rather than escaping the specific punishment, a person may escape the total situation in which he or she is punished. The escape may be only a psychological one by means of alcohol or some other drug that reduces the anxiety aroused by the threat of punishment. Or it could be a physical escape from the location of punishment. If a school uses punishment rather than rewards, the child may simply learn not to go to school. If divorce is punished too severely by costly fees and legal hassles, couples may decide not to get married at all. Among reinforcement theorists, this is known as "escaping the aversive situation."

PROBLEMS WITH REWARDS

For the reasons just outlined, reinforcement theorists generally encourage the use of rewards rather than punishments in treating social problems.[14] But this introduces a new difficulty. What exactly is a reward, and how do we distinguish it from a punishment? On the surface this appears to be a naïve question, but to ask what is a reward is, in a sense, a rephrasing of the age-old question, "What do people really want?" Phrased in this way, the difficulties in identifying rewards become more obvious. Three of these difficulties will be briefly described, and two major problems with rewards will then be treated at greater length.

1. When studying animals in the laboratory, the common procedure is to make them very hungry and then offer food as a reward for doing something. An extremely deprived animal will, indeed, work for a reward of food, water, or some other basic need. However, starving the country's population hardly suggests itself as an appropriate solution to social problems. Free citizens must be rewarded with more subtle manipulations, and these are harder to identify than you might suppose. Money is often advanced as a general reward, but its influence on those who are not deprived is overrated. For example, the President of the United States has an annual salary of only $200,000; Nelson Rockefeller earned a mere $62,500 a year as Vice-President.[15] Some state governors earn as little as $10,000 to $20,000 a year.[16] Many garbage collectors earn more than that. Money is not *the* reinforcer, and many people will forsake money for some other cherished goal, such as power, fame, prestige, a feeling of moral righteousness, and self-respect. These rewards are not nearly so easily manipulated as food for a hungry rat.

2. One of the strongest rewards for most people, as well as most lower animals, is change, variety, stimulation, and excitement. People like the chance to explore, hunt, overcome obstacles, and meet challenges.[17] This creates a great difficulty in finding a proper reward because it implies that a *moderate* amount of anxiety or fear of punishment can be desirable.[18] As John Lofland puts it, there is such a thing as the *pleasantly fearful*.[19] Anyone who has ever tasted the joys of trespassing, being chased by Mr. Snodgrass after sending the baseball through his window, stealing the neighbor's apples, being served alcohol with a phony identification, engaging in forbidden sexual practices, or smoking marijuana for the first time with the shades carefully drawn will not have to be reminded that breaking the law can be delightfully exciting. Taking a chance on punishment can function as a reward. This fact muddies the water considerably.

3. Another difficulty in applying rewards is that the reward soon becomes expected, and when the expected reward does not materialize, the result is frustration, anger, or aggression. In short, rewards create frustration that operates like punishment.[20] Someone who is expecting $100 and is rewarded with only $10 is being rewarded in the strict sense of the term, but he *feels* as if he were being punished. Upon reflection, it becomes apparent that most of the common punishments in our society are not the direct application of painful stimulation so much as the removal of expected rewards. Fines and imprisonment are

removal of rewards, and the use of solitary confinement in prison is the removal of all rewarding stimulation.* It is an extreme version of sending a naughty child to bed without supper.

COMPARISON LEVEL   In order to determine what rewards to expect, you do not have to reflect on your past rewards. You can also notice what rewards other people are getting and determine your proper level of reward on the basis of this comparison. By combining what you have been told to expect, what you received in the past, and what others similar to yourself are receiving, you can arrive at your *comparison level*, which represents your "proper" level of reward.[21] If you are doing better than your comparison level, you feel rewarded; if you are not reaching your comparison level, you feel frustrated. Comparison level is a social-psychological process that has little to do with satisfying physical needs. A poor man who discovers that his total worth has just become $100,000 feels elated; a multimillionaire hearing the same news feels ruined. What may have been the full life for our ancestors—a thatched hut, a few coarse clothes, a little rough food—is considered intolerable poverty today. Comparison level is similar to what social theorists have called level of anticipation, expectancy level, level of distributive justice, or level of relative deprivation. Whatever it is called, we all know that sinking feeling of not getting what we deserve, not keeping up with the people next door.

Keeping up with the folks next door can be quite frustrating, however. As you move up in the world, you will find that the people next door are also moving up. When you finally move into your $100,000 dream house, you can peek out the window, see a $150,000 house down the street, and begin to feel poor again. Students of social problems sometimes cannot understand why the more affluent members of society are not more eager to support programs for the poor. One reason is that the affluent do not think of themselves as wealthy. Their comparison level is formed by observing others just as wealthy.[22] The poor are not salient. The folks next door and the people at the country club are salient, and many of them are a lot richer. So let *them* pay for welfare!

Appreciation of the influence of comparison level helps explain

---

* Reinforcement theorists are frequently unappreciative of the fact that most common punishments are removal of rewards or, as they like to phrase it, "time out from positive reinforcement." In their parlance, this is not a "punishment" society but a "time out" society. The withdrawal of a reward might be defined differently than a punishment, but phenomenologically it is very similar.

why Americans, who achieved record gains in income, education, and other areas from the late 1950s to the early 1970s, also showed a steady *decrease* in professed happiness on questionnaires administered over the same period.[23] When your success is increasing, but your comparison level is increasing even faster, you feel relatively deprived. Comparison level analysis also helps explain why urban blacks rioted in the 1960s, when they "never had it so good." It is precisely *because* their social position had improved that they felt more frustrated and unjustly rewarded.[24]

Revolutions do not occur during times of great economic hardship. They occur when times are relatively good.[25] Perhaps the most fruitful time for civil disturbance is when a steady period of rising expectations is halted by a sudden decrease in perceived rewards.[26] In the case of American blacks, previous to the urban riots of the 1960s, blacks had made substantial gains in income, housing, education, and other measures of social success. But the rise might have been just enough to raise their comparison level to that of the whites, who were doing even better.[27] The result was a feeling of relative deprivation and frustration.

On the whole, rewards are not only important in themselves, they are also important in terms of what they do to our expectations for future rewards and perception of what constitutes a just reward. These two effects work in opposite directions; the reward gives us satisfaction, the expectation sets the stage for frustration. If the frustration increases faster than the satisfaction, the result is increasing anger and feelings of being deprived. Feelings of deprivation are especially likely if the rewards are given unequally, if people are led to expect more than they receive, or if the rewards are subsequently reduced and people suffer a decline to a previous level of reward.

ATTITUDES VERSUS BEHAVIORS   In discussing comparison level, I emphasized the overall level of reward experienced by different groups and its effect on the happiness and social harmony of society. Now our attention will return to the application of rewards in strengthening specific behaviors, which is the major interest of reinforcement theory. Even in regard to presenting specific rewards for specific actions, we will see that an increase in reward can decrease the desirability of the behavior rewarded.

We have previously considered the concept of evaluation or attitude and distinguished it from salience. Viewing social problems from the perspective of attitudes would suggest that solving social problems demands that people develop a positive attitude toward those actions beneficial to society and a negative attitude toward those that are harmful to society. Now, what is the effect of rewarding an activity on the later attitude toward that activity?

Leon Festinger was the first to popularize the idea that rewarding an action can *decrease* fondness for doing it.[28] According to Festinger, if you perform an undesirable behavior for a good reward, you have two relevant thoughts on your mind: (*a*) I am doing something I don't like, and (*b*) I am being rewarded well for doing it. These two thoughts are mutually compatible, or consonant. But if you are not well rewarded for the action, your thoughts are not in agreement: (*a*) I am doing something I don't like, and (*b*) I am *not* getting much of a reward for doing it. This is an uncomfortable situation to be in. There is a psychological conflict between the two thoughts, which Festinger calls *cognitive dissonance*. Why do something you don't like doing unless there is some profit in it? There are a number of things you can do to help reduce this unpleasant cognitive dissonance:

1. Don't think about both thoughts together. (Reduce their salience.)
2. Write the whole thing off as unimportant.
3. Convince yourself that you are actually being forced into doing the unpleasant activity.
4. Find a good excuse, such as a powerful reward, to explain your action.
5. Change your mind and decide that the action is not unpleasant after all.

It is the last possibility that is most intriguing because it implies a general method for developing a positive attitude toward any action. *To get people to like doing something, reward them with the minimum reward necessary to induce them to do it.* It also helps to remind them that they are voluntarily doing it for little reward, and that it is a rather important action. In this way, the other alternative ways to reduce dissonance will be eliminated. Festinger is employing a distinction between the action and the attitude toward the action that should not be lost. The more money you receive for an action now, the more likely you are to do it now but the less likely you are to like the action itself. You must continue to receive rewards in the future if you are to continue to do it. The less you receive for the action, the more likely you are to like it, and that means you need not be rewarded so much to do it in the future. In a free society, it is desirable to develop beneficial attitudes so that appropriate actions are freely given, or else citizens must be constantly rewarded or threatened with punishment.

Festinger's theory of cognitive dissonance might appear to contradict common sense, but if you reflect upon it a while, it will appear less strange. Have you ever found yourself, in an unpleasant situation, trying to find an excuse for being there? When you cannot find the excuse, that sinking feeling you experience is cognitive dissonance. In such a situation, it is often easier to convince yourself that, after all, the situation isn't so bad. A similar case occurs with regard to hazing and unpleasant initiations for fraternities and social clubs. According to the theory of cognitive dissonance, an unpleasant initiation can actually make you like the club more than a pleasant one. If you are voluntarily suffering for something you don't really like, that makes you pretty foolish. It may be easier to convince yourself that the suffering is worthwhile than to accept the thought that you are a fool.[29] The important thing about a theory is not whether it fits common sense, however; it is whether it is supported by research, and in a number of studies in which different amounts of reward were given for a behavior, the prediction of the theory was confirmed. The more reward people are given for doing a voluntary activity, the less positive their later attitude is toward the activity.[30]

So far, we have emphasized the effects of rewards on learning to like something we did not originally like. A related problem is the effect of adding an additional, extrinsic reward to an activity that is already enjoyable in itself. The experimental results suggest that here, too, the effect of the reward is to make the activity less enjoyable in its own right.[31] In one series of studies, preschool children were given expected rewards for doing things they enjoyed doing for nothing—playing with puzzles and making drawings. When given an opportunity to play with the materials later on (when no reward was presented), they played with them less than children who were never given any such rewards. Evidently, the extrinsic rewards made the activities less intrinsically enjoyable.[32]

In another study, male college students were given the task of putting simple jigsaw puzzles together.[33] In one condition, the puzzles were completely blank and the task was relatively boring. In this condition, the students found the task more enjoyable when they were given $1 for doing it. In another condition, the puzzles were not blank but formed interesting and enjoyable pictures, including *Playboy* centerfolds. In this condition, the students considered the task more enjoyable when they were *not* given any money for doing it. At least under some circumstances, if someone is going to do something anyway, giving an additional reward will decrease its attractiveness on future occasions. It is better to leave well enough alone.

THE LIMITATIONS OF REWARDS   This brief review does *not* demonstrate that rewards or punishments will never work in reducing social problems. There are probably many situations in which the principle of reinforcement provides the simplest explanation for socially undesirable behavior and suggests the surest path to eliminating the problematic activities. However, the limitations of the use of rewards that we have been considering should serve to remind us that a complete understanding of social problems will demand an understanding of praise, self-respect, perception of justice, need for self-understanding, and other mechanisms more subtle and various than simple rewards and punishments.

Governmental action aimed at removing socially destructive behavior presently emphasizes punishments or the removal of rewards, such as fines and imprisonment. B. F. Skinner and others have argued that the use of rewards will be much more effective than punishment in providing long-term reduction of unwanted actions.[34] The use of rewards rather than punishment is probably a step in the right direction, but rewards in themselves will not supply a complete answer to the problem of getting people to behave themselves. We should not be surprised if the use of rewards in large-scale programs aimed at reducing social problems occasionally backfires. This does not mean that people are stupid or irrational. It only means that people are much too complex for any simple theory of human nature to handle.

LOOKING FOR BARGAINS

Bargaining or negotiating about various social problem issues is the last of the three major sources of paradoxes and pitfalls we will consider in this chapter. Bargaining related to social problems is a commonplace on the news, and the antics and maneuvers of the negotiators frequently appear completely irrational. As we shall see, that may be the intended effect.

Bargaining involves two or more parties, each of whom has some power to reward or punish the other. If only one of the two parties has power, there is no bargaining; there are only demands. The cat does not bargain with the mouse, nor the king with a slave. It is the essence of bargaining that each side can hurt the other. There also must be some conflict or disagreement between the two parties, or else there would be no need for bargaining in the first place.

LET'S COMPROMISE

In the ideal bargaining situation, the parties attempt to find a solution which achieves both their goals. Trying to find a means for both parties to win is known as a *win–win approach*. This should not be confused with compromise. "Let's compromise" is a fine-sounding phrase, but compromise is actually the opposite of a win–win strategy; it is a *lose–lose strategy* because in compromising neither side gets what it really wants.[35] Nor does compromise solve the problem of the fairness or legitimacy of the various demands.

Prison inmates, college students, and other inexperienced negotiators have been known to make "nonnegotiable demands" which create the appearance of a pigheaded resistance to compromise. Of course, all negotiators have a list of nonnegotiable demands but, by definition, they are not introduced into the negotiations. If a union considers a 5 percent pay raise to be a nonnegotiable minimum, the union representative might begin by requesting 10 percent or 20 percent; then the negotiations can proceed. In the typical negotiations relating to social problems, both sides will begin with such outrageous demands that any final settlement can be hailed as a "statesmanlike compromise." The more desirable win–win approach involves stating goals, rather than demands, and the negotiations attempt to find a way for both parties to reach their goals. In the beginning, each party might attempt to change the other's mind about the proper avenue for reaching their mutual desires, and as Isidor Chein has put it, "Compromise itself entails a compromise of that goal."[36]

Needless to say, bargaining about social problems as revealed in the news does not usually suggest a win–win strategy. The negotiators are often too unsure of their own positions to give the appearance of trying to help the other party achieve its goals. They cultivate, instead, a public image of a "tough" negotiator who adopts a win–lose strategy and is determined to be the one who wins. In order to demonstrate that they are hard-working and determined negotiators, they surround themselves with an air of energy and dedication. This is often for the benefit of their constituents, who are curious about what is happening because the actual bargaining is secret. The image of the Secretary of State furiously jetting from one international bargaining session to another, or of the mayor and union representative emerging disheveled and unshaven from a marathon round of negotiations, helps convince the voters and union members that they are earning their salaries. No one is quite sure what they are doing, but it is clear that they are doing it energetically.

With this as background, we will consider a few of the common tactics negotiators can employ in attempting to achieve their bargaining demands. The logic of many bargaining situations has been analyzed by means of the theory of games.[37] Our present interest is not with the logic, but with the psychological ploys that come into play when the parties adopt a lose–lose or win–lose strategy.

LACK OF RESPONSIBILITY

Claiming a lack of responsibility is one of the themes that runs throughout our consideration of social problems. We will meet it again in Chapter 7 when we consider techniques of decision making. We have already seen it in operation in the attempt to dissociate personal power from the establishment of norms and as a device for reducing cognitive dissonance. Our interest here is with the negotiators' claim of lack of responsibility for their bargaining position. If negotiators can convince the opposition that they are only messengers with no real power, there will be little pressure on them to change their position, because they cannot change it; they have no authority.[38] The claim of lack of responsibility frequently merges with a version of the Mutt and Jeff routine. For example, the union representative might say, "Personally, I think your offer is a good one, but if I were to bring it back to the rank and file, they would skin me alive." The management negotiator might reply, "Personally, I like your proposal, but we've had a bad year and the stockholders would never accept it." In international diplomacy the United States' representative might say, "We like your proposal, but the President could never get it through the Senate." The Soviet representative would answer, "We appreciate your position, but it would never get past the Central Committee." Much of this denial of power by some of the most powerful people on earth would be humorous if the results were not the continuation of social problems.

If a negotiator cannot convince the opposition of his lack of power, he can carry the strategy one step further and actually *make* himself *not* responsible. The often discussed "doomsday device," popularized by the movie *Dr. Strangelove*, provides a good example. If a deadly device goes off automatically whenever the opposition does something considered undesirable, then the opposition must give in. They cannot attempt to talk the opponents out of using the device because they no longer control it. Happily, a doomsday device has not yet been installed, as far as we can tell, but more modest creations of the same variety have been observed. The use of security dogs trained to attack on sight provides a nice example. The dogs can be left at a store overnight, and a sign posted which says in effect:

> Dear potential burglar,
>
> This store is being protected by stupid, mean, vicious animals over which no one has any control. Anyone who enters this store will be torn apart. I realize that it is entirely unfair to lose an arm just for trying to steal a few dollars' worth of merchandise. But don't blame me; I'm a nice guy. You will have to negotiate with the dogs.
>
> > Yours truly,
> > The Management

The use of mounted police in quelling riots is a similar technique. You might trust the police not to run you over in cold blood, but when a 1,000-pound horse is galloping toward you, can you trust the horse?

THE CLAIM OF IRRATIONALITY Going crazy is a variation of the strategy of loss of responsibility. If you are stark, raving mad, the opposition will be tempted to give in to your demands, knowing that you cannot be reasoned with. The real advantage to being irrational lies in the fact that the typical threats that are available involve a loss to both parties. If there is a nuclear war, both sides lose; if the kidnappers kill their hostage, they lose their only bargaining power; if labor strikes, it hurts itself as well as management. One side can expect that as long as the other side is rational, it will not want to carry out its threat and hurt itself, merely to hurt the opposition. It is therefore advantageous to convince the opposition that it is dealing with a completely irrational group that doesn't mind hurting itself. Many stirring slogans have been created for this purpose:

Better dead than red!
>   An anticommunist motto

Live free or die.
>   State motto of New Hampshire

Give me liberty or give me death.
>   Patrick Henry

Negroes are ready to die for respect.
>   A resident of Watts.[39]

One variant of the ploy of madness is the threat of suicide. For this threat to work, the opposition must be convinced that the party making the threat is really beyond reason. Or as Thomas Schelling has phrased it, "If a man knocks at a door and says that he will stab himself on the porch unless given $10, he is more likely to get the $10 if his eyes are bloodshot."[40]

It might appear that the threat of suicide is an absurd bargaining strategy, but it is actually rather common. It is often found between lovers or between husband and wife, and it occasionally appears with respect to social problems. Examples would include hunger strikes by prisoners or protesters and threats of bankruptcy and economic ruin by large corporations. The hint of suicide was one of the major maneuvers used by New York City in 1975 to gain federal funds to help its finances. The suggestion was repeatedly made that the city would be destroyed (and the nation seriously harmed) unless the nation came to its aid. One official threatened that without federal aid, "The flow of blood would be irreversible."[41] Another warned Congress, "I cannot deny that there is a contagion in New York which is about to sweep across the nation. Don't kill us because we are ill."[42] And another implored, "Do we want people 50 or 100 years from now to look back and say that we, here today, sat back and allowed this city to die?" And yet another moaned, "This may be the last day for democracy in New York."[43] In case the argument was still not clear, another compared New York City's default to "stepping into a tepid bath and slashing your wrists."[44] If the nation could be convinced that New York City is irresponsible enough to allow itself to "go down the drain," then it will feel compelled to come to its aid. Not to stop a suicide is a form of murder.

DESTRUCTION OF COMMUNICATION   Another stratagem to make demands more compelling is to make the demands and then cut off all communication. By destroying the capacity to communicate, the opposition is, in effect, incapable of negotiating and will feel more pressure to agree with the demands, especially if they are made by someone irrational to begin with.

Arthur Stinchcombe draws the analogy of a man in a box.[45] The man in the box has a button which he can push to electrocute someone outside of the box, but he does not have any means of communicating with him. Although he holds the power of life and death over the man, he is actually powerless. In order for that button to be of value, he must be able to (a) give commands, (b) receive feedback on whether the commands have been obeyed, and (c) convince the man outside that he does have a button and will use it. Destruction of communication attempts to overcome the advantage of the opponent with the button by destroying the first two requirements. (It would also help the man in the box to have a power control on the button so that the man outside could be given painful shock rather than electrocuted. In some situations, total control is less desirable than partial control, because the more severe the threat, the less believable it becomes.)[46]

Because a failure to communicate can signal the seriousness of one's demands, it is frequently employed as a symbol of determination. During international crises, the governments will call home their ambassadors, not just for "consultation" but also to underscore their perception of the seriousness of the situation. In wartime, all direct communication between the warring parties may be terminated for fear that staying in communication would signal a softening in one's position. During the Vietnam War there were frequent rumors of "peace feelers," which were exceedingly indirect communications. A typical peace feeler would involve a diplomat from Hanoi mentioning something to a Swedish newspaperman, who would pass it along to the Yugoslavian ambassador at a cocktail party, who in turn would mention it to the Pope, and so on. If the diplomat were simply to pick up the phone and call the U.S. State Department, it could be interpreted as a sign of weakness. On the more informal level, the "silent treatment" and "sending to Coventry" serve the dual purpose of being both a punishment and a display of the righteousness of the silent party. If a husband wants to "talk it over" with his wife, that might suggest that he realizes he might be partly to blame himself.

In general, the breaking of communication can signal that a party is not really very interested in the negotiations, and does not care if there is an agreement or not. This can be a good impression for a negotiator to create. The more desperate one party is for an agreement, the more likely he is to give in to the other's demands. This implies that the party that has the smaller need for making an agreement gets the better deal. This is sometimes called the *principle of least interest*. With the principle of least interest in mind, union officials might decide to get a haircut in the middle of the negotiations while management will suggest that if they do have a long strike, it will help reduce their bloated inventory. Similarly, in international disputes, one side might suggest that a war would be beneficial because it would help the economy and increase support for the ruling faction. Like most bargaining ploys, these claims have an element of humor about them, but can also backfire and contribute to social problems. It also must be remembered that many announcements by the bargainers are made for the official records or to protect their public image and are not believed by either party. On the other hand, there is always the possibility that the bargainers might begin to take their public image seriously and fool themselves as well as the public.

THE CASE OF PLEA BARGAINING

Many of the principles we have met in thinking about social problems merge and crystalize in the institution of the criminal trial and sentencing. There is space here to touch on only a few of the more interesting characteristics as they relate to paradoxes of bargaining.

I mentioned before that one of the functions of the criminal law is to serve as a moral affirmation of the justice of the community. This aura of virtue is compromised if convicted criminals, as a matter of course, are dragged off to prison screaming their innocence. A variety of techniques have been developed to avoid this embarrassment to the symbolic function of the law. In the Soviet Union, political prisoners are often declared insane and "treated" in state mental hospitals; their protestations of innocence and cries of persecution can then be dismissed as the ravings of madmen. In Renaissance Europe, accused witches were judged guilty only after they publicly proclaimed their sins and named their accomplices in witchcraft. The fact that the confessions were routinely extracted by torture was not made salient.[47] In contemporary America, the procedure is to extract a confession of guilt without the use of torture. This procedure is so successful that the majority of those found guilty in American criminal trials have waived their constitutional rights and simply declared their guilt. As many as 95 percent of the misdemeanor convictions are due to guilty pleas.[48] A similar pattern exists in felony trials as well. In 1976, for example, 91 percent of the forgery and counterfeiting convictions and 80 percent of the narcotics convictions in federal courts were determined by guilty pleas.[49]

This high proportion of guilty pleas means that the official constitutional rules for determining guilt—trial by jury, cross-examination of the witnesses, presumption of innocence, etc.—are bypassed in favor of determination by informal bargaining. The prosecutor has the bargaining weapon of threatening to bring the accused to trial on more serious charges and requesting the maximum penalty. The prosecutor is supported by the knowledge that those cases that are brought to trial in America usually end in a finding of guilty anyway.[50] The defendant has more than the state's desire for the appearance of justice as his bargaining tool. The defendant's real power is in knowing that the prosecutor wants very much to avoid the time and expense of actually bringing the case to trial. The simple fact is that there are not enough courtrooms, judges, and other resources available in America to hear all the cases that would be brought to trial if all those accused actually demanded their constitutional rights. The court is under great pressure to keep the cases moving along toward some resolution for fear that the whole criminal justice system would grind to a halt.[51] One federal judge described the logic of the situation:

> If in one year, 248 judges are to deal with 35,517 defendants, the district courts must encourage pleas of guilty. One way to encourage pleas of guilty is to establish or announce a policy that, in the ordinary case, leniency will not be granted to a defendant who stands trial.[52]

The stage is then set for serious bargaining. The negotiations typically focus on the precise charge the accused will plead guilty to and the exact sentence the prosecution will recommend to the judge. Hence, these informal deliberations have become known as *plea bargaining*, and their successful completion occurs when the defendant is ready to "cop a plea." Someone originally charged with several counts of burglary may be willing to cop a plea to a reduced charge of possession of stolen goods. Selling narcotics may be reduced to simple possession, statutory rape to contributing to the delinquency of a minor, and aggravated assault to simple assault.

As in any bargaining situation, the usual ploys are used. A defendant who gives the impression that he or she will suffer irrationally rather than plead guilty may get a better offer from the prosecutor.* If you can afford bail, you are in a much better position to bargain because it is generally accepted that delays aid the defense more than the prosecution. As time passes, witnesses die or disappear, evidence gets lost, memories fade, angers subside, and the prosecution is more likely to make a mistake which would result in acquittal.

Anyone who is kept waiting in jail is obviously not in a good position to play a waiting game. Nonetheless, if you are facing, say, a five- to ten-year sentence, it may be worth your while to stall in hopes of gaining an acquittal or at least a better offer from the prosecution. One interesting aspect of this situation is that the time spent in jail awaiting trial can itself become a chip in the bargaining by being counted as time served toward whatever sentence is finally determined. The common folk wisdom is that people go to jail *if* they are found guilty, but in many cases people are kept in jail *until* they plead guilty, and then they are released.[53] The bargaining that results can appear exceedingly paradoxical. The following recounts a conversation between Martin Erdmann, a noted defense attorney, and his client, who had spent ten months in jail awaiting trail on an armed robbery charge.

> "Well, if you *did* do anything and you are a little guilty, they'll give you time served and you'll walk."
>
> "Today? I walk today?"
>
> "If you are guilty of something and take the plea."
>
> "I'll take the plea. But I didn't do nothing."
>
> "You can't take the plea unless you're guilty of something."

*Protesting your innocence is, in a sense, a version of attempting to appear irrational. The jailhouse is a most pragmatic place, and everyone connected with it knows that whether the accused is actually innocent (in the historical or theological sense) is immaterial. The only thing that matters to the rational defendant is the evidence that can be presented at a trial. If the prosecution has ten witnesses willing to swear that they saw you commit a crime, it doesn't matter that you are totally innocent; you had better start bargaining. To refuse to bargain on the grounds that you feel a moral compulsion to proclaim your innocence is to say that you are willing to go to prison in order to save your self-respect. If you can convince the prosecution that you would actually be so irrational, you might get a better offer.

"I want the year. I'm innocent but I'll take the year. I walk today if I take the year?"

"You walk if you take the plea, but no one's going to let you take the plea if you aren't guilty."

"But I didn't *do* anything."

"Then you'll have to stay in and go to trial."

"When will that be?"

"In a couple of months. Maybe longer."

"You mean if I'm guilty I get out today?"

"Yes."

"But if I'm innocent, I got to stay in?"

"That's right."

It's too much for [the defendant]. He lets go of the bars, takes a step back, shakes his head, turns around and comes quickly back to the bars.

"But *man*—"[54]

After the deal has been hammered out by informal bargaining, it is desirable to deny officially that the whole process has ever taken place. This occurs in what is known as the *copout ceremony*, in which the accused officially states before a judge that he or she is guilty of the charge that had been previously agreed upon, and that he or she personally chooses to waive the constitutional rights of a trial without any pressures or promises being applied.[55] (After officially becoming guilty, the defendants typically return to proclaiming their innocence as soon as the ceremony is over.)[56] The copout ceremony serves to rationalize the system, demonstrate that justice has been served, create official records showing that crime does not pay, and make it psychologically and legally awkward for defendants to change their minds and retract their confessions. The dangers in the procedure have been nicely summarized by the President's Commission on Law Enforcement and the Administration of Justice:

The system usually operates in an informal, invisible manner. There is ordinarily no formal recognition that the defendant has been offered an inducement to plead guilty. Although the participants and frequently the judge know that negotiation has taken place, the prosecutor and defendant must ordinarily go through a courtroom ritual in which they deny that the guilty plea is the result of any threat or promise. As a result there is no judicial review of the propriety of the bargain—no check on the amount of pressure put on the defendant to plead guilty. The judge, the public, and sometimes the defendant himself cannot know for certain who got what from whom in exchange for what.[57]

SUMMARY

This chapter considers three families of paradoxes concerning social problems. The first paradoxes center on what is salient about social problems. Because the changing and conflictual are more salient than the stable and continuous, we tend to exaggerate the amount of disorder and conflict within society. Those employing social norms to their advantage try to make the norm salient and not their creation and use of it. This disguises the actual operation of power in society and focuses attention toward an abstraction. Terrorism is an attempt to manipulate salience which can be successful because salience is separable from evaluation.

The second family of paradoxes centers on the limitations of rewards and punishments in controlling complex social behavior. People do try to maximize their rewards, but these are subjective rewards determined by subtle social factors. The injudicious use of rewards can increase frustration and hostility by increasing expectations. Rewarding an action can also create a more negative attitude toward the action due to the need to justify ourselves and reduce dissonance.

Lastly, bargaining relating to social problems produces a number of paradoxes. In order for negotiators to demonstrate their determination and discourage pressures on them to change their position, they might destroy communication, deny they have any social power, or appear completely irrational. All of these attempts are rational within the limitations of a win–lose strategy. Plea bargaining in the criminal justice system provides a good example of bargaining regarding social problems.

SIX

Approaches to Understanding Social Problems

Now that we have considered some of the sources of information and misinformation, we can face two broad questions: (*a*) exactly what are social problems, and (*b*) what are the common approaches to understanding them?

It is traditional to present the key definitions and theories at the very beginning of most textbooks. This is the proper procedure from a purely logical point of view. But from a psychological perspective, it helps to have at least some insights into an area before deciding on exactly what the area covers. The way you define any division of knowledge will determine much of your later thinking. This is especially true in areas like social problems, which can be loaded with emotional preconceptions. Definitions, in a sense, are arbitrary, but they commit you to consider some things and ignore others. A good definition should tell you where to look; it should not tell you what to see.[1]

Most people have a tendency to define a social problem so that their pet problems are given high priority, and the problems they contribute to are ignored. This is just another example of the general rule that everyone likes to think that someone else *is* the social problem. A steel company executive is probably more anxious to see that "welfare cheats" and "labor goons" are included in the definition of a social problem than pollution or monopoly capitalism. A college student might be more interested in a definition that includes unemployment and problems in education than one that stresses premarital sex and marijuana use.

DEFINING A SOCIAL PROBLEM

Perhaps the easiest way to approach defining a social problem would be to present a few typical examples. Below are a half-dozen definitions taken from recent texts on social problems. Take a minute or two to look them over.

1. Simply put, social problems are conditions of society which have negative effects on large numbers of people. [2]
2. Social problems, in the context of our discussion, are viewed as those significant discrepancies between cultural prescriptions and present-day conditions which influential leaders and involved persons believe should be ameliorated by appropriate social action. [3]
3. A social problem is a condition that has been defined by significant groups as a deviation from some social standard, or breakdown of social organization. [4]
4. Sociologists usually consider a social problem to be an alleged situation which is incompatible with the values of a significant number of people who agree that action is necessary to alter the situation. [5]
5. A social problem is a condition affecting a significant number of people in ways considered undesirable, about which it is felt something can be done through collective action. [6]
6. A social problem exists when a significant number of people, or a number of significant people, perceive an undesirable difference between social ideals and social realities, and believe that this difference can be eliminated by collective action. [7]

One characteristic of these definitions should be obvious. They separate a social problem from a personal problem. If you have a toothache, that's your personal problem. If millions are demanding a national program of dental insurance, there is a social problem. If you can't find a job, that's your problem. If millions cannot find a job, and they are going hungry and marching in the streets, that's a social problem. All common definitions stress that a social problem has to be social; it deals with society collectively rather than with a few individuals.

There are two major ways a social problem can be distinguished from a personal problem. A social problem can either (*a*) *harm* a large number of people or (*b*) *worry* a large number of people. These two ways are not at all identical, and there is substantial disagreement among sociologists on which to prefer. To say that a condition *hurts* a large number of people is an *objective* statement. To say that it *worries* a large number of people is a statement about how people *feel* about something, a *subjective* condition. It is possible for people to be collectively hurt by something and not worry about it, like the proverbial frog that was contentedly boiled to death when the temperature of its water s-l-o-w-l-y rose to the boiling point. From the objective viewpoint, a society that smokes hundreds of billions of cigarettes a year has a social problem even if it doesn't recognize it. On the other hand, sometimes a society is aroused by a subjective social problem that has no objective foundation. The "witch" problem in Salem, Massachusetts, and the "Jewish" problem in Nazi Germany provide two good examples.[8]

It can be seen from our definitions that different sociologists take different sides on the subjective–objective distinction. Definition 1 is objective. Definition 6 is subjective; a social problem is based on how people *perceive* the situation. One of the major difficulties with a purely objective definition is that it is often difficult to determine scientifically and objectively what exactly is hurting people. It is usually much easier to determine what they *think* is hurting them. It is easier to agree that people are concerned about recreational drug use than to agree on exactly what the effects of the drugs might be. Another difficulty is that even if we could construct a list of things that objectively hurt people, the list would contain an endless litany of practices, beliefs, attitudes, institutions, and objects that would bear little resemblance to what people in our society normally call social problems. In order to escape these difficulties, most contemporary sociologists adopt a more subjective approach. Some consider a social problem to contain both an objective condition *and* a subjective response to that condition. Any approach that stresses the subjective nature of social problems has its own difficulties.[9]

IMPLICATIONS OF A SUBJECTIVE DEFINITION

There are at least five characteristics of a subjective approach to social problems that are worth mentioning.

1. *Popular interest is fickle.* Although the underlying facts (the objective condition) are constant, popular concern about the problem can vary tremendously. A few highly publicized incidents can drastically increase the level of popular interest in a problem. For instance, it has become a predictable feature of American life that every year that is divisible by 4 will show a substantial increase in popular concern over the adequacy of our national defense. This concern usually diminishes rapidly after the Presidential elections.

Similarly, public outcry over crime, unemployment, drug addiction, pollution, racism, and other items on the typical list of social problems is quite fickle and often bears little relation to objective measurement of the extent of the problems. Therefore, it is often desirable to measure the *extent* of the problem objectively when its *existence* is defined subjectively. Even those scholars who advocate a subjective approach usually reserve the right to tell people that a social problem is not as bad as, or is worse than, they believe.

2. *A social problem represents an evaluation.* To perceive a condition as "undesirable," as in definitions 5 and 6, is to express an attitude or evaluation. A social problem reflects a gap between the world as it is perceived to be and the world as it is "supposed" to be. Such a gap can be closed by either of two actions: (*a*)the *objective* conditions (or the popular perception of them) can change or (*b*) the *evaluation* of them can change. Some social problems, therefore, can be "solved" by simply deciding that, after all, things are not as bad as we thought. The social problem of drinking alcohol decreased remarkably when people decided it was not all that bad, and Prohibition was repealed. One of the paradoxes of the subjective approach to social problems is that problems can be removed by a mere change of attitude.

3. *Somebody has to complain about the problem.* Who are the people who decide there is a social problem? Are they necessarily the majority of the population? Or is a small but vocal minority sufficient? If you look over the definitions, you will notice that they do not really answer this question. Definition 2 refers to "influential leaders and involved persons." Definition 3 speaks of "significant groups." How can we determine who these significant groups might be? A significant group of

"influential leaders and involved persons" to one observer may be a band of "rabble rousers" and "professional troublemakers" to another.

Definition 6 refers to a "significant number of people, or a number of significant people." If those significant people happen to be the scientists whose job it is to measure and report the existence of social problems, the subjective definition of a social problem becomes indistinguishable from an objective one. In either case, a group of specialists study a social situation, decide it is harmful, and this establishes a social problem. Once again, we can see that the distinction between the objective and the subjective can be quite fuzzy.

4. *Social problems are things that we do something about.* Social problems do not have to be indicated by opinion polls. They are also indicated by petitions, pickets, political action, and other collective efforts. We do not need an opinion poll to tell us that a "significant number of people" think racial discrimination or unemployment are social problems; they are marching in the streets to let us know. Some definitions explicitly mention the hope for change through collective action as an indicator of a social problem. According to this conceptualization, until people decide we should do something about it, a problem like bad weather, which affects a large number of people, is not a social problem; it is merely a common misfortune. We do not cry, "They ought to do something about it" unless we feel it is the type of thing that society *can* do something about.

5. *Social problems reflect optimism.* The use of collective action to indicate a social problem implies that the more faith people have in government and other institutions aimed at improving social conditions, the more social problems there will be. A country like the United States will have more than its fair share of social problems because (*a*) many Americans have been told to expect freedom, justice, free education, and other advantages; (*b*) they think the government can do something about a problem if it really wants to; (*c*) they have faith in progress—a belief that things are supposed to be getting better and better; and (*d*) America is full of economists, sociologists, journalists, government officials, and others who have a professional interest in detecting and dealing with social problems. For these reasons, America can be said to have a "social problem consciousness."[10] Other cultures which lack these characteristics will show less social interest and collective action because they have no great hope that things can or should be better. As long as misery is the accepted condition of mankind, there is only collective misfortune; there are no social problems. From this

perspective, social action, including marches, picketing, demonstrations, and the like, is a sign of hope.

In summary, when forming a definition of a social problem, four levels of reality could contribute to the definition: (*a*) the physical reality—what the facts are; (*b*) the perception of the reality—what people think the facts are; (*c*) the evaluation of the perception—whether the situation is considered good or bad; and (*d*) the social action that follows the evaluation. Although each of these levels is somewhat independent of the others, they all could be thought of as part of a "complete" social problem. Or the definition of a social problem could use just one level. A purely objective definition would take the physical reality as the defining factor and disregard the others. A subjective position might stress the existence of collective action and ignore the objective situation.

I have not stated one definition that is *the* best definition to use. There is no need for you to choose among these different approaches either, but you should be aware of the possible levels of reality that could enter into a definition. To clarify this point, we will now consider an objective social problem that is not on most people's list of major social problems.

MISTREATMENT OF THE UGLY: A SOCIAL PROBLEM THAT ISN'T

Americans are familiar with many kinds of prejudice and discrimination. There is prejudice against women, blacks, browns, Indians, those with Latin surnames, Jews, Orientals, the retarded, ex-mental patients, ex-convicts, the young and the old, to mention a few. But one of our most thorough prejudices is rarely mentioned. I am referring to our prejudice against the ugly, the homely, the fat, the disfigured, the short—our prejudice against all those who are not well-formed, tall, dark (but not too dark) and handsome. We tend to assume that someone who is ugly or misshapen will work on the assembly line or in the back of the warehouse and not in the executive suite. Many who would never think of telling a "dumb Polack" joke would not hesitate to make fun of someone who is short or overweight.

I am not referring to those who have a physical handicap so that they cannot do the work of someone normally endowed. For some years, we have had a strong public relations program aimed at hiring the physically handicapped. I am referring to those who have no physical handicap at all and who can do the same work as anyone else. Their only handicap is aesthetic; they just don't look nice.* There is no campaign to hire the ugly. Studies of a number of different groups, including adults and children, blacks and whites, and lower- and middle-class subjects, have shown that, in general, those who are facially disfigured or obese are considered less attractive than those who are crippled or missing a limb.[11]**

It is amazing how little discrepancy from the normal figure or physiognomy we tolerate before someone is labeled "deformed."[12] Someone whose eye is oddly cast, or whose nose is somewhat off-center, or who has a harelip is considered clearly deformed. Disfigured persons, to use Erving Goffman's cogent term, carry a public *stigma;* they have the "wrong" identity.[13] Or as the Bible tells us:

> And the Lord said to Moses, "Say to Aaron, none of your descendants throughout their generations who has a blemish may approach to offer bread of his God. For no one who has a blemish shall draw near, a man blind or lame, or one who has a mutilated face or limb too long, or a man who has an injured foot or an injured hand, or a hunchback, or a dwarf, or a man with a defect in his sight or an itching disease or scabs, or crushed testicles; no man of the descendants of Aaron the priest who has a blemish shall come near to offer the Lord's offering by fire. . . ."
>
> (Leviticus 21:16–21)

In spite of the frequent claim that it is the inner self that matters, Americans spend an estimated $7 *billion* a year on products and services to make their faces prettier, and endure up to a million cosmetic surgeries annually.[14] If you cannot afford a nose job or a face lift, you can always turn to prayer. *Little Talks to Boys and Girls,* a children's inspirational reader, tells how it works:

> Do you know the surest way to have a beautiful face? You do not need to buy creams and powders. Your face can become beautiful and stay

---

*It can be argued that much of the prejudice against various outgroups is actually an aesthetic prejudice. Orientals and women could be considered too short, blacks too dark and lacking the "correct" physiognomy, etc. It might be that the greatest handicap of some retardates is not a low IQ but a low forehead.

**There are some exceptions. Lower-class Jews, for instance, apparently do not find the obese to be unattractive. It would be interesting to see if they have a greater than average prejudice against those who are thin.

beautiful, with a new light all its own, if you take time every day to get alone with the Lord.[15]

Examine television commercials or magazine advertisements and you will see what Americans feel is really important in getting ahead—a good figure and a handsome face.

A group of nondisfigured persons were shown a photograph of a thirty-one-year-old man who managed to become an executive in a chemical corporation. This man was successful and highly intelligent, but he suffered from a congenital malformation. His face was asymmetrical; he had large buck teeth, a receding, pointed chin, and a narrow forehead. Some of the responses to the photo:

He is mean and small—not bright.
He looks mean and nasty.
He might be a follower in a gang.
He's a dope addict.
Man seems to look like a maniac. Has a desire to kill.
Below average intelligence—probably an IQ slightly above or even in the moron group.
Appears to be an imbecile; very low intelligence.[16]

These comments provide an excellent example of our need to associate physical disfigurement with moral and intellectual disfigurement. It is hard for us to imagine someone who is kind, sensitive, intelligent, creative, and—DEFORMED. If we can convince ourselves that the physically deformed are also morally deformed, then things are as they should be—bad goes with bad; good goes with good. The depraved have been given their well-deserved punishment.

Convincing ourselves that unfortunate victims actually deserve their fate is called the *just world* phenomenon or *blaming the victim.*[17] Belief in this kind of just world helps to assuage our guilt over not aiding the unfortunate as well as to relieve anxiety about the misfortune befalling us.[18] If misfortune is due to pure luck, then it could happen to you tomorrow. But if you can convince yourself that the victim actually did something to deserve misfortune, then you don't have to worry. You, being kind and smart, do not deserve tragedy, and therefore you will not receive it. Blaming the victim might have a lot to do with our general insensitivity to others' misfortune and our reluctance to aid those who are victims of social problems.[19]

Perhaps it was a "just world" that the Chicago City Council had in mind in 1939 when it passed an ordinance banning anyone from appearing in public "who is diseased, maimed, mutilated or in any way deformed so as to be an unsightly or disgusting object."[20] Nor could a disfigured person hide behind a mask. The City Council thought of that one too. Another ordinance forbade anyone from wearing a mask or hood unless "taking part in carnivals, mask balls . . . [or has] a written permit issued by the mayor."[21]

The need to believe in a just world is illustrated by our treatment of the obese. It is an article of faith in American folklore that the overweight are lazy gluttons who roundly deserve their fate. According to Harvard nutritionist Jean Mayer:

> We are rapidly creating a new minority—the obese. It is no longer fashionable to look down on people because of the color of their skin or the length of their names or the shape of their noses. It is unfortunately very fashionable, however, to look down on the obese as weak-willed individuals. The prejudice is very strong, and is expressed in every way possible.[22]

There is no evidence to support the belief that overweight is a sign of moral depravity. Research indicates that the overweight usually eat about the same as those of normal weight.[23] Obesity is caused by a variety of genetic, constitutional, temperamental, and personality factors which have little to do with virtue or vice. Moreover, with the exception of those who are tremendously overweight, being fat does not substantially reduce health or longevity.[24] Nonetheless, obesity, especially in women, is considered a sign of moral weakness.* Those who are overweight are less likely to find a good job or be admitted to college.[25] (One university official explained the disdain for heavy applicants by claiming they "would have trouble climbing the hills.")[26] At least one American university suspends overweight students who refuse to reduce.[27]

Even those who are merely unattractive and who have no notable deformity meet with a variety of prejudices.[28] In one study on the effects of looks on school grades, female college students were asked to evaluate the teacher's behavioral reports on a number of children. All of the background and behaviors described in the reports were experimentally controlled; the only thing that varied was the attractiveness of

* Our contemporary American conception that fat is unsightly is a relatively recent development in Western aesthetic attitudes. Look at the classical statuary of the Greeks and Romans, and you will see that the traditional Western idea of beauty is our conception of fat. The proud, naked beauties in Rubens' paintings would be ashamed to appear in a bathing suit in present-day America.

the child whose photograph was attached to the report. The students who evaluated the reports showed no systematic bias when they contained only minor transgressions in behavior. But when the child committed a more serious disturbance, the attractive child was considered much more forgivable. An attractive child who misbehaved was seen as a "good kid" who was having a bad day, while an unattractive child was seen as a real troublemaker, even though they had committed the same offense.[29] In a similar study, a group of fifth-grade school teachers evaluated report cards. The teachers considered the attractive children to be brighter, to have better social relationships with other children, and to have parents who were more interested in their education. Because all the information except the photos was the same, the teachers were actually evaluating the children on the basis of their looks.[30]

One of the more interesting prejudices about looks in American culture is our disdain for the short. It is considered proper to be a big person, someone who thinks big, who has a big heart, who never would do a small thing. Tall men get the better jobs, and some jobs, like fireman and policeman, are entirely closed to short people.[31] One of the best predictors of who will win the American Presidential election is not party or platform but height. The taller candidate almost always wins.[32]

Not only do short people get shortchanged in social relations. The process also seems to work in reverse; successful people are perceived as taller. The Australian psychologist Paul Wilson introduced some students to a man he described as a professor from Cambridge. To other students, he introduced the same man as a college student. In each case after the man left, the students were asked to estimate his height. The man was perceived as being about 2½ inches taller when he was thought to be a high-status professor.[33]

As with other forms of prejudice, our association of goodness with being tall, lean, and well-formed is deeply implanted in our popular culture. In nursery rhymes the bad witches are ugly, the heroes are handsome, and the heroines are gorgeous. The monsters in fairy tales are both ugly and bad, and the charming princes are handsome and good. (It is interesting that we have the same word, *monster*, for someone who is terribly misshapen or terribly immoral.) In westerns the hero is presented as tall and lean, even if he actually has to stand on a box to kiss the leading lady. When Dr. Jekyll is transformed into Mr. Hyde, he becomes both ugly and cruel. When Robert Bruce Banner turns into the Hulk, he becomes both ugly and stupid.* Dick and Jane in children's readers might be black or brown. Jane might even be a leader once in a while rather than always tagging behind. But would Jane ever have a harelip? Would Dick be a midget?

The prejudice against the homely and deformed is very similar to other prejudices in our society. It is simply more thorough and less conscious. Nevertheless, the same unfortunate effects of prejudice occur even if it has not yet developed into a social problem in the subjective sense. Many people are made needlessly miserable because of disfigurements. Many lives are wasted. Society is denied the talents of those who could be of great benefit if they were given a fair chance. Costs to the public for welfare, mental health treatment, and other costs of discrimination are needlessly increased. In terms of many objective measures, it could be demonstrated that we do have a social problem. But by the subjective definition, there is no problem of prejudice against the ugly and deformed.** There is little public outcry or collective action; there are only lots of isolated pockets of frustration and defeat.

APPROACHES TO SOCIAL PROBLEMS

Now that we have considered the definition of a social problem and an example of what might be called a "potential" social problem, we can discuss the ways sociologists have developed for understanding and solving social problems. There is no *one* way to understand a social problem, any more than there is one way to understand light or matter. There are a number of different approaches, each with its own strengths and weaknesses. In this section, I will present an overview of

---

*The literature of monster fiction and horror movies provides a fascinating example of blaming the victim. Immoral creatures are almost always ugly as well. (There are a few exceptions, such as Count Dracula, who is rather handsome except for the problem of an uncorrected overbite.) In the original *Frankenstein*, by Mary Shelley, the monster was at first intelligent and kind, and became cruel by people hating and mistreating him because he was ugly.[34] In the film versions, the monster is usually cruel and stupid right from the start. In this way, the story matches our prejudices rather than enlightens them.

**In forming the National Association to Aid Fat Americans (NAAFA) and similar groups, overweight Americans have begun to fight back. They have their work cut out for them. When NAAFA complained to the New York City Commission on Human Rights about cases of housing discrimination against fat people, the Commission said it dealt only with discrimination due to age, sex, race, religion, and national origin. Discrimination due to body build was apparently allowed.[35]

four popular approaches. There is nothing magical about these four approaches; others could be added. But these four are all popular among social scientists, and taken together should provide a good introduction to the different conceptualizations developed by specialists in understanding social problems.

DEVIANT BEHAVIOR

Perhaps the easiest way for most people to begin to understand social problems is to concentrate on the rules, or *norms*, of society. In a legalistic society like America, many of these rules have been made into laws—laws against theft, rape, discrimination, public intoxication, the use of heroin, corporate monopoly, etc. In order to include a broader variety of social problems, most sociologists prefer to speak of norms, the rules of proper behavior, rather than laws. Being unemployed, having more children than one can afford, repeatedly getting drunk at home, and being addicted to prescribed medication can represent social problems even though no specific laws are being broken. In such cases, it is the more general norms of society that are being violated. Social problems then can be construed as the result of people deviating from norms. This *deviance* approach, as it is called, suggests some questions. Who are the people who are violating the norms? How do they violate them? How do these violations constitute a social problem? What causes these people to act this way? How can we change their behavior?

Concentrating on the deviant behavior of individuals is probably the approach most commonly used by the public in understanding social problems, and sociologists who take this view usually strike a responsive chord in the general population. However, too often people use the deviance approach to avoid thinking about social problems rather than as the beginning of serious thought. Their error is to adopt an extremely moralistic stance in confronting deviant behavior. This leads to a conceptual shift from deviant *behavior* to deviant *people*. Social problems are no longer actions, they are people. Some inherent weakness in the deviants is then assumed to be the cause of the problem. This weakness may stress free will ("She chose a life of crime") or some inherent character or biological flaw ("He was a bad seed"). The solution to a social problem has degenerated into a never-ending search for the "bad guys" who *are* the social problem. Even if they could be found, there is little that can constructively be done with them, because the focus is on the person and not the behavior.

A hypothetical illustration will help explain why this error leads to the abandonment of serious thinking. Imagine you have a ten-year-old son who stutters. You take the child to a speech specialist, who gives him a complete battery of diagnostic tests. Two weeks later, after analyzing all the test results, the specialist calls you back for the diagnosis. "Your son," he proclaims, "is a born stutterer, and that's all there is to it. That will be $300."

That is not the way it is supposed to be! The professional, whose job it is to solve problems, is the one person who is not allowed the excuse, "That's the way it is, and there is nothing to be done about it." To take another example, a bishop might be a firm believer in free will, but when half of the congregation gets up and walks out in the middle of his sermon, he doesn't tell himself that they freely chose to leave, and "that's all there is to that." He will be looking for an *explanation* for their behavior, and "freely choosing" is not an explanation. As a theologian, the bishop may believe in free will, but as a teacher and administrator, he believes in explanations. In the same way, sociologists have the responsibility to look behind deviant behavior, to find its cause, and to discover ways of reducing or eliminating social problems. The sociologist is not allowed to say, "The community freely chose to riot, and that's all there is to that."

The first step in seriously applying the deviant behavior approach is to focus on the behavior of individuals and refer to *stealing* rather than thieves, *polluting* rather than polluters, and *using drugs* rather than "dope fiends." The problem then is to locate the cause of the behavior. There are any number of potential causes of deviant behavior, but many sociologists feel that the most common reason for the violation of norms is that people *learn* to do it. Those who violate norms have learned to be deviant just as those who obey the norms have learned to obey them. There are several ways this can come about.

One common social learning conception, popularized by the noted sociological theorist Robert Merton, focuses on the frustration of social goals.[36] According to this view, a deviant learns the goals approved or encouraged by society but has no socially accepted means of achieving these goals. The deviant then learns to violate the norms of society in order to achieve the goals of society. For example, in a variety of ways, contemporary American society encourages sexual activity, sexual conquests, and sexual delights. This is particularly true for a large number of young persons, who are simultaneously discouraged from getting married. The result is the deviant behavior known as premarital intercourse. [37] Premarital intercourse, in turn, leads to a variety of undesirable consequences, including illegitimacy, venereal disease, abortion, and hasty marriages; hasty marriages, in turn, lead to family problems, divorce, and so on.

Another example would be the goal of economic success, which is frequently frustrated by prejudice, discrimination, and other obstacles. A poor, uneducated man who has accepted the goal of economic success but feels the legitimate paths to that goal are blocked could become a thief, pimp, or drug dealer. In other people's eyes he is contributing to a social problem, but in his eyes he is achieving the success that he was taught to cherish. Similarly, executives who engage in ecological destruction, political bribery, and other shady practices might not worry about it because the practices increase the profits they were taught to expect. They are achieving the culturally prescribed goals even if their methods are violating the norms. Those who are removed from the operation of social norms are said to be in a state of *anomie*. Social problems can then be seen as the result of anomie in conjunction with frustrated goals.

Another social learning approach to deviant behavior concentrates on the existence of deviant subcultures. This conceptualization is more closely associated with the criminologist Edwin Sutherland and his theory of *differential association*. [38] This theory emphasizes the importance of learning more or less specific patterns of deviant behavior by associating with those who themselves practice the behavior. For example, the prostitute's daughter learns to be promiscuous and manipulative with her sexual favors in much the same way that the banker's son learns finance. In Sutherland's words, "Since criminal behavior is thus developed in association with criminals it means that crime is the cause of crime. In the same manner war is the cause of war, and the Southern practice of dropping the 'r' is the cause of the Southern practice of dropping the 'r'." [39]

The differential association and the anomie approaches more often complement each other than conflict. It is likely that the subcultures in which certain criminal behaviors are most common are also those in which the normal routes to success are blocked. Those who feel trapped in poverty might well have a number of role models available for learning prostitution, robbery, drug dealing, and other forms of deviance. The businessmen, who feel frustrated in their desire to increase profits by the constantly increasing network of regulations and laws, might have plenty of teachers available for learning price fixing, rigging union elections, dubious accounting practices, and other violations of norms.

It is not necessary to think of *the* criminal subculture—the hypothetical underworld where the most notorious evil-doers congregate and plot their nefarious schemes. There are a number of subcultures, each teaching its own particular class of norm violations. Nor should you think of a teacher of deviance as necessarily explicitly telling others exactly how to behave. It is possible that this sort of teaching of deviance occurs more often than many people believe. But the more typical teaching of deviant behavior is similar to the way most other behavior is taught—learning by imitation. By observing the way executives operate in some companies, the junior executive may have many role models available for learning norm violations. The young boy in the slums learns that some norms are highly regarded, such as the norm against letting others take advantage of you. Other norms, such as the norm against stealing, might be thoroughly ignored by his role models.

The deviant behavior approach is reminiscent of many of the concepts we have considered in previous chapters. It points out the importance of comparison level and frustration. It reminds us that people are often reinforced for behaviors in unexpected ways, and that the behaviors we think we are teaching might be quite different from what is actually being taught. It also reminds us that the salient norms are not the only ones important for understanding social problems. It might be that one of the most important norms for understanding deviant behavior is the norm of getting ahead at all costs, being a success no matter what. This norm is not usually salient when we think of the rules of American society.

It is frequently said that deviant behavior is antisocial; that it is action *against* society. According to either the differential association or the frustrated goal approach to deviance, what we would call deviant behavior in fact is the result of social influences. Deviant behavior, therefore, springs from the same social actions as any other behavior. It is not against society; rather, it is the effect of a different kind of social pressure. In the same way, the anomie that causes deviance need not be interpreted as the complete lack of social norms. Some norms may be weakened in the development of deviance, while other social standards are just as strong or stronger than ever.

Philip Zimbardo provides a nice illustration of the way supposedly deviant behavior can actually be the result of ordinary social influence processes. Zimbardo was interested in the particular form of deviance known as "car stripping." He left an old car on the street in New York City with the hood raised, suggesting it might be abandoned. Then he secretly watched what happened:

> What happened in New York was unbelievable! Within ten minutes the 1959 Oldsmobile received its first auto strippers—a father, mother, and eight-year-old son. The mother appeared to be a lookout, while the son aided the father's search of the trunk, glove compartment, and motor. He handed his father the tools necessary to remove the battery and radiator. . . . In less than three days what remained was a battered, useless hulk of metal, the result of 23 incidents of destructive contact. The vandalism was almost always observed by one or more other passersby, who occasionally stopped to chat with the looters. Most of the destruction was done in daylight hours and not at night (as we had anticipated), and the adults' stealing clearly preceded the window-breaking, tire-slashing fun of the youngsters. The adults were all well-dressed, clean-cut whites who would under other circumstances be mistaken for mature, responsible citizens demanding more law and order. [40]

In this case, imitation of adults, the authority of the family, and other aspects of stable social structure are clearly contributing to the development of delinquent patterns of behavior. Zimbardo's observations also suggest that the norms of car stripping might vary widely from one section of the country to another. When he tried the same study in Palo Alto, California, no one touched the car except one kind passerby, who lowered the hood when it started to rain. [41]

Some forms of deviance may be the result of the failure of social norms to guide an individual's behavior properly. Retarded persons who have difficulty learning norms might provide an example of those who would violate a norm out of ignorance. Some people intellectually know that the norm exists but still feel an overwhelming need to violate it. Examples of this source of deviance might include the alcoholic, the drug addict, the nymphomaniac, and the kleptomaniac. But most violations of norms are likely to be due to the operation of social influences rather than their lack, and the retarded and nymphomaniacs are exceptions to this general principle.

It is encouraging to think that deviance is still under the influence of social processes. This suggests that by taking the appropriate social action, deviant behavior can be reversed. It then becomes a matter of discovering the appropriate action and convincing those concerned to follow that course. This is possible only because the focus is on the behavior and not on the people who perform the behavior.

VALUE CONFLICT

The second approach to understanding social problems, the value conflict approach, is an extension and elaboration of the deviant behavior approach. In a sense, it begins where the deviant behavior approach ends—with the existence of different subcultures with different norms or experiences. The emphasis, however, is now on the clash between the groups themselves, and not on the deviant behavior of individuals.

According to the value conflict approach, several factors are necessary to generate a social problem. (a) *There must be different groups.* Groups or subcultures are seen as the transmitters and generators of the social values that precipitate conflicts. (b) *The groups must be in contact.* There will be no social problem created if Greenland Eskimos believe in monogamy and North African Moslems practice polygamy. It is only when close contact occurs between the groups that a social problem could occur. (c) *The groups hold different cherished values or interests.* If I believe in wearing white socks and you believe in wearing black socks, there is little likelihood of a social problem resulting. However, if a large, well-organized group feels it is very important for everyone to wear white socks and another group feels equally strongly about black socks, a problem is on the way.

When these conditions are met, social problems can result, either through competition for scarce resources or due to attempts to enhance group values. When most people think of social problems resulting from group conflicts, they think of wars, bread riots, labor-management conflict, and similar clashes. These would be examples of competition for such limited resources as land, oil, bread, or money.

There are other equally important but less obvious ways that group conflicts can cause social problems. In addition to a desire for resources, a social group also has values, which extend beyond the group's purely economic interest. Values are basic attitudes or estimates of worth that are important to the life of the group. A group not only wishes to cherish its values, it desires to extend them. When these group values are extended, the group gains in prestige, and perhaps social power as well. This suggests the second way in which group conflicts can cause social problems. A group will attempt to enhance its own values by forcing them upon another. Fifty years ago, for instance, many Americans were not satisfied with their own personal abstinence from alcohol; they lobbied for Prohibition, which forbade everyone to drink. Other groups with different values came in conflict with the values of Prohibition, and the result was a whole complex of social problems. Many social conflicts, including those surrounding drug use, sexual practices, sexism and racism, can be thought of as conflicts between groups with different values.

Social problems can also result from a conflict of values within one individual. This can occur due to the operation of different *reference groups*. A group to which you feel allegiance and whose values, opinions, and attitudes you cherish is known as a reference group. Most of us are under the influence of various reference groups throughout our lives, and these groups frequently support conflicting values.* A teenage boy, for example, may wish to support both the ideals of his family, which stress restraint and a dignified decorum, and those of his peer group, which stress a hedonistic, free-swinging life-style. The teenager can be said to be faced with *intrapersonal* value conflict—a conflict within the same individual. Sometimes the conflicting values are proposed by the same group, as when parents tell their children to (a) become financially successful, (b) value their honor above all else, (c) never let anyone make a fool out of them (d) never get in trouble with the law, and (e) be popular with their friends. They usually forget to explain how to do all these things simultaneously.

In countries like America, which contain a great diversity of potential reference groups and potential value conflicts, most people feel a moderate amount of intrapersonal value conflict much of the time. These conflicts create a double bind within the individual that mirrors the conflict found among groups in the total society. They can lead to guilt, depression, alcoholism, and other neurotic or escapist behavior.

The conflicts between groups can reside in deep-seated interests

---

* A nice illustration of the existence of varied reference groups in our society can often be observed on the television talk shows. All of the guests on these shows are presumably popular, enjoyable, or at least "interesting" personalities. A typical show might have a noted minister, a famous football player, a movie actress talking about her third divorce, and a professor who just wrote a book about fraud in the funeral business. It becomes an interesting parlor game to discover some value they all hold in common.

rather than cherished values. It is doubtful, for example, that many people would defend prostitution as a cherished value, but many do have an interest in maintaining it. Among those who benefit from prostitution are the prostitutes themselves, their clients, pimps, procurers, motel managers who can make a greater profit by selling the same room five or ten times a night, politicians and policemen who receive protection money, and businessmen who like to "entertain" their out-of-town clients.

The value conflict approach reminds us that even though many groups might complain about a problem, other groups (or perhaps even the same group) will have an interest in supporting it. The supporting groups might not be as vocal as the offended groups, and their personal gain may be less obvious, but if we look hard enough we may be able to find the groups that are maintaining a social problem. The sociological theory that advocates an analysis of a social institution or condition in terms of its functions for various groups in the total operation of society is called *functionalism*.*

Most people would accept the hypothesis that there are various groups that indirectly or directly benefit from capitalism, marriage, the educational system, the legal system, and similar institutions in our society. In fact, as some functionalists would argue, because these groups are interconnected in the total operations of society, in a sense society, as a whole, benefits from these institutions. However, many people become uncomfortable when it is suggested that many groups, or even society as a whole, benefit from the institutions that are a part of social problems. One source of discomfort is the fact that functionalism has a knack for finding all sorts of unexpected beneficiaries of social problems besides the supposedly selfish perpetrators of the problems themselves. For example, it has been suggested that illegitimacy is functional in American society because it provides the "raw material of the adoption process."[43] Without this surplus of unwanted babies, many sterile couples would remain unhappily childless. This kind of explanation can be uncomfortable.

Functionalism, like any sociological theory, should not be judged on whether its position is flattering or insulting to any particular group. Nor does a theory have to agree with our conscious feelings about social problems. It also should be stressed that functionalism is

---

Functionalism is a term that has seen more than its fair share of service in social science theory. Perhaps because it sounds so nice (what American would be against a *functional* explanation?), it has been used to refer to a number of things that may have very little in common.[42]

not a "conspiracy" theory; there is no assumption that people are even aware of what they are doing, let alone working in explicit cooperation.

Functional analysis is usually most convincing when it is applied to a stable, well-entrenched problem. Prostitution, for instance, has been around for so long, and has triumphed over so many well-publicized campaigns to remove it, that even those with the most charitable impression of our antiprostitution efforts must begin to wonder how serious we really are about getting rid of it.

Poverty is another persistent social problem. Can there be functional reasons for keeping poverty? Columbia University sociologist Herbert Gans has suggested a number of possible functions for poverty.[44] Among Gans' suggestions:

1. The existence of poverty creates a relatively cheap labor supply for the dead-end, dirty, demeaning and unhealthy work that must be performed in any society.
2. The poor, by paying higher taxes, subsidize the affluent and allow them to pay less for the governmental programs they enjoy.
3. The poor support medical innovation by furnishing the patients for teaching hospitals and medical experimentation.
4. The existence of a number of poor men increases enlistment in the armed services and thus provides a relatively inexpensive army without recourse to military conscription.
5. Poverty supplies jobs for the police, social workers, and others who "serve" the poor.
6. The poor supply a market for inferior goods that otherwise would be wasted, such as day-old bread, deteriorated housing, and secondhand clothes.
7. The poor help maintain the salience and legitimacy of social norms by supplying a group against whom they can be applied.
8. The continued existence of poverty helps create the surplus capital that funds high culture, art, and other intellectual activity.
9. Poverty provides an occasion for the affluent to express their social conscience by funding hospitals, charity drives, research foundations, and similar philanthropy.

Gans' examples indicate that it is not difficult to find people who benefit from poverty.

At least two items on the list merit elaboration because they have application well beyond the specific problem of poverty. Item 5 refers to the interest of various professional groups in gaining a livelihood from social problems. This function has been alleged of many social problems in addition to poverty. In discussing the news in

Chapter 2, I quoted Howard Becker's suggestion that rule enforcers find it advantageous for us to be worried about the existence of social problems. In general, it has been argued that all professional groups have an interest in maintaining the problem they are supposed to be trying to erase.* If physicians actually did cure all disease, their income would be greatly reduced. If teachers could teach in four years what now takes ten, the unemployment rate among them would soar. On the whole, it is functional for many professionals not to try too hard. As more people are employed in these service industries, we might expect that social problems will grow apace. As John Lofland has put it,

> The growing army of social workers, psychologists, psychiatrists, police, etc., constitutes a stratum with a precise interest in ensuring a flow of persons defined as deviant. The training undergone by such specialists creates a stratum whose aim it is to discover "out there" in the empirical world those sorts of people they have been trained to see. As more of them become better trained and organized—that is, more professional—their sensitivity could well increase. [45]

Item 7 on the list of possible functions of poverty argues that the existence of deviant groups increases the importance of the very values that are being challenged by that group. This, too, is a general principle with applications well beyond the specific area of poverty. We have previously encountered the importance of salience as a construct in analyzing norms and attitudes. The present line of thought suggests that by having a few handy deviants to condemn, a social group can increase the salience of its commitment to the values those deviants are challenging. Although groups generally want their values to be endorsed by others, they may also appreciate a few weak, but well-publicized, pockets of deviance in order to increase their group solidarity. [46]

You might think of this social process as analogous to the effect of contrast in visual perception. [47] A strong contrast can increase the perceptual reality of a figure by enhancing the contours between the figure and its background and bringing the figure into sharper relief. The television screen normally appears gray, but by activating parts of the screen so that they appear white, the unactivated parts appear black by contrast. In an analogous fashion, the existence of deviant persons brings into sharper relief the very values they reject. Kai T. Erikson describes this function of the deviant:

---

* Writers of books on social problems provide a clear example of this rule.

As a trespasser against the norm, he represents those forces excluded by the group's boundaries: he informs us, as it were, what evil looks like, what shapes the devil can assume. In doing so, he shows us the difference between kinds of experience which belong within the group and kinds of experience which belong outside it.

Thus deviance cannot be dismissed as behavior which *disrupts* stability in society, but is itself, in controlled quantities, an important condition for *preserving* stability.[48]

The classic example of a threat to a group increasing its solidarity is the "rallying round the flag" that occurs during war. Similarly, a well-staged and well-publicized criminal trial has the power to force a reaffirmation of the values challenged by the criminal more than any abstract discussion. It is likely that many middle-class Americans were never so convinced of the virtues of short hair and cleanliness as when they meditated upon the existence of "dirty, long-haired hippies." Deviants can be said to provide a *negative* reference group. Just as a positive reference group establishes the values to be emulated, a negative reference group sets an example of what should be avoided. The virtue of chastity might best be taught by creating both a positive reference group of virtuous women to idealize and a negative reference group of promiscuous women to ridicule and scorn.

SOCIAL DISORGANIZATION

In discussing value conflicts, we saw that social problems can represent practices which are functional for certain groups within society, or for society as a whole. However, as Robert Merton has argued, there is no need to assume that *all* functions are planned or deliberate.[49] A problem can be the unplanned function or result of actions taken without any expectation that a social problem was being created. The approach to social problems that emphasizes the unanticipated effects of social actions is known as the *social disorganization* approach. According to this perspective, we tend to forget that social actions do not occur in a vacuum. They take place in a *plenum*—a space that is completely filled. You can put something in a vacuum and move it about as much as you please, and the only effects are on the thing moved. In a plenum, you cannot put something in unless you also take something else out, because all spaces are filled. You cannot move one thing unless you move other things as well. Any action is transmitted throughout the space, because everything is interconnected.

Society is a plenum composed of interconnected parts. We have an unfortunate tendency to focus on isolated parts of society in a way that ignores this interconnectedness. Birth control, eating pork, pornographic literature, chemical fertilizers, highways, and other aspects of society tend to be seen as good or bad in themselves without consideration of the situation in which they occur. So when the total situation changes, the old conception of one part of the total is not changed because it was never seen as only one thread in the fabric of society.

What *behavior* is for the deviance approach, and *groups* are to value conflict, the concept of *structure* is for the social disorganization approach. Social problems are seen as the distortion of the normally correct structure of society. This approach argues that a change in society can upset the harmony, equilibrium, and balance of the social structure so that things no longer fit together. More specifically, society is a structure of attitudes, habits, values, and things. If we change a thing, we have to change the attitudes, habits and values associated with that thing or else social imbalance and social problems will result.

As our awareness of ecology has increased in recent years, our appreciation of the wisdom of the social disorganization perspective has also increased. In a sense, ecology is to the physical and health sciences what social disorganization is to the social sciences. They are both built on the same general principle: *You cannot do just one thing!* [50]

Student riots furnish an example of a social problem that can be interpreted from the social disorganization perspective. Over a period of years, increases in unemployment, economic affluence, and the presumed technological complexity of work have led to an increase in the amount of schooling expected of young Americans. This has led, in turn, to the growth of university communities where 20, 30, or 40 thousand students were brought together in a small area and subjected to common experiences and frustrations. As a result, a student subculture was formed. Common rituals, drugs, music, dress, and language helped mark off a member of this subculture from the general society. A sense of in-group solidarity developed among the students, who found pride and strength in their shared experiences. Eventually, students organized to riot over the draft, university regulations, and other common frustrations. University administrators were startled; parents were shocked; politicians were outraged. In creating the huge universities, they forgot that you cannot do just one thing.

There are many kinds of imbalance that disrupt the social structure and create social problems. The Industrial Revolution, urbanization, immigration from abroad, and the movement of rural Southern poor to Northern urban centers are among the factors that have caused dislocation of social structures in America. Similar processes have taken place throughout the world. Yet one factor is generally considered to stand out above all others as the creator of unanticipated social problems. That factor is technological change. In the Western hemisphere, technology has developed at an unprecedented pace since the beginning of the Industrial Revolution several centuries ago. It is impossible to determine precisely the magnitude of these technological developments, but the estimates of biophysicist John Platt may provide an indication of their scope:

> In the last century, we have increased our speeds of communication by a factor of 10^7; our speeds of travel by 10^2; our speeds of data handling by 10^6; our energy resources by 10^3; our power of weapons by 10^6; our ability to control diseases by something like 10^2; and our rate of population growth to 10^3 times what it was a few thousand years ago.
>
> Could anyone suppose that human relations around the world would not be affected to their very roots by such changes?[51]

William F. Ogburn has emphasized the concept of *culture lag* as a tool for understanding the social problems created by such massive technological shifts.[52] The concept of culture lag states that culture—the norms, expectations, and institutions out of which we construct our daily lives—changes much more slowly than technology. Social structures, therefore, are growing more and more out of balance, and our culture is falling further and further behind the accelerating pace of technological development. A technological revolution demands a revolution in morals, law, and the art of conducting our daily lives which we are reluctant to supply.

In Chapter 4, it was pointed out that technological innovations are adopted in such a way as to maintain the traditional informal methods and the existing social structure. The social disorganization perspective argues that although that might be the intention, even the best laid plans may go astray. Because society is a plenum, the ultimate effect of the introduction of technological change might appear in completely unexpected places. The groups that introduced the change may have been thinking only of their own interest, but their action affects a number of groups far removed from their immediate concern. Many years ago, Ogburn pointed out 150 plausible social consequences of the development of the radio. These included such unplanned effects as the favoring of the contralto voice over the soprano (due to better transmission), quicker detection of criminals (through police radio), and drastic alterations in the nature of political campaigning.[53]

It is easier to understand the vast extent of culture lag if you think in terms of generations rather than years. A year is an astronomical, not a cultural unit. A generation, which can be roughly estimated at twenty-five years, is the length of time it takes an infant to grow up, learn what has to be learned about living in society, have children, and begin to teach his or her children what was learned. A generation can be thought of as a unit of cultural transmission.

The automobile, computer, radio, television, airplane, the electronics industry, and the atomic bomb have all been introduced into society in the last one to three generations. Yet they are discussed in universities patterned after those developed twenty-five to thirty generations ago. They are controlled by an economic system developed four to ten generations ago. They are regulated by a legal system developed eight to fifteen generations ago. They are moderated by a moral system that developed sixty-five to one hundred generations ago, and thrust into a family structure that developed countless ages ago. Culture does lag behind technology!

Consider the example of war. Until recently, as history is measured, war was an ageless, unpleasant, inefficient but tolerable social institution. With the Napoleonic wars, the development of universal military conscription, and the rise of the modern nation-state about seven generations ago, war became decidedly worse. Two generations ago, World War I introduced the battle tank, the rapid-fire machine gun, poison gas, aerial bombardment, and the submarine, and war became truly horrible. A little over one generation ago, World War II gave us the guided missile and the atomic bomb, and it became apparent that, as a social institution, war was no longer functional. But there has not been enough time for many of us to learn to tell our children anything about war other than what we were told by our parents.[54] In the plenum of society, we have yet to develop a replacement for it.

The deviant behavior approach stressed the violation of norms. The social disorganization approach reminds us that the norms themselves might be out of date. As a result, the social disorganization perspective can be rather pessimistic. It challenges one of the basic beliefs of Americans—the belief in progress. It might be that we cannot progress technologically until we are willing to progress in other aspects of our culture as well. We have yet to come to grips with the extended life span provided by medical technology, so that we have the social problem known as the population explosion. How long will it be before our culture catches up with safe abortion, organ transplants, new definitions of death, sperm banks, and sex change?

LABELING

Labeling, the last approach to social problems we will consider, has developed out of the thought of George Herbert Mead, a noted American social philosopher.[55] Mead explored the way in which interaction with other people allows someone to develop a sense of what he or she is—a *self-concept*. According to Mead, it is only by dealing with other people that we understand what kind of person we are. By treating you a certain way, people make it possible for you to figure out what your self really is.

You will recall that the deviance approach stated that society can encourage deviance by providing role models, frustration, anomie, and other causes of deviance. According to the labeling perspective, this is correct as far as it goes, but it does not go far enough. It does not really explain how a person comes to think of himself as a certain kind of deviant, how a person adopts a deviant life-style, a deviant commitment, a deviant self-image. Labeling theory, like most approaches to social problems, is not terribly concerned with single, bizarre acts of deviance, like that of Charles Whitman, the Texas sniper, who started shooting people one day. Labeling stresses long-term patterns of deviance, what Howard Becker called a *career* in deviance.[56] For prostitutes, burglars, forgers, drug users, and the like, deviance is not a one-time thing; it is an intimate part of their lives.

What, then, is deviance? In his book *Labeling Deviant Behavior*, Edwin Schur defines it this way:

> Human behavior is deviant *to the extent that* it comes to be viewed as involving a *personally discreditable* departure from a group's normative expectations, *and* it *elicits* interpersonal or collective reactions that serve to "isolate," "treat," "correct" or "punish" *individuals* engaged in such behavior.[57]

Howard Becker puts it more bluntly:

> . . . *social groups create deviance by making the rules whose infraction constitutes deviance,* and by applying those rules to particular people and labeling them as outsiders. From this point of view, deviance is *not* a

quality of the act the person commits, but rather a consequence of the application by others of rules and sanctions to an "offender." The deviant is one to whom that label has successfully been applied; deviant behavior is behavior that people so label.[58]

From these definitions, it can be seen that labeling theory is interested less in someone's possible deviant behavior and more in what society does about it. The focus now is on what society calls the person and what these names or labels do to shape the person's self-image and later behavior. By deemphasizing the deviant and deviant behavior itself, and concentrating instead on what society does to the potential deviant, labeling theory makes the following generalizations:

1. Almost any behavior could be considered either deviant or nondeviant.
2. Hence, everyone, in some way or other, could be labeled deviant.
3. Some people in society are in the habit of calling others deviant.
4. Those name-callers, or labelers, have great flexibility in whom they chose to call deviant.

Recalling the position of Mead that the way people treat you determines the kind of person you will become, labeling theorists draw an important conclusion from the above generalizations: *By choosing to label some people "deviant," certain groups in society work to create in those people the deviance they claim to deplore.* Labeling theory argues that, contrary to the implications of the deviance approach, society is not just indirectly causing deviance by providing role models or frustration; it is directly causing deviance by putting the label "deviant" on certain people. Deviance doesn't exist until society creates it. To put it another way, deviance can be encouraged not only by rewarding deviance but also by the methods society uses to *punish* deviance.

There are two general ways in which society's label becomes a reality. First, the label acts directly to change people by telling them what kind of people they are. Just as a little boy is told by his parents what kind of person he is going to be when he grows up, so also a man is told by society what kind of person he is *now*. People look into a glass mirror to find out what they look like; they look into the mirror of other people's eyes to determine what they *are*.

Second, labeling works indirectly to create deviance by structuring a person's social relations so as to encourage behavior likely to be labeled deviant in the future. The criminal court is one important labeler in our society. When the judge says, "I find you, the defendant, guilty," the judge is actually applying the label of "criminal" to you. As a consequence of that label, you are sent to a prison, where you are thrust into a deviant subculture. When you are released, the label of "criminal" will follow you from the prison. All of this is likely to encourage you to become a criminal; in other words, the label of "criminal" is creating criminality.

Martin Gold and Jay Williams studied the effects of apprehension of juvenile delinquents on their later behavior.[59] For a group of apprehended delinquents, Gold and Williams found matching controls who performed comparable amounts of delinquency but were never caught by the police. They then analyzed the later delinquency of all the subjects and observed that those who were apprehended committed *more* delinquency than those who got away with their initial delinquency. Gold and Williams conclude, "It appears, unfortunately, that what legal authorities now commonly do upon apprehending a juvenile for his delinquent behavior is worse than not apprehending him at all."[60]

One or two additional examples will help clarify how labeling can create deviance. Another noted group of labelers in our society are the teachers and professors who specialize in the label *stupid*. In accord with their professional status, they do not actually say "stupid," but with the help of educational psychologists they employ a variety of euphemisms, including "dull normal," "hyperactive," "culturally deprived," "learning disability," "developmentally handicapped," "retarded," "antisocial personality," and "minimal brain disfunction." Some of these terms are close to meaningless behaviorally, but they can decide what school the child attends, what grade, track or program the child is entered into, and in general, how the teacher and the school will relate to the child. By treating the child as "stupid," the labeler might, in fact, deprive the child of the encouragement and assistance necessary to avoid actually becoming stupid.[61] Thus, the application of the label could create a career in deviance.

One of the most important sources of labels in our culture is the psychiatric profession. According to Thomas Szasz, a noted critic of psychiatric practice:

> Wherever we turn, there is evidence to substantiate the view that most psychiatric diagnoses may be used, and are used, as invectives: their aim is to degrade—and, hence, socially constrain—the person diagnosed. . . .
>
> Thus, when a psychiatrist declares that Senator Goldwater is unfit to be President, he does not do something unusual; his act is not the

miscarriage of some other, fundamentally different sort of psychiatric performance. On the contrary, it is indistinguishable from declaring one person unfit to stand trial, another to execute a will, a third to drive a car, a fourth to serve in the Peace Corps. In each of these instances, the psychiatrist plays his characteristic social role: he brands as illegitimate the roles or role-aspirations of certain people.[62]

The most important social constraint at the disposal of the psychiatric profession is the power of involuntary commitment—placing people in mental hospitals. When the psychiatrists apply their euphemisms for "crazy," the result is similar to when a judge says "guilty." The person so labeled may be incarcerated among those who have been given a similar label under frustrating and dehumanizing conditions. When placed in a mental hospital, the danger is created that a behavior can turn into a career.

In a noted study on the use of the label "insanity," D. L. Rosenhan had eight quite sane persons admitted to a number of mental hospitals.[63] These pseudopatients all feigned hearing voices in order to get in, but otherwise were truthful about themselves. As soon as they were admitted to the hospital, they acted perfectly sane. It is interesting that although none of the pseudopatients was ever detected as a fake by any staff member of the hospitals, a large number of the real patients realized that the pseudopatients were not actually insane. Several suggested quite accurately that they must have been journalists or professors "checking up on the hospitals."

Rosenhan's study does *not* prove that there is no such thing as schizophrenia or other "mental" disorders.[64] It does indicate that professional labelers in our culture can be easily fooled in applying their labels. Moreover, once a label of "mental illness" has been officially applied, it sticks. "Having once been labeled schizophrenic, there is nothing the pseudopatient can do to overcome the tag. The tag profoundly colors others' perceptions of him and his behavior."[65] Each pseudopatient was finally discharged with a lebel of schizophrenia "in remission."[66] In psychiatric parlance, the phrase "in remission" means roughly "temporarily in abeyance." In other words, even when they were released, the pseudopatients were never actually considered "cured." As Kai Erikson has pointed out, there are elaborate rituals, such as the copout ceremony, for placing a person into a deviant category. But once placed, there are few, if any, comparable rituals for removing the label.[67] The label follows the deviant as a part of his or her self-image.

A related point is that once the label is placed, there is little the person labeled can do that cannot be perceived as compatible with the label. Labels like "schizophrenic" are so ambiguous that almost any action of the person labeled could be interpreted as additional evidence for the truth of the label. For example, as a part of the study, the pseudopatients kept notes on their experiences in the hospital. Several times this note-taking was itself considered indicative of the pseudopatient's illness. "Patient engages in writing behavior" was one nurse's cryptic comment. [68]*

There may have been occasions when you were unfairly accused of being drunk or under the influence of some drug. If so, you know the problem of trying to erase an incorrect label. Should you stand up for your rights and let them know they can't push you around? (Suspect became hostile and abusive.) Should you simply sit back and smile? (Suspect was in a silly stupor.) Should you attempt to prove logically that you couldn't possibly be drunk? (Suspect became argumentative and irrational.) How do you erase such a label?

Fortunately, there are good biological tests to determine if you are under the influence of alcohol and some other drugs. But there are no tests for many of the powerful labels that are used in our society to categorize and defame. How do you prove you are not a confidence man, a prostitute, a homosexual, a liar, a schizophrenic, or a fool?

USING THE APPROACHES

Several characteristics of these four approaches should be mentioned. First, all of them have implications about society beyond the area of social problems. They are not necessarily as pessimistic as our problem orientation might suggest. Unanticipated functions of social actions, for instance, can be good as well as bad. A society may prefer tea to water solely on the basis of taste, but the process of boiling the water for the tea would also help prevent disease. In the same vein, social disorganization is not always bad. A little disorganization may provide a beneficial stimulus for social development.

It should also be mentioned that no approach is inherently mor-

---

*Putting the redundant "behavior" after descriptions of activity is a device, especially popular among behavioristic psychologists, for adding an air of objectivity and scientific analysis to an otherwise drab assertion. In creating an impression of scholarship, "I scratched" is not nearly as powerful as "I engaged in scratching behavior."

alistic. All the approaches could be made to appear righteous and accusatory by the proper choice of language and examples, but their basic positions attempt to be objective and nonmoralistic. Nor is one approach necessarily "liberal" while another is "conservative." It is probably best to think of them as without political philosophy. It should also be apparent that you should not choose the *one* approach you wish to use. They are all useful.

What do these approaches do? They should do four things:

1. They should recommend a set of concepts or ideas to use in thinking about social problems.
2. They should indicate what data, facts, or relationships to look for, and which to ignore, in thinking about social problems.
3. They should suggest the situations, conditions, and causes that give rise to particular problems.
4. They should suggest solutions to particular problems.

There are several things these approaches will *not* do:

1. They will not guarantee a solution.
2. They will not guarantee understanding.
3. They are not mutually exclusive. To some extent, several approaches, taken together, might be needed to understand a social problem.
4. They will not guarantee a value-free interpretation of a problem. It might still be necessary to make a personal decision as to what is correct for society before these approaches can suggest an action to be taken.

Because of these limitations, I have used the awkward phrase "approaches to understanding" social problems rather than "theories" of social problems. These approaches are not, strictly speaking, scientific theories. A theory must be either true or false, and these approaches are too broad to be proven true or false.* It is better to think of them as helpful and useful, rather than correct or incorrect. Avoid the habit of thinking, "Is this approach correct for this problem?" Ask yourself instead, "Is it useful to think this way?" Approaches are tools, and just as a good mechanic knows how to use many tools, so also will a serious thinker about social problems be familiar with a number of approaches. Any one job might require only one tool. It may even be possible to make any automotive repair with only a screwdriver and a pair of pliers, but except as an exercise in mechanical virtuosity, there

---

* According to a common viewpoint, a scientific theory is never proven true, but it *may* be proven false. These approaches could never be proven false.

is no reason to try it. If you can think with all four approaches, you will find that sooner or later, all of them will be helpful in understanding social problems.

Let me extend the simile slightly and say that attempting to understand and deal with a social problem is like trying to fix an automobile. Thinking in this way suggests several parallels.

1. *A number of things can require fixing.* A neglected car might have a dead battery *and* an empty gas tank *and* dirty spark plugs. In the same vein, a thoroughly neglected social condition can have many things that need fixing. We too often fall into the habit of looking for *the* solution to a problem. It may be, in fact, that any number of things must be done to get a car, or a society, in proper shape. This is one reason why a number of approaches can be helpful for the same social problem.

2. *Tests can be made to reduce the number of possible explanations.* A good mechanic does not go haphazardly through all the questions he could ask about a problem. He applies a series of tests to help him focus on the real problem. Does the engine turn over? If so, the problem is not with the battery or the starter. Is fuel getting to the carburetor? If so, the problem is not with the gas line. In the same way, a social problem fixer can apply tests that can drastically reduce the number of plausible explanations. It is one of the purposes of an approach to suggest what those tests could be. For example, the value conflict approach reminds us to look for hidden groups that might be benefiting from the problem.

3. *Maintenance is easier than repair.* If you wait until your car cannot move at all, you have waited until it is too late. It is easier to keep it going if you supply standard maintenance, even when nothing appears to be wrong. In the same way, if a society waits until the economy is in shambles, people are rioting in the streets, and no one has any faith left in the government, it has waited too long. The four approaches we have considered not only suggest causes of social problems, they also suggest standard maintenance of society. If we wait until it is clear to everyone that there is a serious social problem, the repair bill might be a lot higher than if we corrected the problem the first time we heard a slight squeak.

4. *Trying to fix things can cause problems.* One of the more interesting parallels suggested by the automotive simile is that the very process of attempting a solution can itself create additional problems. An unskilled mechanic might overcome one problem and in the process flood

the engine and kill the battery. Is it possible that an unskilled social problem fixer might turn a minor problem into a major one by well-intentioned but foolish actions? The social disorganization and labeling approaches, in particular, argue that this is exactly what might happen. It may be better to do nothing than ask a lout with a sledgehammer to make some fine adjustments.

It is, perhaps, most appropriate to end our consideration of approaches to social problems by recognizing that, like anything else in life, they can be misused.

SUMMARY

There is no general agreement among social scientists on exactly how to define a social problem. Some definitions stress the objective reality of the social situation that makes it a problem. More commonly, sociologists emphasize the anxiety and discontent of the public in changing an unpleasant situation into a true social problem. This subjective approach implies that a social problem is removed if people decide that there is nothing to be done about it or that it is not a problem after all. Discrimination and prejudice against the homely and unattractive provide an example of a situation which has the objective component of a social problem but is not often considered one because people generally accept the situation.

Four different approaches to understanding the cause of social problems are worth considering. The *deviance* approach emphasizes the role of frustration and deviant subcultures in teaching individuals to behave in a socially problematic fashion. The *value conflict* approach focuses on the role of different social groups in generating social problems. The groups can do this by competing for scarce resources, attempting to force their values on others, and causing conflicts within the individual. The *social disorganization* approach highlights the imbalance and disharmony among elements in society caused by social change. When culture lags behind technological change, numerous social problems can develop. Lastly, the *labeling* approach stresses the role of social groups in categorizing various individuals as deviant. By applying the label, a self-fulfilling prophecy can result, so that the individuals act in accordance with the label and in the process contribute to social problems. These four approaches are mutually complementary, and taken together provide valuable insights into the nature of social problems.

SEVEN

Decisions, Decisions

So far, we have been concerned with figuring out what information we should have, getting that information, and interpreting it. We will now turn to the task of putting the information together to form a conclusion. This is the problem of selecting among alternatives, choosing a course of action, or simply making decisions. The aim of this chapter is to highlight some of the major difficulties faced in rational decision making and to discuss some of the means to overcome them. In the next chapter, we will consider more directly some effects of incorrect decision making on creating social problems.

It is interesting to note that the science of decision making is a rather recent development in the history of human thought. Because rational decision making is of greatest importance, one might expect that it would be one of the first intellectual challenges our ancestors confronted when they first decided to use their heads for something besides a hatrack or wig stand. But it was not so. Even now, there is little about the techniques of decision making that is not disputed by one expert or another. Nevertheless, during the last several decades, a large literature about the proper ways to make decisions has been slowly accumulating in mathematics and economics, and we can only hope to cover a few of the major points of this literature.

ACCEPTING THE DECISION

For many people, the most fundamental obstacle to becoming a good decision maker is their failure to admit that they do make decisions. As we saw in Chapter 5, from the perspective of cognitive dissonance theory, decision making can be quite unpleasant. If you deliberately and knowingly make a choice, and it turns out to be a disaster, you not only suffer the disaster, you also suffer the greater shame of being responsible for your misfortune. How can you constantly criticize your political representatives when you voted for them? Some people avoid this hazard by refusing to admit that they make decisions. At least they will not admit to making a choice until they have had a chance to see if they made the correct one. If they did, they gladly take the credit; otherwise, it wasn't their fault.

On the political level, this process leads to what Erich Fromm called "escape from freedom"—the desire to avoid the responsibility that accompanies freedom by rejecting freedom itself and embracing a dictator who will make your decisions for you.[1] On the philosophical level, refusing to recognize your freedom of choice is similar to what the existentialist philosophers call "inauthentic living" or "living in bad faith"—the shallow, empty life that results from a failure to accept the frightening openness of your existence.[2] Regarding social problems, there are some clues to look for in determining if someone is living in bad faith. Those who express positions like the following are good candidates:

My union has absolutely no power. Or alternatively, *I have absolutely no influence on my union.*

There is nothing I can do in my neighborhood that would substantially alter anything.

I know the company I work for is contributing to social problems, but there is absolutely nothing I can do about it.

All candidates in the election are equally bad.

Another tactic is to admit that a choice exists but to act as if it is actually no choice at all. This approach either stresses the obviousness of the solution or the idea that there is no possible solution. The best alternative is perceived as patently clear, or there is no way of finding it. Either a fool could see the right thing to do, or else there is no right thing. Such dichotomies admit no middle ground for conscious decision making which might help find the better alternative without removing the possibility of being wrong. A related escape from deliberate decision making is the ploy of converting all choices into absolute moral confrontation. People who use this trick admit to making choices, but all their choices somehow turn out to be choices between total good and complete evil. Some examples of this strategy regarding social problems:

> *It would be nice to do something about my company's polluting, but I have an obligation to my wife and children not to risk my job. I can't let them starve, can I?*

> *There may be no good reason for this war, but we all have the moral obligation to defend our country, right or wrong.*

> *I personally have no objection to renting the apartment to that black family, but we all have an obligation to keep peace in the neighborhood.*

Using this kind of moral absolutism, one can quickly decide that only immoral people would even have to think about the decision. If the morally demanded course of action just happens to be the personally advantageous one—as it usually is—then so much the better. A version of this escape from responsibility is often heard from politicians who claim that any failure to increase their own authority would be an immoral and unconstitutional denial of their "sacred oath of office."

In contrast to making excuses, rational decision making recognizes that making a choice about social problems almost always involves choosing among a number of alternatives, each of which is neither totally good nor totally bad. *Decision making* is the phrase we use for describing those operations we use to weigh the good against the bad and decide which alternative is the most good or the least bad.

WEIGHING THE GOOD AGAINST THE BAD

We will consider a hypothetical decision regarding unemployment. To keep matters simple, we will consider only two alternative programs for decreasing unemployment: a federal job creation program

HOW TO THINK ABOUT SOCIAL PROBLEMS

and simply doing nothing. We will assume there are five important factors relevant to our decision for which our two alternatives have different effects, and that we can put an asterisk next to the alternative that
has the advantage for each factor. All of this is summarized in Table 7.1.
Which alternative is better? Doing nothing is better in terms of taxation, inflation, and freedom from governmental interference.* On the
other hand, doing nothing is not as good as the job creation program
for the "target" goal of reducing unemployment, nor as good in increasing the Gross National Product. Decision making involves finding a
way to juggle these goods and bads in order to determine the overall
better approach.

One attempt at a solution would be to focus on the particular
problem that is being addressed in the first place—unemployment. You
might argue that because the job program does what it is supposed to
do—create jobs—it is more desirable than the alternative of doing nothing. While there is something to be said for this line of thought, there is
also something very wrong with it. Another one of the factors might be
more important than the target factor of unemployment. As our discussion of social disorganization indicated, it is certainly possible inadvertently to create a large problem while successfully combating a small
one. It might be better to look for the crucial factor, the most important one of the five, and decide on the basis of this one factor alone.

TABLE 7.1   COMPARISON OF TWO APPROACHES FOR REDUCING
UNEMPLOYMENT

| | PROGRAM | |
FACTOR	Doing Nothing	Federal Job Program
Unemployment		*
Inflation	*	
Taxation	*	
Freedom from governmental interference	*	
Growth of Gross National Product		*

* We are also assuming that for each factor there is a general agreement on which direction is
desirable. (For example, a *decrease* in unemployment is good, a *decrease* in taxation is good, and so
on.) There is probably more agreement on these matters on the level of public rhetoric than in actual fact. As our consideration of value conflict suggested, there are probably a number of groups
that benefit from increased taxation, inflation, unemployment, and the like.

But using the most important factor has its own problems. Assuming we did have a means of selecting the most important factor, it might well be that a combination of lesser factors is collectively more important than the single crucial factor. Maybe unemployment is more important than any other individual factor, but is it more important than taxation, inflation, and freedom from governmental interference taken together?

In order to avoid the problem of how to weight the different factors in terms of their relative importance, you might simply assume that each factor is equally important. The solution to the problem could then be determined by totaling the number of factors in favor of each alternative. In our example, doing nothing "wins" by three to two. The problem this technique presents is that we could count the "areas of concern" in a number of different ways in order to create any number of factors we wished. We could break down unemployment into rural, small town, and urban unemployment. In this case, doing nothing "loses" to the job creation program by a score of four to three. Manipulating the number of advantages and disadvantages is a common trick. You can probably recall a number of instances when speakers have enumerated the factors so that there are always more pros than cons for their pet program.

All of the approaches to the unemployment problem we have considered have serious drawbacks. Moreover, these difficulties become increasingly severe when we have more than two alternative actions to choose from. Even in the case of two alternatives, we must conclude that a clear solution will not emerge unless we have more information than we have been working with. If we are only trying to find inspiration, putting the information together as in Table 7.1 is often helpful. But to find a good solution to the problem we must go beyond Table 7.1 and find a way to weight the advantages and disadvantages of an action more precisely.

DEVELOPING A SCALE OF VALUES

The jobs that are specifically developed by a job creation program are salient. But jobs can also be lost due to the increase in taxes which finances the job program. The taxes take money away from consumers who would use it to buy goods and thus create jobs. If it could be shown that a "job creation" program actually lost more jobs than it created, most people would probably agree that doing nothing would be superior to instituting the program. They could easily make this decision because they are placing jobs lost against jobs gained on the same scale of measurement. The decision is then determined by simple arithmetic. In order to work other factors besides jobs into the decision making, they too must be placed on the same scale of value and measured in the same units of measurement.

Because money is the standard medium of exchange in our culture, this common scale is usually called a monetary scale and the unit of measurement of the scale is the dollar. But the particular name we give to the scale or the unit of measurement is unimportant. Once we adopt a common scale, anything measured on that scale can be converted to anything else measured on the same scale.* If we can evaluate both bananas and refrigerators in terms of dollars, we can speak in terms of dollars, bananas and refrigerators interchangeably. In the same way, when we know the rate of exchange, it doesn't matter if we measure in U.S. dollars, French francs, or German marks. If considering the measurement scale to be a monetary scale appears too mercenary to you, call it a banana scale. What is important is that each cost and benefit associated with the decision end up on the same scale of measurement so that we can directly compare them.

Determining the value of any good in terms of dollars and cents is not always easy. How can we measure health, beauty, justice, or freedom in terms of money? How can we place orgasms and sirloin steaks on the same scale? In order to answer questions like these, a number of techniques have been developed. In one way or another, they are all variations on simply asking a person what value he or she puts on the things to be measured. If someone were to ask you what you would be willing to spend for, say, a dozen oranges or a recording of Beethoven's Seventh Symphony, you would have no great difficulty in giving at least a rough estimate. But when someone asks you the value you place on your eyesight or your good name, the questioning gets rather sticky.

It is easier to think of what value you would place on these things for someone else. Approached in this way, it can be seen that people make decisions like this all the time. It is routine for juries to determine a monetary award in cases of wrongful death or personal injury

* It is usually also necessary to assume further that the scale be at least an equal interval scale and not a mere ordinal scale. An equal interval scale would be like the temperature scales of Fahrenheit and Celsius; an ordinal scale would give only the order of the measurements: cold, cool, warm, hot. You can add degrees of temperature; you cannot add "hots" and "colds."

involving the loss of an eye or an arm.[3] In the same manner, the loss of a person's good name is routinely measured in libel cases. The free market mechanism provides a means of measuring the value of an endless number of goods and services. It might be argued that an irreplaceable painting is truly "priceless." But if the painting were actually auctioned off to the highest bidder, a price would, in fact, be found. It might be considered silly to compare sexual intercourse with sirloin steaks, but sex has been traded for food more than once, and the rate of exchange actually determined.

On a moral level, some actions might be wrong and no amount of money can justify them. Finding a common scale of value does not imply that we would be so immoral as to murder a child if the price is right. However, it is a curious characteristic of human sensibility that what is clearly immoral on the level of personal commission often becomes a matter of money on the level of social omission. The bills legislators deliberate often are matters of life and death for many people, and governmental decision makers, like physicians, learn to balance saving lives with cost as just another part of their job. Would you be willing to increase your taxes by $1 to fund a program that would decrease infant deaths by one? How about a $100 increase to save the life? $500? $1,000? In a way, the point at which you begin to say "No" indicates the value you put on that life. When the question is one of probability rather than certainty, we even make these decisions about our own life. If you ever decide to sacrifice a small probability of dying for comfort, convenience, or money, as in choosing to take an automobile rather than ride a train, you are supplying the kind of information that allows a decision maker to determine the value you put on your own life.

While few people make decisions by using paper and pencil and actually estimating the conversion rate from one kind of benefit to another, it should be obvious that a rough approximation of this procedure does happen all the time. Qualitatively different payoffs are subjectively weighted against each other in numerous ordinary decisions, such as buying a house or car, choosing a job, deciding on a career, and selecting a date or mate. The process is merely not as objective and open as I have made it. In buying a house, for instance, monetary considerations must be balanced with attractiveness, space, neighborhood, quality of schools and shopping available, and a number of other qualitatively distinct considerations. Somehow all of these get weighed in the same balance.

There are complications to finding the common scale of value that we will not go into here. For now, we will assume that we can, at least in rough terms, put all the benefits and costs in making a decision on the same scale of value.

Returning to the example of choosing a program to decrease unemployment, if we could estimate the monetary value of the various factors, as we have done in Table 7.2, the decision is easily made. We would choose the job program because its total gain of $10,000 is better than the $0 of doing nothing. If we were comparing two different programs rather than one program with doing nothing, the column on the left would not be a series of zeros but would contain a different set of costs and benefits, and we would choose the program with the greatest total gain. If we were choosing among alternatives, all of which were bad (had a negative total effect), the same procedure would be followed. In situations in which every possible alternative is bad, people are most tempted to reject the decision and refuse to make their estimates and calculations. These situations are often exactly the ones in which rational decision making is most useful in order to hold losses to a minimum.

COMPARISON LEVEL AND SATISFICING

It is time to complicate matters somewhat by considering a major difference between our unemployment example and many common, everyday decisions, such as buying a house or finding a job. In the unemployment case, we arbitrarily considered two alternatives; in

TABLE 7.2   DECIDING BETWEEN TWO APPROACHES FOR DEALING WITH UNEMPLOYMENT

| | PROGRAM | |
FACTOR	Doing Nothing	Federal Job Program
Unemployment	$0	$100,000
Inflation	$0	−$25,000
Taxation	$0	−$50,000
Freedom from governmental interference	$0	−$25,000
Growth of Gross National Product	$0	$10,000
Total effect	$0	$10,000

everyday life, our choices typically are much more numerous. If there are only a dozen alternatives to choose from, there is no difficulty in expanding the procedure to cover them. But in finding a house or a job, there might be thousands of alternatives. And in the process of choosing among them, some will no longer be available, while others will develop. Finding the best one can be a never-ending process. Furthermore, it must be recognized that the actual process of looking for a job, house, car, date, etc. itself costs time and money. To put it another way, one of the costs that must be considered in making decisions is that making decisions itself costs something.

In situations like these, people usually do not search for the best solution to the problem; they learn to settle for one that is merely "good enough," a process Herbert Simon called *satisficing*. [4] When satisficing, the decision maker recognizes that there are too many alternatives to choose from and does not bother to compare all of them. The decision maker instead estimates what would constitute a satisfactory payoff and keeps looking at alternatives until one is found that hits the mark. In the example of looking for a job, an applicant might decide to take the first job that comes along that offers more pay than the last one. By this procedure, the best payoff among all the alternatives considered is selected, but all possible alternatives are not considered. Of course, the danger is that an uninvestigated alternative might actually be much more attractive than the one that was selected as good enough.

Although satisficing is logical, it does introduce a very subjective element—determination of the payoff that is good enough. On the psychological level, a number of personality variables are likely to influence the choice, including optimism, need to achieve, and the comparison level of the decision maker. It is to be expected that a poor person with fewer resources to support the selection process and a lower comparison level would settle for a job that someone well-to-do would never seriously consider.

On the level of national decision making about social problems, determination of satisfactory payoffs involves national aspirations analogous to an individual's level of aspiration. Should a 4 percent level of unemployment be defined as *full* employment? Is a 1 percent illiteracy rate good enough? What amount of racial prejudice is satisfactory? What level of pollution is tolerable? Should we move in small steps or hold off until we have discovered an ideal solution? [5] In answering questions like these, it is only natural to seek perfection, but in the process of seeking, nothing is being done at all. Sometimes it is possible to determine mathematically whether it is optimal to go on looking or take what is available for the time being. But on the level of national aspirations, it is rarely possible to do this. Some nations, like people, will settle for what others would not tolerate.

DECISION MAKING WITH UNCERTAINTY

We can now consider yet another complication. Often we do not know what nature has in store for us until after we have made our decision. In the unemployment problem, we simply assumed that the program would create a precise number of jobs, measured in dollar units. We disregarded uncertainties like the weather, the growth of the economy, the actions of other nations, and so on, even though these might have a great deal to do with the number of jobs the program can create. In actual decision making, this disregard is not justified. We are usually faced with some uncertainty as to what the results of our action will be. In decision terminology, we might know the payoff for any state of nature and yet not know which state of nature will actually occur once we have made our decision. A simple illustration would be the choice of whether or not to carry your umbrella to work. You might be able to estimate the cost of carrying your umbrella when you don't need it as well as the cost of not having it when you do need it. But there is still something else you would like to know. Is it going to rain?

PROBABILITY

The weather forecast typically reports the likelihood of rain in terms of a percentage: 10 percent chance of rain, 60 percent chance of rain, and so on. Social scientists prefer to use probabilities, which are simply the percentage divided by 100. An event that occurs 100 percent of the time has a probability of 1.0; it is a certainty. An impossible event occurs 0 percent of the time or has a probability of .0. Any event with a probability between .0 and 1.0 may or may not occur, and as the probability approaches 1.0, the event becomes more and more likely. The easiest way to establish a probability is to determine the percentage of time over the long run that an event occurs. This is the way the weather forecast makes its prediction. If past weather records reveal that today's meteorological conditions have resulted in rain one-half of the time, then the probability of rain is .50. If there is insufficient past experience to guide you, you might simply have to make your best subjective estimate of the probability.

Sometimes we can figure out the probability of a complex event by breaking it down into a number of simple, independent events. A pair of events is said to be independent when the occurrence of one event does not influence the occurrence of the other. Your getting heads on a flip of a coin and a snowfall on Christmas in Moscow are a pair of independent events. In such cases, the probability of both events happening is simply the product of the probabilities of the simple events. If the probability of heads is .5 and the probability of a Christmas snowfall in Moscow is .4, then the probability of *both* happening together is $.5 \times .4 = .20$. By the way, this principle helps explain why the scenarios one frequently meets in the news are often completely inaccurate. For instance, around election time candidates are fond of reporting scenarios that will result in their victory. If candidate X loses the New Hampshire primary, *and* candidate W withdraws from the race, *and* the AFL-CIO endorses candidate Y, *and* so on, *then* candidate Z will win. Do not be fooled by the fact that each individual event has a fairly high probability. If these events are independent and *all* must happen for candidate Z to win, the probability of each single event may be quite high, but the probability of their product is quite small. The probability of six independent events each with a probability of .7 occurring together is $.7^6$ or .12—a rather unlikely occurrence.

MINIMAX

In order to see how uncertainties alter the nature of decision making, look at Table 7.3, which describes a simple, two-alternative decision. The element of uncertainty exists because you do not know the state of nature that will apply. If you choose alternative X, you get a $0 payoff regardless of the state of nature. But if you choose Y, you either lose $1 or win $100,000, depending on whether A or B is the state of nature.

One strategy to use in situations like this is to think pessimistically and try to avoid the worst thing that could possibly happen. For the decision in Table 7.3, the worst payoff is the loss of $1 when you choose Y and nature is in state A. If you choose X in order to avoid this loss, you have used the decision strategy known as Minimax-Loss, or Minimax for short. *Minimax* stands for *Mini*mize your *Max*imum loss, and is a common decision strategy. To apply a Minimax strategy, simply assume that no matter which alternative you choose, nature will give the worst possible result for that action, and then select the action for which that worst possible result is least bad.

If you are more of an optimist, you might decide that this is your lucky day and attempt to *Maxi*mize your *Max*imum profit; this would be a *Maximax* strategy. In our example, Maximax would dictate choosing Y in hopes of getting the $100,000 profit. Another possible approach would be to assume that each state of nature is equally likely and choose the alternative that gives the best payoff averaged over all states of nature.

There is something to be said for any of these approaches, as well as a number of others that could be considered, but interest among decision makers has focused more often on the Minimax strategy. One reason for this interest is that Minimax works nicely with strategies in playing various games. Playing a game is very much like making any other decision except that there is another player who takes the place of nature in determining the payoffs. Many common gambling games are called *zero-sum games* because the sum of your loss and the other player's loss (remembering that a profit is a negative loss) always equals zero. In playing a zero-sum game like poker, whatever you win someone else has to lose to keep the sum equal to zero. A Minimax strategy for poker would be simply not to play the game at all. Not playing has a loss of $0, while playing the game always runs the risk of a greater loss.

TABLE 7.3   PLAYING A GAME WITH NATURE

		State of Nature	
		A	B
Alternative Action	X	$0	$0
	Y	−$1	$100,000

In general, following a Minimax strategy reduces gambling, avoids risks, and leads to an overall conservative approach to life. There are considerations for and against this aversion to risk, but there is one situation where it is generally agreed that a Minimax approach is most appropriate: when playing a hostile, all-knowing opponent. In a zero-sum game with one other player, he or she is not just another player but a competitor, an opponent, an *enemy*. Whatever you lose, your opponent wins, so your opponent wants you to lose as much as possible. If your opponent is also all-knowing as well as hostile, the wisest thing to do is stay out of the game. Don't play poker with the Devil. In general, if a state of nature is going to be deliberately chosen to do you the most harm, Minimax is called for, and to the extent that your opponent is both hostile and clever, Minimax is preferred over other strategies.

There are many areas related to social problems which approximate to a greater or lesser extent a two-person, zero-sum game between clever, if not all-knowing, opponents. These situations contain some very interesting bargaining and strategic encounters, including national defense against enemy nations, labor against management, Democrats against Republicans, buyer against seller, and cops against robbers. In such conflicts, the most conservative course of action—not playing the game—might not always be available. If you must play the game, a Minimax-like strategy can still be followed by avoiding all risk, settling for a safe return, and not being tempted by the chance for a big profit.

Adopting a Minimax strategy in decision making is analogous to adopting a win–lose strategy in bargaining. Many theorists do not like to think of common social conflicts like those between labor and management or buyer and seller as zero-sum games or win–lose encounters. They would prefer to think of life as composed of non-zero-sum games, where several players are jointly playing a game against the forces of nature and everyone can win. For example, by acting to improve the economy, both labor and management could benefit. Similarly, both buyer and seller can benefit by improving efficiency in production. In these cases, presumably there is some factor of nature, such as the laws of physics or the actions of the total economy, that both players are playing "against." In many bargaining and mixed-conflict situations, the bargainers are both opponents and partners simultaneously, and which role is salient will determine which strategy is most appropriate.

EXPECTED VALUE

In choosing an alternative in conjunction with the uncertainties of nature, it is unwise to assume that nature is out to get you. Nature is not a hostile opponent. In situations like the one described in Table 7.3, where the state of nature is to be determined by some random process, the Minimax strategy seems overly pessimistic. Why give up a chance to win $100,000 in order to avoid the risk of losing a mere $1? Many people would choose alternative Y and hope for the big profit. Of course, it might be that X actually is the best choice even in a random selection. What if state of nature B represented getting a bridge hand that was all hearts and A represented getting any other possible combination of cards? In this case, actually getting all hearts is so unlikely—about 1 chance in 635 billion—that you might as well forget about winning the $100,000 and save your dollar. Many games of chance, such as lotteries, roulette, and slot machines, are structured like the payoffs in Table 7.3. They contain enormous payoffs associated with very unlikely events in order to entice the player away from the conservative strategy of not playing. While such games might be games against nature in a sense, they are also zero-sum games against the house, and the Minimax strategy is wisest. Don't play against the house.

One of the advantages of the Minimax strategy is that you don't have to bother to figure out the probabilities of the various states of nature. On the other hand, when the probabilities are known, Minimax ignores this valuable information. It is obviously advantageous to know how likely the states are and to use this information in your decision about playing the game. In fact, if the probabilities can be estimated with some assurance, there is another strategy that is generally recognized as the best: *Choose the action with the greatest expected value.*

To understand why this strategy is best, you must know what is meant by the expected value of a choice. Briefly, in order to know the expected value of an action, you must know (*a*) the different states of nature that might occur with that action, (*b*) the probabilities of the states of nature, and (*c*) the payoff of each state of nature on the common scale of value. To get the expected value for an action, you multiply the value of the state of nature by the probability of its occurrence and sum each of these products over all possible states of nature. This is a verbal way of describing the mathematical formula:

$$EV = \Sigma P_i \, v_i$$

where *EV* is the standard abbreviation for expected value; the Greek letter sigma (Σ) stands for the sum over all *i* states of nature; P_i is the probability of the *i*th state, and v_i is its value. For example, if you bet on a flip of a fair coin, heads you win $5, tails you lose $5, the expected value is

$$EV = .5\ (\$5) + .5\ (-\$5)$$
$$= \$2.5 - \$2.5$$
$$= 0.$$

As you probably anticipated, the *EV* of the bet is 0. To take a more interesting example: You draw a card from a well-shuffled deck. If it is a heart, you win $10; a spade, you win $20; a diamond or club, you lose $7. The expected value of this wager is:

$$EV = .25\ (\$10) + .25\ (\$20) + .50\ (-\$7)$$
$$= \$2.5 + \$5.0 - \$3.5$$
$$= \$4.0.$$

It must be remembered that the expected value is not the result you would expect on any particular wager; it is the result you would expect on the average wager over the long run. In the coin-tossing example, if you made the wager 1,000 times, you would expect to neither win nor lose. A wager like the coin-tossing one, with an expected value of 0.0, is said to be a fair bet. One with a positive expected value, like the card-drawing example, is a good bet which you would expect to win *over the long run*.

Knowing the expected value of an action gives a handy measure of its worth, and finding the best action under conditions of uncertainty merely demands finding the action with the highest expected value. It can be shown that as long as you have assurance in your estimates of the probabilities, and that they do not change as a result of your actions, the decision rule of maximizing your expected value is the correct one, and might be called the *rational* decision strategy.

PSYCHOLOGICAL VALUE

Now that we have come so far in analyzing decision making, it is time to add another complication by reconsidering the basic scale of value we have been using in the analysis. I said earlier that in order to compare values, they must all exist on the same scale, and that we would arbitrarily call that common scale the monetary scale. We now must consider an additional wrinkle in this scale, and to help you appreciate the wrinkle, consider the following problem.

Imagine you are at the local bank to put a few dollars in your account, and you bump into Crazy George, the local eccentric. Crazy George is noted for three things: (*a*) he never lies; (*b*) he is fabulously wealthy, and (*c*) he is likely to do almost anything on a whim. George hands you $1 and tells you it is yours to keep. He then offers a gamble that allows you to make even more money. He challenges you to flip your own coin, and if it lands heads, you will give him back the dollar, but if it lands tails, you can keep the $1 and he will give you an additional $2. Of course, you quickly compute the expected values:

$$EV \text{ (not betting)} = 1.00 \ (\$1.00)$$
$$= \$1.00.$$

If you don't bet, you keep the original dollar with certainty. And if you do bet,

$$EV \text{ (betting)} = .5 \ (\$0) + .5 \ (\$3.00)$$
$$= \$1.50.$$

Since the bet has a greater *EV* than not betting, it is rational to take Crazy George up on his offer. So far, so good.

Now let's change the situation somewhat. Rather than giving you $1, imagine that George gave you $1 million. After you recover from the shock, he offers you a bet. You can flip your own coin, and if it lands heads, you will give him back the $1 million, but if it lands tails, he will give you another $2 million. The expected values can be easily calculated:

$$EV \text{ (not betting)} = 1.00 \ (\$1,000,000)$$
$$= \$1,000,000$$

and

$$EV \text{ (betting)} = .5 \ (\$0) + .5 \ (\$3,000,000)$$
$$= \$1,500,000.$$

The expected value analysis clearly indicates that you should take the bet. But if you are like most people when asked what they would actually do in this situation, you would agree to take the first bet and reject the second bet (and run to the deposit window before you changed your mind). This discrepancy is curious because both bets are good bets; they are of the same general form, and the advantage of the second bet is much greater than that of the first. Why are people so irrational according to the expected value analysis?

When asked to defend their choices, most people respond something like this: If you take George's second bet, you are running a good risk of losing almost everything you have (assuming you were not a millionaire to start with). Now you have $1 million to buy all the things you dreamed of having. Why risk losing that for another $2 million, which really won't give all that much more pleasure than the first $1 million?

This argument suggests that people should not only consider the bet itself but also how much money they have to start with. The general rule that is suggested goes something like this: If you have lots of money, take any good bet. But if you don't have much money, do not risk what little you have unless it is a very good bet indeed. Behind this rule is the interesting assumption that doubling your wealth does not double your happiness. This seems to make sense. Having two cars does not bring twice the happiness of having one car. Having two houses does not bring twice the happiness of having one house. It would be silly to bet your house "double or nothing" even though it may be a fair bet in terms of expected value. What, then, is the relationship between money and happiness?

For a variety of theoretical and empirical reasons, many authorities believe that the relationship is something like the one depicted by the curved line in Figure 7.1. In this figure, the horizontal axis represents the payoff in money; the vertical axis is the happiness or utility the money actually brings (in some arbitrary unit of measurement); and the dashed line represents the relationship that would exist if the value of money were independent of how much you had to start with. It can be seen that as one goes farther out on the horizontal axis, the curved line or utility function departs more and more from the simple, direct relationship of the dotted line. To put it another way, an increase in money close to the zero point increases utility more than the same increase farther to the right. This represents graphically the assumption we have been pursuing—that any specific additional amount of money is less psychologically valuable the more you have to start with.*

If we could determine the exact mathematical relationship be-

---

* In economics, this relationship is sometimes called the "law of the diminishing marginal utility of money."

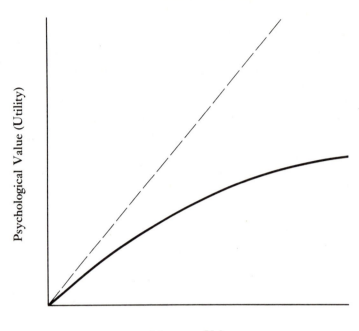

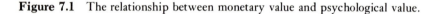

Figure 7.1   The relationship between monetary value and psychological value.

tween money and utility, we could also determine the exact utility of Crazy George's bets. The Swiss mathematician Daniel Bernoulli, who first popularized the utility function we are considering, suggested that utility was proportionate to the log of the monetary value.[6] This is one of the many relationships that would yield a curve like the one in Figure 7.1. There is no general agreement on the exact definition of the curve, so we will assume that the relationship is utility $= \sqrt{\text{money}}$. This relationship will also yield a curve like the one in Figure 7.1 and will simplify our calculations.

Now we can determine the expected utility (EU) of Crazy George's second bet. We will assume that before he gave you $1 million, your total worth was $1,000. Then:

$$\text{EU (not betting)} = 1.00\sqrt{\$1,001,000}$$
$$= 1,000.5$$

and

$$\text{EU (betting)} = .5\sqrt{\$1,000} + .5\sqrt{\$3,001,000}$$
$$= .5 \ (31.62) + .5 \ (1,732.34)$$
$$= 881.98.$$

In terms of units of utility rather than money, *not* betting is preferable. To see if this kind of utility analysis fits common sense, we can also apply it to the first bet, where the stakes were $1 and $3. Again we will assume your initial worth was $1,000.

$$\text{EU (not betting)} = 1.00\sqrt{\$1,001}$$
$$= 31.638$$

and

$$\text{EU (betting)} = .5\sqrt{\$1,000} + .5\sqrt{\$1,003}$$
$$= .5\,(31.623) + .5\,(31.670)$$
$$= 31.646.$$

We see that according to the utility analysis it is still wise to accept the first bet, because it is a small bet relative to the total amount you started with.

GAMBLING

Utility analysis helps to clarify some interesting paradoxes in decision making. Buying insurance, for example, is a kind of wager or zero-sum game with an insurance company. And because the insurance company has a thorough knowledge of the rate of various events, they make sure that any insurance they offer is a good bet for them. Unless you know something your insurance company does not know (e.g., you like to sleep with rattlesnakes or drive with your eyes closed), insurance will be a bad bet for you. By means of expected utility analysis, we can see if it makes sense to buy insurance in spite of its poor expected value.

We will assume you have a $20,000 house as well as an additional $10,000 in savings and want to insure your house against fire for one year. The insurance company's statistics indicate that the probability of a house like yours actually burning down in the course of the year is .01. Given this probability, a fair bet would be $200 against the $20,000 cost of the house. Or in terms of expected value for the insurance company:

$$\textit{EV} \text{ (offering insurance)} = .99\,(\$200) + .01\,(-\$19,800)$$
$$= \$198 - \$198$$
$$= 0$$

However, the company will not make any money offering fair bets, so it will add an additional $20 for overhead and profit. The $220 cost of insuring your house from fire for a year is now a good bet for the insurance company and a bad bet for you in terms of expected value. What about expected utility? Looking at it first from your perspective, a charge of $220 will guarantee against the greater loss of $20,000 of your total $30,000 worth.

$$\text{EU (not buying insurance)} = .99\sqrt{\$30,000} + .01\sqrt{\$10,000}$$
$$= .99 \,(173.205) + .01 \,(100)$$
$$= 172.47$$

and

$$\text{EU (buying insurance)} = .99\sqrt{\$29,780} + .01\sqrt{\$29,780}$$
$$= \sqrt{\$29,780}$$
$$= 172.57.$$

So from your point of view, buying insurance offers the best expected utility. How about the insurance company? Let's assume the company has $1,000,000 in assets. If they do not offer the insurance, they will have the utility of $1,000,000 with certainty, or

$$\text{EU (not offering insurance)} = \sqrt{\$1,000,000}$$
$$= 1,000.$$

And if they do offer the insurance, they will have the utility of the additional $220 no matter what and lose $20,000 in the one chance in 100 that the house burns down, or

$$\text{EU (offering insurance)} = .99\sqrt{\$1,000,220} + .01\sqrt{\$980,220}$$
$$= .99 \,(1,000.11) + .01 \,(990.06)$$
$$= 1,000.01.$$

Therefore, you should buy the insurance, and the company should offer it. Everyone is happy! Of course, in terms of expected value, the rich insurance company is getting richer, and you are getting poorer, but that is the price you pay for having so little to begin with. If you had lots of money, like the insurance company, it would not pay to buy insurance. It might not seem fair, but it is quite rational.

POVERTY AND GAMBLING

People buy insurance as a protection against the risk of great loss. In general, an expected utility analysis indicates that rational people avoid risks of all kinds. We should try to keep the money we have because it is worth more, and not get infatuated with the chance of making a big profit. In short, we should avoid gambling. This analysis certainly does *not* describe the way people actually do behave when faced with a pair of dice or a $2 window at the race track. People throughout the world love to gamble. Americans spend tens of billions of dollars annually on illegal betting alone.[7] Bingo, Friday night poker games, betting on the horses, dogs, football and basketball games, casino betting, legal lotteries, and numerous other games of chance are an integral part of the American way of life. Most of these gambles are not even fair bets; they are "sucker" bets that are sure to lose over the long run.* Moreover, many of those who bet are the poor, who can least afford to lose. This does not agree at all with the expected utility analysis.

We have already seen one reason why people might gamble in spite of its negative utility. In Chapter 5, we saw that people have a need for excitement, stimulation, adventure, and the pleasantly fearful.[8] It is possible that the poor especially lack sufficient stimulation in their lives and therefore would show a greater desire for the stimulation of a poker or numbers game. A second approach toward explaining why people, especially the poor, gamble focuses on the utility function itself. It can be argued that although the function generally is the smooth concave curve depicted in Figure 7.1, for any particular individual it might have a number of distortions or irregularities in it. Presumably the curve is never going to slope downward (an additional amount of money would never have a negative utility), but the steepness of the curve might vary markedly according to a number of factors.** A rather unlikely example would be a man who has $2,000 and is suffering from a fatal disease. If the cost of treating the disease is $4,000 paid in advance, the man's utility curve might look something like the one drawn in Figure 7.2.

The figure shows that to this particular man the only amount of money that really matters is $4,000, and it would be wise for him to

---

* All casino gambles, legal lotteries, and gambling associated with organized crime have negative expected values. It is possible for a player with sufficient skill and stakes to have a positive expected value for poker, pari-mutuel betting at the race track, and a few other gambles. It should be recognized that some gambles, such as at church carnivals and bingo games, are but thinly veiled charitable contributions.

** Even this assumption is somewhat doubtful. It is possible, given the idiosyncrasies of tax rates, welfare regulations, eligibility for college scholarships and the like, that an additional small sum of money could actually decrease the total income, and therefore the total happiness of an individual.

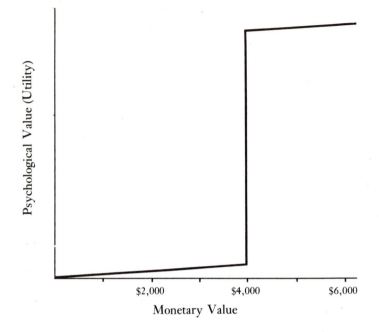

Figure 7.2 Utility function for a man who needs $4,000.

bet his $2,000 double or nothing even if the odds were against him. If he loses his $2,000 it doesn't really matter, because he will be dead and have no use for it anyway. While this example is somewhat far out, it is less implausible that a person could have a utility function something like the one drawn in Figure 7.3.

The curve in this figure is the familiar concave curve throughout most of its length except the area around zero, where it is flattened. For someone with such a utility curve, it is rational to both buy insurance or bet on a lottery, depending on how much money the person has to start with. The curve indicates that amounts around the zero point have a different psychological "feel" to them than higher portions of the curve.[9] For example, a rich man might see little difference between losing all his money and losing all but $100. In either case, he would feel "wiped out." This means that to him there is very little difference in utility between having nothing and having $100, which is exactly what the flat portion of the curve around zero dollars indicates. Similarly, a poor person who has only 25¢ to spend until the welfare, social security, or paycheck arrives might feel there is nothing he or she can do

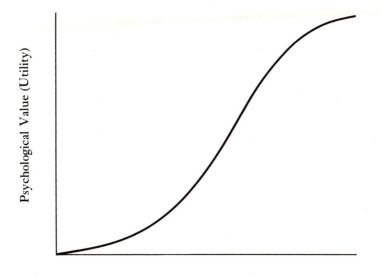

Figure 7.3   A hypothetical utility function.

with 25¢ anyway. If the 25¢ is bet on the lottery and wins $100, *that* would mean something.

Viewed from this perspective, government sponsored lotteries are not terribly unfair, although they do have a negative expected value. The real tragedy may be that there are some people so poor that 25¢ has little meaning.

SUMMARY

There is no strict dichotomy between rational and irrational decision making; they are the two extreme poles of a continuum, with most decisions being neither wholly one nor the other. The first thing one must do with a decision is accept it as something to work with. Making a *wise* choice does not guarantee a *correct* choice, but it should increase the probability of success over the long run, if indeed there is a long run. Rationality is not contrary to or to be contrasted with subjective factors in making a decision. A rational approach to decision making uses subjective elements, including your personal scale of value, level of aspiration, and awareness of how much you are willing to lose. As a result, two people faced with the same decision, but with different values, resources, or aspirations, may choose different alternatives even though both are acting quite rationally.

From a decision-making perspective, much of life is a gamble; it is an attempt to maximize one's values or utilities in the face of uncertainty. One very important aspect of the situation is whether you are facing a hostile opponent. If so, it is often best to avoid risk, be conservative, and adopt a Minimax strategy. If you are not facing an opponent, but only the uncertainties of an unpredictable future, it is better to try to maximize your expected utilities by considering the psychological value of the possible outcomes weighed by their probability of occurrence. People may be more rational than would appear at first glance when the psychological value and not the monetary value of the outcome is taken into consideration.

Even if *the* correct strategy cannot be discovered, a decision analysis can be of value by excluding at least some of the possible alternative courses of action or by suggesting what additional information you require to make a better choice.

EIGHT

Mistakes in Social Decision Making

We saw in the last chapter that the rational approach to making decisions against the uncertainties of nature is provided by the general rule: maximize your expected utility (EU). In the case of so much in life, however, it is one thing to state an ideal rule; it is quite another to apply the ideal in specific representative life situations. Some of the problems in applying ideal decision making have already been mentioned in the last chapter. Now we can go further and point out that in most cases of major social decision making, the actual application of a precise formula to arrive at the solution is totally impractical.

One obvious difficulty is that frequently the necessary probabilities can only be wildly guessed at. Sometimes it is possible to apply devices for improving your probability estimates, and in a sense this is exactly what experimentation is all about.[1] If you are wondering how many lives would be saved by a proposed health care system, you need not wonder forever; you can try a pilot program and see. Unfortunately, getting these probabilities is often costly and time-consuming and demands a severe limitation on the number of alternatives that can be investigated. Because of the expense of feasibility studies, pilot programs and the like, only a few alternatives involving limited changes from the traditional approach are usually seriously considered. Another great difficulty in applying rational decision-making rules to social problems involves finding common agreement on the utilities of the various states of nature.[2] If everyone has his or her own formula to solve a problem, whose formula do we choose? (We will pursue this difficulty further in the next chapter.)

For these reasons, expected value or expected utility analysis cannot often be applied precisely, as a formula, in solving major social problems. Nonetheless, consideration of these formulas is of great value in understanding social problems because they provide the *form* of correct decision making. Expected utility determination functions as a sort of template or benchmark to hold against your actual thinking about social problems. This allows you to see if your approach to social problems has at least the general form of rational decision making. A noticeable lack of correspondence between ideal and real decision-making methods should prompt the question, "Am I missing something very important?" In this chapter, we will consider several of the more likely ways in which your approach and the approach of contemporary American society, in general, may be departing from the form of proper decision making.

ACCENTUATION OF THE NEGATIVE

The EU formula combines both profits and losses to achieve a single utility estimate which represents the psychological value of an action in the face of uncertainty. Even in the simpler case of decision making without uncertainty, it is necessary to weigh profit against loss in making a decision. For instance, in choosing between A and B where

Action A = no change in the present situation, and
Action B = a gain of X and a loss of Y,

the decision basically revolves around determining if the gain of X is large enough to offset the loss of Y. If you only consider the loss and ignore the gain, this is analogous to using Minimax when it is inappropriate to do so. To focus on the loss to the exclusion of the gain will result in a systematic distortion of your decision making away from the ideal form. Such negative thinking is reminiscent of the stereotypic "Jewish mother," who is found under a variety of labels in most ethnic groups. It is the essence of the Jewish mother to detect tragedy in whatever happens, no matter how good it appears on the surface. If her son gets a good job, the Jewish mother moans, "What if he gets fired?" If her daughter wins $1 million, she complains, "Think of the taxes she'll have to pay!" [3]

There is a fair amount of evidence that decision makers in our society, especially professional social scientists, are collectively a group of Jewish mothers. They accentuate the negative and disregard the positive. The result is that only half of the effects of any particular course of action are seriously considered. Accentuation of the negative is reflected indirectly in a variety of ways. For example, the 1975 edition of *Books in Print* lists 19 titles starting with *anxiety* (*Anxiety and Education*, *Anxiety and Neurosis*, etc.) and only 5 starting with either *tranquility* or *calm*; there were 378 beginning with *war* and only 113 beginning with *peace*. [4] The professional social science literature is even more lopsided toward the negative. One recent enumeration of the doctoral dissertations produced by social scientists found that there were more than seven times the number of dissertations on war as there were on peace. [5]

Most major sociological research is indexed in the *Sociological Abstracts*. In the 1974 *Abstracts* there were 15 references under *war*, but only 1 under *peace*. There were no references under *tranquility or calm*, but a total of 36 for *riots* and *aggression*. [6] The *Psychological Abstracts*, which index the literature for professional psychology, show the same pattern, as summarized in Table 8.1. [7]

For two reasons, the psychologists' overwhelming emphasis on negative experiences, indicated in Table 8.1, is probably an *underestimation* of the actual discrepancy. First, many of the studies listed under

TABLE 8.1   NUMBER OF REFERENCES TO PSYCHOLOGICAL STUDIES, 1974

NEGATIVE EXPERIENCES		POSITIVE EXPERIENCES	
Pain	90	*Pleasure*	7
Hate	2	*Love*	16
Hostility and *Aggression*	337	*Friendship* and *Hope*	17
Grief and *Sadness*	21	*Happiness* and *Joy*	6
Anxiety and *Fear*	451	*Tranquility* and *Peace*	0

"positive" experience are really "negative" studies in the sense that it is the *dangers* of the positive experience that are the concern. For example, listed under *pleasure* is an article entitled, "Drug Use for Pleasure: A Complex Social Problem," and under *happiness* is one on the "Urban Malaise." Much of the literature on *love* is not a study of the joys of love; it is a study of the tragic effects of romantic love, such as unhappy marriages and divorce.[8]

Second, the negative literature in the indexes is more dispersed than the positive literature. The number of studies on *aggression* and *hostility*, for instance, does not include many studies listed under *war, violence, riots, conflicts, arguments*, etc. There are many more of these negative headings than positive ones. In fact, it is difficult to even think of positive opposites to the vast number of miseries, frustrations, horrors, and disasters studied by contemporary American social scientists. As the philosopher William Warren Bartley has argued, even our language accentuates the negative:

> The case of psychoanalysis is also instructive. Tending as it does to concentrate on abnormal behavior, it reflects a general tendency in most languages to develop a more refined, precise, and differentiated terminology to deal with the abnormal, the deviant, the illegal, the "bad" than with what is normal, ordinary, legal, good. Words like "nice" and "good man" are indeed virtually meaningless in most contexts. In English words like "guilt," "sin," "shame," and "vice" have no true positive counterparts, or at any rate are far more definite in their meanings than are their nearest positive counterparts, which more often indicate the absence of negative characteristics than anything definitely good. . . .
>
> *On the whole*, then, with some exceptions, language tends to fuse pro-words, but to differentiate among various con-words. Thus the significance of moral evil is cast into higher relief.[9]

This does *not* mean that bad words are more numerous in English and other languages; in fact, just the opposite is the case. In the typical text, words with good connotations are substantially more common than those with negative ones (*friendly* is more common than *unfriendly*, *good* than *bad*, *honest* than *dishonest*, etc.).[10] The infatuation with negative concepts reflects not their frequency but their power, drama, impact, and ability to hold our interest. We saw in Chapter 2 that the news too often is seduced by the attraction of the negative. We see now that social scientists fall into the same trap. Their concern with what is wrong rather than with what is right is probably both a reflection of our general social orientation and a reason why this orientation is maintained.

One aspect of our accentuation of the negative regarding social problems is our greater interest in death than in life. Our nation does not really have a health care system; it has instead a disease care and death prevention system. The medical profession's emphasis on disease rather than health has reached a point where substantial increases in health and longevity are no longer being produced by disease care. To further increase the nation's health, the interest must shift from an accentuation on treating disease to a positive appreciation of maintaining health and safety.[11]

It is amazing how much we are willing to pay to prevent death. By denying free abortions to women on welfare who desire them, the state, in effect, is willing to pay an estimated $2,000 for prenatal, postnatal, and delivery care for each baby rather than $150 to $250 for an abortion. These costs do not include the additional billions necessary to provide subsistence for those children who are raised on welfare, the estimated $2,500 per patient for women requiring hospitalization as a result of botched illegal abortions, or the costs associated with the estimated one out of fifty patients that die.[12] The concept of *death*, even of a fetus whose mother strongly wishes the pregnancy terminated, has a powerful impact in our society. Another example would be the movement among suicidologists (a typical, negatively oriented, social science group) to erect a suicide barrier on the Golden Gate Bridge in San Francisco. The proposed barrier would consist of a series of nine-foot-high stainless steel spikes and cost at least $3.5 million.[13] If a sum that large were invested at 7 percent annual interest, the revenue alone, without touching the principal, would be sufficient to pay each of the fifteen suicides a year more than $16,000 not to jump.

The point is not that we should show a callous neglect of the despair of potential suicides or that there are no ethical considerations other than money involved in abortion. The point is that the government's willingness to tax average citizens to deal with acute problems may well be an example of decisions influenced by accentuation of the negative. What we need to know is the effect of shifting tax money from Medicaid to educational programs that highlight the joys of mature sex. It may be that a concentration on the joy of responsible family life can do as much for the maintenance of healthy families as the reluctance to provide money for abortions. In the same vein, it is necessary to evaluate the extent to which removing tax money from the citizens' pockets contributes to frustration and even suicide before the wisdom of multimillion-dollar suicide barriers is established.

Following the lead of the medical profession that specialized in the problem of disease and the clergy that specialized in the problem of sin and guilt, the social sciences found their own special problems. Psychologists became specialists in "mental illness." Sociologists became authorities on "social pathology." Marriage counselors focused on "problem marriages." (This is why people see a marriage counselor when they are anticipating a divorce rather than before getting married, which would be the more logical approach.) It is only in recent years that serious interest in positive mental and emotional experiences has become vaguely respectable in social science. Due mostly to the so-called third wave in psychology, which emphasizes growth, happiness, and creativity, a serious psychological work entitled *Joy* was finally published in 1967.[14]* After decades of dissecting antisocial behavior, sociologists and social psychologists are beginning to study altruism, helping, and cooperation.[15] The fact that people such as myself lecture and write books on social problems rather than social happiness may, in itself, be a kind of objective social problem.

THE CASE OF EDUCATION

The American educational system provides a clear example of the accentuation of the negative. Within education there is an applied field known as *special education* which treats the education of "exceptional" children. Because "exceptional" is defined as a deviation from the average, by definition there must be as many exceptional children who are exceptionally good as there are ones who are exceptionally bad. But the bulk of interest and money in special education has been aimed at those with problems.[16] Writing in 1958, Willard Abraham summarized the situation:

> We have (1) only two colleges and universities which offer full sequences of courses to help prepare teachers of gifted children; (2) one state that certifies teachers in that area (30 states certify teachers in speech, 27 in hard-of-hearing, 22 in mental retardation, and a total of 122 colleges and universities offer specialized sequences in preparation

* The first two major "waves" in American social science were the Freudian and the behavioristic approaches to understanding man.

related to exceptional children); (3) *no* state that has a full-time person in its department of education devoted to the education of the gifted; and (4) *not one* faculty member in 122 colleges and universities was reported to be devoting full-time to the area of the gifted. No one begrudges the dozens of college and university training programs to prepare those who teach the mentally retarded, speech handicapped, blind, and other exceptional children—but are the gifted *less* important? [17]

From our perspective, it should be noted that today's gifted children are precisely the ones we will be turning to in the future to solve our social problems, including finding cures and treatment techniques for mental retardation and other handicaps. They deserve the best education available, even if they do not present a "problem."

The accentuation of the negative in education also helps explain the traditional disdain for sex education. Even when a school has the courage to install a sex education class, it is usually organized around how to avoid problems rather than how to use sex to create a happier and more fulfilling life. Thus, there is extended treatment of venereal disease and the dangers of promiscuity, and little mention of techniques in foreplay and the pleasures of oral sex. Eating, the other notorious human pleasure, is given similar treatment. High school food and cooking courses concentrate on avoiding problems—injuries, food poisoning, imbalanced diets, etc., and downplay the fact that eating can be quite enjoyable. The typical textbook has a lot to say about beriberi and rickets, but very little awareness of garlic or curry powder. From the treatment given them in American schools, one would think that sex and eating were necessary inconveniences, like cleaning your teeth or wearing an athletic supporter, rather than pleasures to be enjoyed. [18]

Similarly, the study of juvenile pathology, rather than juvenile excellence, has dominated sociology and child psychology. As one authority put it:

> It is something of a paradox that a nation which has exulted in its rapid expansion and its scientific-technological achievements, should have developed in its studies of childhood so vast a "problem" literature; a literature often expressing adjustment difficulties, social failures, blocked potentialities and defeat. . . . In applying clinical ways of thinking formulated out of experience with broken adults, we were slow to see how the language of adequacy to meet life's challenges could become the subject matter of psychological science. Thus there

are thousands of studies of maladjustment for each one that deals directly with the ways of managing life's problems with personal strength and adequacy.[19]

An example of what could be done in accentuating the positive is the work of University of Minnesota psychologist Norman Garmezy on psychologically healthy children. Garmezy's research focuses on those who come from disadvantaged environments—broken homes, poverty, alcoholic mother, father in prison, etc.—*who turn out all right*.[20] It is a refreshing change in American social science to study those who overcome hardships rather than those who fall victim to them. Might not the successes tell us as much about how to succeed as the failures?

DITHERING

To *dither* is to excite, agitate, shake up. Someone who is in a dither is all excited. This is usually considered to be an unpleasant state, but dithering also has its positive aspects. In the world of business, a new president can take over a company and "shake up" top management. Haphazardly shifting jobs might get workers out of a rut and help them see things from a more productive perspective. In the same vein, someone with a radio or watch that does not work might grab it firmly and do a little dithering. For some reason or other, this often gets the device working again. If everything is working fine, it is obviously unwise to try serious dithering; there is too much to lose and little to gain. But when things are not going very well, even random agitation can be worth a try. Another problem with negative thinking is that it discourages dithering because the tragedies that could develop are more salient than the advantages that could also result.

In a sense, many of the actions available to deal with social problems are forms of dithering. They shake things up with the possibility of increased effectiveness and the possibility of making things worse. Psychotherapy provides a nice illustration. Studies on the outcome of psychotherapy indicate that with some kinds of therapies and certain kinds of clients, there is both an increase in the probability of getting better *and* an increase in the probability of getting worse.[21] Avoiding therapy yields a higher probability of no change at all. Because the probability of improvement may be greater than the probability of getting worse, it may be quite rational to enter psychotherapy from an expected utility perspective. However, someone who focuses on the negative would look at the probability of getting worse and avoid therapy. Such a person might go through life being moderately miserable for fear of getting completely ruined. Focusing on the negative aspects of any treatment, change, or shock can blind a society as well as an individual to the greater possibility of triumph and joy. The expected utility approach does not mind a little dithering now and then.

In summary, the accentuation of the negative is pervasive in the social sciences. By maintaining a problem orientation rather than one that tries to maximize the total positive utility, a problem solver may solve some problems but not achieve real success. Accentuation of the negative can lead to frustration and unhappiness that indirectly causes many social problems. It also causes a waste of talent and resources by ignoring those with potential instead of problems. Lastly, like other Minimax-like strategies, it is too conservative and avoids too many opportunities for success due to timidity and fear of failure.

THE LEAP INTO THE INFINITE

What I like to call the "leap into the infinite" is a distortion of rational thinking that often accompanies negative thinking. Unlike the stress on the negative, to which social scientists and professionals are more liable, the leap into the infinite is more often found in the average citizen. To see how this confusion works, we will go back several centuries and review an old theological argument.

PASCAL'S WAGER

The seventeenth century French thinker Blaise Pascal became famous both as a mathematician and as an apologist for the Christian religion. He combined his two great devotions in an interesting argument for leading a holy life that has become known as Pascal's wager.[22] Pascal's goal was to demonstrate that people should believe in God and follow His will even though His existence cannot be proven, and may, in fact, be quite improbable. To do this, Pascal employed an expected utility argument containing two kinds of utilities. First, there is the utility to be gained by enjoying immoral pleasures on earth. Presumably there must be some positive utility to lying, stealing, cheating, fornicating, getting drunk, etc., or else they would not be so popular. The total utility of these sinful pleasures we will call S for sin. Second, there is the pleasure of joining God in heaven (and avoiding hell), which comes from leading the good life and giving up S. The utility of heaven is greater than all the pleasures on earth and lasts forever. Therefore, we will designate the utility of heaven as $+\infty$. Letting P be the probability that there is a God, we have the expected utilities:

$$EU \text{ (of rejecting God)} = +S$$

and

$$EU \text{ (of accepting God)} = 0 \ (S) + P \ (+\infty)$$
$$= +\infty$$

Regardless of how small the probability of God's existence, when multiplied by infinity, it creates a utility infinitely greater than any finite utility of sin, no matter how energetic the sinner. Therefore, one should always do the will of God no matter how unlikely it is that He actually exists. This is not the place to review the whole theological debate surrounding Pascal's wager.* The bet is of interest here because people use a similar trick in dealing with social problems.

The trick is to overcome the inability to specify an important probability by hypothesizing an infinite utility which overwhelms everything else under consideration and dictates the preferred action. For this trick to work, the key utility does not have to be really infinite, it just has to be large enough to overwhelm everything else. The result is to go through the motions of an expected utility analysis but actually to adopt the extremely moralistic stance that was described in Chapter 7 as the enemy of rational thought.

You have probably heard people speak like this:

There is no price too great to pay for liberty.
The sanctity of the home is without price.
I would do anything for my country.
Life is not worth living without art.

If you have, you were being set up for Pascal's wager. You were probably tempted to reply in kind by creating an opposite infinite utility to

---

* There are two main counterarguments. First, it could be that the God described by Pascal is a self-contradiction, and therefore $P = 0$. Second, Pascal's argument assumes that God does not want us to lie, cheat, steal, etc., and this assumption could be challenged.

put on "your" side. If your opponent says that allowing abortion would destroy the *sanctity of life*, you can counter with the *precious heritage of personal freedom*. If you are defending pornography and the charge is *corruption of the youth of America*, you can come back with *government tyranny over a free press*. A cry of "communist" can always be countered with "fascist."

CATASTROPHIZING

Either something unthinkably bad or something unthinkably good is sufficient to stop thinking and start a shouting match. But in keeping with the accentuation of the negative, the unthinkable is usually a horrible loss rather than an overwhelming gain. (Somehow hell is easier to imagine than heaven.) To focus your energies on avoiding unspeakable evils rather than sifting through the more commonplace pros and cons of a true expected utility analysis is called *catastrophizing*—living in fear of the ultimate horror. Albert Ellis, the American psychologist and sexologist, has shown how catastrophizing lies at the heart of much neurotic behavior.[23] On the level of social problems, it is equally disastrous. There are three techniques which, taken together, can help reduce the drift toward catastrophizing.

1. Find the positive counterpart of the catastrophe and stress that. If you must think of a great loss, think of it as the *lack* of a great gain. It is often easier to see great goods rather than great evils in human perspective. When you find yourself thinking about a term on the left, switch to its pair on the right:

totalitarianism	democracy
slavery	freedom
depression	productive economy
violent crime	personal safety
discrimination	equal opportunity
war	peace

2. Try to see how the catastrophe can be associated, to some extent, with any alternative action. The trick of Pascal's wager is to get the opponent to think that the ultimate horror could only occur given one particular action—the one to be avoided at all costs. To take the example of tyranny and the Vietnam War, supporters of the war argued that it would avoid tyranny by

(*a*) protecting the freedom-loving people of South Vietnam,
(*b*) giving the "free" nations of the world inspiration in their fight against totalitarianism, and
(*c*) crushing the tyranny of Soviet expansionism.

Of course, those who were against the war argued it would *advance* tyranny by

(*a*) supporting the totalitarian government in South Vietnam,
(*b*) exhausting our resources, which could be used to fight tyranny all over the world, and
(*c*) increasing tyranny in America due to the draft.

A fair and rational argument would recognize that the issue of freedom does not fall neatly on one side or the other of the issue. As we saw in Chapter 7, the choice between heaven and hell is no choice at all.

3. Try to break the catastrophe into smaller, more manageable units. Do not let one enormous payoff rest in the same equation with ordinary likes and dislikes, or it will overwhelm everything else.* The utilities must be *bounded;* that is, they should all be roughly of the same degree of importance. Such concepts as freedom, justice, and equality must be dealt with, but they must be kept to manageable proportions.

With effort, it is possible to develop the habit of thinking in terms of delimited degrees of freedom, brotherhood, justice, and the like. For example, rather than thinking about "justice," think about how *many* Americans are being denied how *much* they are due for how *long*. Rather than concentrating on "religious freedom," you might ask: How *many* people would be denied how *much* of their religious freedom for how *long?* It is unlikely that you could put a precise estimate of worth even on mundane amounts of freedom and justice, but at least they are no longer overwhelming.

LITTLE THINGS STILL MEAN A LOT

On a number of occasions, we have run into the insidious effects of accumulating little things. We will approach this subject again in the next chapter from the point of view of social organization. Now it

---

*A classic example among decision makers goes something like this: Assume that you prefer turkey to chicken. Then you should logically prefer being given a turkey sandwich and being shot at sunrise to being given a chicken sandwich and being shot at sunrise. It is doubtful that many people would bother to make the "rational" choice in such a situation.

would be appropriate to consider it from the perspective of decision making. In the expected utility formula there are two factors—the probability or the utility—that can be quite small. If the utility is small in absolute value, this indicates that it is of little consequence *unless* lots of these small utilities are accumulated over individuals or time to yield a large total payoff.

If someone stole 10¢ from you every day for a year, you would be much less likely to notice than if the thief took $36.50 on December 31. Although the losses are the same, the single theft of $36.50 is likely to be above your threshold of awareness. In previous times, the threshold for losses and its subsequent distortion of decision making was less of a problem than it is today. A nineteenth century peasant who kept his gold in a stocking under his mattress was not likely to be robbed in subthreshold installments. It is too inefficient to steal one gold coin at a time.

Today's buying and selling are conducted by signed notes and plastic credit cards, and "money" is a magnetic trace on a computer tape. With a few moments' programming time, a computer programmer can steal 10¢ from each of 10,000 savings accounts and deposit the $1,000 in his account. It is unlikely that you would notice that your yearly interest of $29.53 should have been $29.63, and if you did notice, you would probably not get excited about it. Much of the new field of computer crime relies on the accumulation of numerous subthreshold losses and is exceedingly difficult to detect.[24]

The broad dispersion of the losses associated with white collar and institutional crime is probably greatly responsible for our lack of outrage at this form of crime relative to more salient forms, like purse snatching and burglary. The same dispersal of loss is observed in reverse when someone robs a bank or large company. Interview studies have shown that many people who would never think of stealing from a person would give serious thought to stealing from a large business or the government.[25] Their rationale is that "no one is really hurt" by such thefts. More correctly, lots of people are hurt but beneath their threshold of concern.

DEALING WITH SMALL PROBABILITIES

When the little thing influencing a decision is not a utility but a probability, things get even trickier. The expected value formula tells us that the effect of a small probability of a modest gain or loss is negligible, but a small probability of a large gain or loss can be crucial. In expected value terms, a certain gain of $1 is equivalent to one chance in a thousand of a $1,000 gain, or .001 ($1,000)= $1. Finding solutions to many social problems is complicated by our inability to *feel* the plausibility of an equation like this. It is as if the smallest real probability the average person could consider is .01. If a very small probability is salient, it is considered at least a 1 chance in 100 possibility. If it is not salient, it is considered "practically" impossible. The vast difference between probabilities of .01 and .001 or .001 and .0001 is unappreciated, although it is crucial in making wise decisions about many social problems.

The decision to build nuclear power plants exemplifies a social decision of vast importance complicated by very small probabilities of great catastrophes. If a reactor accident were to cause a major release of radioactivity, it could kill tens of thousands and result in billions of dollars in property damage and the contamination of thousands of square miles of valuable land. On the other hand, the probability of a major accidental release of radiation may be as low as 1 accident per 100,000 reactors per year.[26] It is difficult for the average person to sift calmly through such small probabilities of great horrors.

The construction of dams provides another example. It is quite unlikely that any particular dam will fail, but if it does, it can create a major disaster. The failure of the Teton dam in Idaho in 1976 killed 11 people and caused between $400 million and $1 billion in damage.[27] Even though the probability of a major dam failure has been estimated at .0001 or less per dam per year, if more consideration were given to such unlikely events in calculating the costs of construction, fewer dams might be built.[28] A similar expected utility structure is created by research on Recombinant DNA, which involves the creation of new strains of microorganisms by altering their genetic structure. Incalculable gains can result from the development of organisms that produce insulin or "eat" oil spills, and incalculable miseries may result if the scientists inadvertently create and release a new form of disease-producing germ. In cases like these, there is no easy way to determine the exact probability. An auto manufacturer can build and test a new brake system without any great difficulties. But building dams or nuclear reactors and searching for exceedingly small probabilities does not lend itself to pilot projects. Often such probabilities can be determined only by going ahead with the full project, accumulating enough experience over the years, and keeping your fingers crossed. Of course, this approach necessitates that whatever we learn, we learn the hard way.

It might be that our inability to deal effectively with small probabilities of great utilities also relates to the maintenance of the total economic structure of American society. It has been argued that one reason average citizens are relatively unmoved by the great inequality present in our society is that they are hoping some day to make it to the top themselves.[29] From the point of view of expected utility, most people would be substantially better off if tax loopholes were closed, inheritance taxes increased, and the aged and disabled supported by income taxes on unearned income rather than the present social security tax on earned income. In other words, there are more poor and middle class than rich, and so anything that would decrease the difference in income between the needy and the affluent would help more people than it would hurt. And yet, even though America is a popular democracy, there has been little popular outcry for the reduction of inequality. The situation is like the lottery or roulette game, which has a negative expected value and yet lures many people to bet on the slim chance of winning big. It has been estimated that less than one-half of 1 percent of the families in America earn more than $100,000 a year.[30] And most of them had a head start and were not born poor.* So the probability of a poor person becoming rich is exceedingly small. Yet we are constantly reminded of the rare immigrant who becomes a millionaire or the unusual black woman, daughter of sharecroppers, who strikes it rich. This is reminiscent of the way gambling casinos publicize the occasional big winner at the slot machines. Or as economist Joseph Schumpeter has put it:

> Spectacular prizes much greater than would have been necessary to call forth the particular effort are thrown to a small minority of winners, thus propelling much more efficaciously than a more equal and more "just" distribution would, the activity of that large majority of businessmen who receive in return very modest compensation or nothing or less than nothing, and yet do their utmost because they have the big prizes before their eyes and overrate their chances of doing equally well.[32]

---

* You will probably recognize that expectancy of success not only reflects on the estimation of small probabilities, it also circles back to the tendency to blame the victim. Opinion polls indicate that most Americans believe that success is due to one's own efforts and not accidents of birth or other circumstances beyond our control.[31] Thus, blaming the victim not only excuses the middle class from helping the poor; it also may trick them into not helping themselves.

SEPARATING VALUE FROM FACT: STEREOTYPING

We have previously seen that common social stereotypes are often misleading. With the help of expected utility analysis, we can see what is really wrong with the use of stereotypes.

A social stereotype can be thought of as a set of interrelated attributes that are attached to a particular racial, religious, ethnic, or sexual group. Table 8.2 presents lists of such traits for several ethnic groups derived from a recent study by Marvin Karlins and his colleagues at Princeton University.[33] The traits are the five attributes most often associated with their respective social group by a sample of white American college students. For anyone familiar with American culture, these characterizations will not be particularly surprising. Italians are "passionate"; Jews are "ambitious"; blacks are "musical." Standard American stereotypes.

The most obvious and often deplored characteristic of such stereotypes is that they lump all members of a group into the same conceptual category, which leads to the incorrect conclusion that it is fair to treat them all the same. The next Italian you meet will be passionate, the next Jew will be ambitious, and the next black, of course,

TABLE 8.2 TRAITS ASSOCIATED WITH SELECTED ETHNIC GROUPS

BLACKS	ITALIANS
Musical	Passionate
Happy-go-lucky	Pleasure loving
Lazy	Artistic
Pleasure loving	Impulsive
Ostentatious	Quick tempered

GERMANS	JEWS
Industrious	Ambitious
Scientifically minded	Materialistic
Efficient	Intelligent
Extremely nationalistic	Industrious
Aggressive	Shrewd

will have rhythm. Thus, people are judged before we meet them and before they have a chance to demonstrate what they really are. This is certainly unfair and leads to numerous errors. But as Roger Brown has argued, though overgeneralization is wrong, it is not the greatest danger created by the use of social stereotypes.[34]

In justification of overgeneralization, it can be argued that at least *some* generalization is necessary, and it is not easy to distinguish a helpful generalization from a dangerous *over*generalization or unfair stereotype. Without generalizations about social attributes, we would have to meet all strangers as if they were entirely unique. This may be exciting upon occasion, but more often it is confusing and even frightening. Is it really so foolish to have different expectancies about, say, an Irish-American bartender and a Baptist minister or a fifty-year-old Marine drill instructor and a twenty-one-year-old rock musician?

Yet there is something terribly wrong about social stereotypes. Look again at the traits listed in Table 8.2. Traits like *lazy, impulsive, industrious*, and *ambitious*, as they are usually applied, are doubtless extreme overgeneralizations from very limited experience. But they are more than that; they are also *evaluations* or *moral judgments*. And as evaluations, stereotypic traits are *not based on experience at all*. The real danger in stereotyping is that it confuses values or utilities, which are personal estimations of worth, with the objective, actual actions of social groups and individuals. This tendency to fuse values and facts, like the tendency to overgeneralize, may be a natural habit of human sensibility.[35] But it should be avoided as much as possible when the goal is clear thinking.

The expected value and expected utility formulas are composed of terms that express probabilities and evaluations, either monetary evaluations in the case of expected value or psychological evaluations in the case of utility. Determining the first component, the probability, requires an estimation of the likelihood of something occurring in nature. This is a statement of fact to be determined by polls, experiments, pilot studies, and personal experience. It has nothing to do with what you personally like or dislike. The second term, the value or utility, is an estimate of worth. It has nothing to do with the probability of anything actually happening. It is your personal response to what may or may not happen. To put it another way, a probability is a judgment on the *world;* a value or utility is a judgment on *yourself.*

When people invoke a social stereotype, they are letting their judgments on themselves masquerade as observations of the world. It may be true that common stereotypes have a "grain of truth" about their factual component. But there is no way of factually demonstrating the truth of the evaluative component. Therefore, two social groups can agree on a behavioral trait, but their stereotypes will have quite different evaluations. If your in-group is noted for being reserved, you can stereotype it as "respecting privacy" and "keeping a proper distance." But if an out-group is reserved, look out! It is "snobbish" and "clannish." Similarly, a group that describes itself as "friendly" and "outgoing" will be described by its enemies as "pushy" and "intrusive." An original and independent person you like is "creative" and "imaginative," but one you dislike is a "weirdo" and a "poor team player."

By means of this *moral alchemy*, to borrow Robert Merton's phrase, a group can change its stereotype as easily as the ancient alchemists dreamed of changing base metals into gold.[36] The group need not actually change its behavior at all; people can simply put a different evaluation on the old behaviors. An out-group, therefore, does not have to change to be accepted into American society; only the evaluation others place on it has to change.

It is instructive to note that two of the traditional out-groups of white, Christian, American society, the Jews and the blacks, have "opposite" stereotypes. Blacks are *lazy*, but Jews are *ambitious*. Blacks are *happy-go-lucky*, but Jews are *scheming* and *grasping*. Blacks are *hedonistic*, but Jews are *sourpusses*. You're damned if you do, and you're damned if you don't. The way to stop this silliness is to make your judgments about the facts and *then* make your judgments about whether the facts are good or bad. If you determine that one ethnic group averages 3.6 baths per week and another averages 5.2, it is up to you what to make of this in terms of morality. You can call the first group "dirty" or the second "compulsive" as you choose. Being aware of such evaluations and how they differ from facts should make it easier to apply them consistently and also to change them if you choose to do that.

VALUES AND VALUE CLARIFICATION

Throughout the last two chapters, we have been concerned with utilities—measures of the psychological value someone places on something. Although this approach to values has an honorable tradition in social science, many people feel it is at best a misplaced conception of values, and at worst, it is downright immoral. They feel that the "ultimate concern" should not be some vaguely mercenary number on a utility scale but rather powerful, humanistic values which express deep, personal commitments like *love, justice, brotherhood*, and *peace*. All I have said about these kinds of values is that they lend themselves to Pascal's wager and should be broken up into smaller, more "workable" units. Now that we have discussed utilities for a while, it would be worthwhile to return to consider more exactly what utilities are and are not. Perhaps we can find a common ground between these two approaches to values—the scientific and the humanistic.

VALUES AS COMMITMENTS

One of the foremost educators to explore the importance of humanistic values is Louis E. Raths. In *Values and Teaching*, Raths and his co-workers note seven basic characteristics of a value.[37] A value is

1. freely chosen
2. from among alternatives
3. after thoughtful consideration;
4. it is prized and cherished,
5. openly affirmed and
6. acted upon
7. repeatedly.

While one can quibble about one or another of the items on Raths's list as well as additional characteristics that could be added, in sum these attributes do aptly describe a deep personal commitment. They summarize what racial equality meant to Martin Luther King, Jr., what social justice meant to Jane Addams, and what political freedom meant to Tom Paine.

In what way does the scientific conception of value as utility conflict with these attributes of humanistic values? Certainly the scientific approach agrees that values (or utilities) must be the result of careful consideration, selected freely from alternatives. Moreover, the whole idea of determining utilities is to act upon them and act consistently. It is not an appropriate use of an expected utility formula to place a positive utility on, say, drinking beer when I do it (it helps me relax) and a negative utility on it when you do it (you're a drunk). This would be using a pseudoscientific formulation to justify prejudice and stereotypes. The whole idea behind any rational decision strategy becomes a travesty if the utilities are deliberately chosen to ensure the "right" choice you have already decided on. Because honest utility estimates determine your actions and are a personal judgment on yourself, they can be said to be prized and cherished. What greater way is there to cherish something than to live by it? Lastly, although there is no need to openly state your utilities, it is certainly not contrary to the scientific approach to do so. To the extent that you act on your utilities, you are at least indirectly proclaiming them. Therefore, the attributes of humanistic values do coincide with the scientific concept of utility.

Nonetheless, the two approaches do seem to have quite different flavors. The scientific approach is couched in mathematical symbols, and the very idea of putting numbers on *peace* or *justice* bothers some people. How can a social scientist actually put a scale value on *love* or *freedom?* The honest answer must be "Not very well." If we can succeed in breaking humanistic values into "workable" units as they apply to any particular social problem, we have accomplished a great deal. At the present time, there is very little agreement on the techniques for finding specific numbers for humanistic values, and the goal of doing so remains a dream.

All that most advocates of the scientific approach to values would wish to argue is that this is a good dream. It does not deserve the stereotype of cold, inhuman, manipulative, valueless science that some would give it. The scientific approach would argue that the more precisely we can weigh humanistic values as they are found in complex existential situations, the more wisely we will be able to decide social issues when they come in conflict. Those who express the humanistic approach do not face as often as social scientists the unpleasant fact that frequently we must decide between values. It may, in fact, be true that in the mind of God, love, peace, and justice are one and indivisible, but here on earth we have yet to find the great fusion that unites them. In deciding on an affirmative action program to hire women in state schools, a bill to legalize abortion, a vote to turn a section of farmland into a recreational park, or a bill to institute capital punishment, legislators consistently find that either side of the issue would affirm some cherished values and deny others. In order to encourage a proper balance among important values, we should bear in mind that they can be compared and weighed, at least in theory.

Thinking about values as divisible also reminds us that they are gained or lost by slow degrees, one step at a time. It is a staple of political rhetoric to claim that a proposal will destroy one value or guarantee another. But in serious thinking about the goals of society, we must recognize that our values advance or decline by small steps. This is meaningless unless we appreciate the fact that values can be actualized in degrees.

VALUE CLARIFICATION

In order to help students understand their own values better, Raths and his co-workers have developed a number of devices known collectively as value clarification techniques.[38] These techniques all involve some form of questioning which is followed by an encouragement to reflect on the answer. For example, you might be asked to choose between going to a rock concert or going to the movies or decide between reading a novel or listening to a record. How you answer the questions should reflect on the value you place on music, and reflecting on your answers should help clarify this value. It goes without saying that when properly conducted, value clarification is not a device for telling people what they *ought* to feel. It is a mechanism for encouraging insight about how they actually do feel. In terms of the scientific approach to values, such techniques can help you understand the personal utilities you associate with various states of nature.

By extension, value clarification techniques can help us understand how the decision makers of a society on the whole feel about certain occurrences. That is, we can speak of collective utility clarification as well as personal value clarification. One obvious way to assess a society's collective utilities would be to poll a representative sample and generalize the results to the total population. But there is another approach of interest related to expected utility. Rather than merely asking people what they would do in a choice situation, we could actually present them with a decision and see how they act. From this point of view, any action of a social group might reveal something about its utilities. Up to now, we have been considering expected utility as a *normative* rule which describes how an ideally rational person would behave. I am now suggesting that we can use expected utility as a *descriptive* rule that clarifies how people actually do feel. If we are willing to assume, for the sake of utility clarification, that people are acting rationally, we can then argue back from their actions to what their utilities *must* be in order to justify their actions.

Let us see how this might work in a particular case. In 1971 the

State of New York instituted a mandatory system of identification cards for welfare recipients.[39] It was hoped that these I.D. cards, which carried a photograph of the recipient, would substantially reduce the level of forgery of welfare checks. However, the Human Resources Administration charged with overseeing the program estimated that (a) losses due to forgery ran about $150,000 a year and (b) the new program would cost about $900,000 a year to run, in addition to $2,000,000 to begin.[40] Even if we assume that all forgery would be eliminated by the program and ignore the start-up cost, the decision would appear irrational. Why spend $900,000 to save $150,000?

As an exercise in utility or value clarification, we can assume that the decision makers involved had all the necessary information and were acting perfectly rationally. Then it appears that forgery must have a value of −$750,000 a year beyond the direct cost to the welfare system. This additional cost of forgery could reflect the desire on the part of decision makers to stop forgers from leading a life of crime, protect those from whom the checks might be stolen, and so on. One interesting possibility is that the close scrutiny of welfare recipients might reflect the distrust of those in power toward those who receive and cash welfare checks. In such a case, making those who receive welfare carry a special means of identification would indicate the value society places on the nobility of work and the ignobility of the poor receiving money when not working. This suggestion is supported by the fact that when people are asked which they prefer, welfare or a work incentive program, they overwhelmingly choose the work incentive program, *even if it costs the taxpayer more than simple welfare.*[41] If this utility analysis were borne out by other analyses, it would indicate that it is improper to consider the I.D. system a cost to welfare as reflecting the utility our nation places on helping the poor. Rather, it would express the utility our nation places on the work ethic and the amount we are willing to spend to enforce that value system on those who are presumed to be unappreciative of the value of honest labor.

On the basis of only one or two observations, we cannot tell which of many possible explanations for a social decision is the correct one. But by observing a large number of actions by the same persons, we can often slowly begin to reduce the number of plausible explanations until either their utility or their irrationality is established.

At the end of our consideration of departures from rationality, it is fitting that we return to the question that has appeared often in attempting to understand social problems: Are people rational? The departures from rationality we have considered indicate that people often do fail to make social decisions in a rational manner. But this does not indicate that all social decisions or even all disastrous ones are irrational. As the functionalists have argued, even the most disastrous occurrence for one group may have a high positive utility for another. It is probably safest to assume that social problems reflect a complex combination of both irrational thinking and value conflict.

SUMMARY

Using the expected utility model, not as a formula to be followed compulsively but as an ideal form to be followed in outline, we can detect several common mistakes in decision making about social problems. First, there is a tendency, especially among professional social scientists, to accentuate negative utilities. In rational decision making, a positive utility cancels out a negative utility of the same absolute size. To ignore this principle leads to a fear of taking risks and a failure to maximize one's potential. Second, many people unnecessarily create enormous utilities, usually catastrophes, which they associate with a particular course of action. This overwhelms rational decision making and should be corrected by breaking down the overwhelming utility into more manageable units. Third, very small probabilities and utilities are all too often ignored. Small utilities can become important when they are accumulated over many persons or occasions. Small probabilities can be crucial if they are associated with large utilities. Fourth, the expected utility formula reminds us to make separate estimations of the probability of an event occurring and the personal evaluation of the worth of the event if it, in fact, occurs. To confuse the two is to engage in stereotyping in which a judgment on nature is confused with a judgment about yourself.

This scientific approach is *not* in essential conflict with the expression of humanistic values. We can use the expected utility approach as a utility clarification device similar to value clarification techniques. In this way, we can determine what the utilities of social decision makers must be if they are rational.

NINE

Individual Intelligence and Social Intelligence

In the last two chapters we considered some important aspects of decision making and how we often deviate from the proper course when making important social decisions. Hidden beneath the surface was the assumption that societies should be rational in the same way that individuals should be. When confronting some social problems this assumption is probably rather safe, and it is appropriate to generalize from ideal individual decision making to ideal national decision making. However, there are situations in which it is foolish to think of a nation as a sort of big person whose utilities should be maximized in the same way that any ordinary person's should be. A nation is not a large organism composed of people in the way a human being is a large organism composed of cells. A person has a psychological and existential unity that a nation lacks. Nations are composed of lots of selfish individuals and interest groups that are capable of consistently subverting the common good for their personal satisfaction. Our failure to develop robust mechanisms for fusing individuals and interest groups into a true national purpose lies at the heart of many deeply entrenched social problems, including prejudice and discrimination against minorities, the

198

SOCIAL INTELLIGENCE

dominance of special interest groups, the devastation of natural resources by waste and pollution, and the population explosion.

It can be easily shown that traditional democratic procedures do
not guarantee the ultimate good of the total society. Table 9.1 describes
a very simple society with only three members—X, Y, and Z. Each of
the citizens is faced with three alternatives—A, B, and C, and reports
the order of preference for each pair of alternatives as indicated in the
table. The symbol > can be read "is greater in utility to" or simply "is
preferred to." For example, citizen X prefers alternative A to B, B to
C, and A to C. A study of Table 9.1 shows that there is some disagreement among the citizens about the most advantageous course of action.
The democratic approach to resolving the disagreement would be to
take the opinion of the majority for each pair comparison. The majority
opinion is given in the last row.

Looking closely at the last row of the table, you will observe
that an interesting thing has happened. The majority opinion is *intransitive;* that is, it is self-contradicting.[1] A *transitive* set of preferences
would have a form like the following: A is preferred to B, B to C, and
the chain is completed by preferring A to C. If instead C were preferred to A, the chain of preferences would be intransitive, self-contradicting, and irrational. It can be seen that each of the three citizens
of the hypothetical society has a transitive set of preferences, although
the preferences of the democratic majority are intransitive. The problem this creates can be easily understood if you imagine that A, B, and
C are islands and that the society starts by owning island C. Because B
is preferred to C, the government is willing to give C plus some small

TABLE 9.1 A SMALL SOCIETY WITH A PROBLEM

CITIZEN	PREFERENCE BETWEEN ALTERNATIVES		
	A versus B	B versus C	A versus C
X	A>B	B>C	A>C
Y	B>A	B>C	C>A
Z	A>B	C>B	C>A
MAJORITY	A>B	B>C	C>A

additional amount, say $1, to get B. But it also prefers A to B, so it trades B plus another $1 for A. Now the stupidity of the intransitivity is revealed because it will then trade A plus another $1 to get back C. Our government is now exactly where it started except that it is $3 poorer and ready for another round of trading.[2] The emergence of irrational intransitivity in the majority opinion reveals how combining the preferences of perfectly rational individuals can create an irrational social policy.

In this chapter, we will be concerned with two interrelated problems: How can a society develop large collective social problems when all its members are acting rationally? And how can we determine a set of national goals that can meaningfully evaluate the actions of the total society? There is no consensus on precise answers to these problems, but a general knowledge of their implications should lay the groundwork for developing workable solutions. First, we will consider the problem of determining national goals. Then, we will consider the three general kinds of abuse which hinder achieving these goals. Finally, we will consider some possible solutions to the abuses.

DETERMINING NATIONAL GOALS

COST-BENEFIT ANALYSIS

One way to determine the value of a social policy for the whole society is to extend the basic expected utility analysis we have been pursuing to larger national projects. Such a practice is called national cost-benefit analysis or welfare economics. Unfortunately, all the problems with utility analysis we have met so far get more and more intractable the more massive and complex a project becomes. It is exceedingly difficult to avoid catastrophizing when dealing with the loss of the Everglades or a serious erosion in our national defense. The positive utility of clean air or racial peace is often difficult to break down into manageable units or evaluate through a free market auction. A second difficulty is that welfare economics brings into focus a problem I have so far avoided—the comparison of utilities across individuals.

A project that will cause a person to move and give someone a job creates decidedly different challenges to utility analysis, depending on whether the two events are experienced by the same person or different persons. If you had to move to take a job, you could simply weigh the pros and cons of the present home and the proposed job and make your best judgment. You would have no reason to lie; misstating your utilities would only hurt yourself. But in the typical case in welfare economics, a project helps some people and hurts others, and the positive and negative utilities occur across people who have every reason to exaggerate them. If those who are faced with moving can cry loud enough, the social planners might decide that the "cost" of the job creation program is too great to justify its implementation.

It would not solve the problem to give everyone a lie detector test because that would measure selfishness and shortsightedness as well as honesty. The six-year-old who screams that he cannot live without the electronic space robot in the toy store's window might very well pass a lie detector test. His parents would more correctly estimate that the child would forget all about it in a day. The temptation for national decision makers is to think of themselves as good parents, disregard our protests, and decide our utilities for us. The course of action is then decided by the utilities we are *supposed* to have and not the ones we have personally chosen.

The classic case of cost-benefit analysis involves the decision to build a dam. If the dam is built, it will put some people to work and put others out of their homes. The construction will probably injure some workers, but the electricity generated will allow a widow 300 miles away to enjoy her Bach records less expensively. The loss of farmland will increase the price of beef, and the lake behind the dam will bring joy to sport fishermen. And so on, for a thousand other effects. The challenge to cost-benefit analysis lies in putting the varied experiences of so many different individuals on the same scale.

Large social projects like dams often reveal the wisdom of the social disorganization or ecological approach to social problems. Biologist Garrett Hardin has argued that the construction of the Aswan dam in Egypt created a number of far-reaching, unexpected consequences.[3] These include the decrease in fertility of the flood plain due to the loss of silt-bearing floods, the devastation of the Mediterranean sardine catch, and the rise of schistosomiasis, a dreadful disease borne by snails living in the irrigation ditches.

The hazards of cost-benefit analysis are probably greatest when the proposed action involves such alterations in ecological systems.[4] Even our present rudimentary understanding of the delicate harmony of natural systems is enough to discourage many projects our ancestors would have leaped into with foolhardy abandon. It can further be argued that when the alteration of natural systems is permanent, even a small negative utility per year becomes staggering when accumulated over all the future generations that must suffer the loss. For these reasons, some social scientists have come to doubt the feasibility of honest, scientific cost-benefit analyses of major national projects.

Nevertheless, dams do get built. Somebody is making the decision even if the procedures behind the choice are unconscious, selfish, and irrational. Other social scientists argue that it is better to make a cautious, honest attempt at cost-benefit analysis and hope for the best than to yield the decision making to even more irrational procedures.

SOCIAL INDICATORS

Those who have given up determining the ultimate social value of any particular project can still attempt to measure objectively the overall quality of life in society. The goal now is not the evaluation of a specific project or program. Rather, it is an attempt to measure the general drift of society as a whole. By means of objective measures of the quality of life, we should be able to gauge overall social progress or potential problem areas.

Many objective measures relating to the well-being of the nation are published annually in the *Statistical Abstract of the United States*.[5] These include statistics on population, health, income, energy use, transportation, agriculture, education, and social welfare. With such measures available, many people have become interested in organizing and correlating them to create a kind of national system of accounting. They have come to agree with Raymond Bauer that "For many of the important topics on which social critics blithely pass judgment, and on which policies are made, there are no yardsticks by which to know if things are getting better or worse."[6] Realization of the need for social yardsticks has given rise to the *social indicators* movement to monitor objectively the quality of life.[7]

Measures of social well-being do not have to be dreary recitations of how many telephones, automobiles, toilets, and television sets we are blessed with. We are all familiar with these simpleminded lists that have done little to enlighten trends in national development. Table 9.2 presents a simplified illustration of one approach to measuring the overall quality of life. On the left are nine areas relevant to the state of the nation, and on the right are two examples of specific measures for each area. These statistics would have to be controlled for technical complications, such as inflation and population growth. Exactly how the individual statistics would be weighted and combined to yield overall measures would also have to be determined.

In forming a meaningful overall measure, we would have to be wary of paradoxical statistics. For example, the more hospital beds, doctors, and medical insurance programs are available, the more people are likely to become officially sick. The misleading average could also emerge. When half of the population is overfed and half is under-nourished, on the average they have a fine diet. A great deal of dis-agreement can be expected on both the values to measure and the spe-

TABLE 9.2   MEASURES OF THE QUALITY OF LIFE

AREA	STATISTIC
Wealth	Median income Percent below the poverty level
Health	Life expectancy Number of work days lost to illness
Knowledge	Median years of schooling Number of books sold
Advancement of knowledge	Number of patents issued Total research expenditures
Environmental quality	Composite air quality index Composite water quality index
Agriculture	Median farm income Total agricultural production
Shelter	Percent living in substandard housing New housing starts
Psychological stability	Number of mental hospital admissions Suicide rate
Family stability	Divorce rate Number of illegitimate births

cific statistics used to measure each value. In spite of all these difficulties, most people would agree at least on which direction of change is desirable for the statistics listed in Table 9.2. There is probably also a general agreement that if all the measures in Table 9.2 are getting worse, something is seriously wrong with the nation.

SUBJECTIVE MEASURES OF NATIONAL GOALS

One unfortunate aspect of most lists of social indicators like Table 9.2 is that they fall into the trap of accentuating the negative. Social progress is seen as a *lack* of problems rather than a growth in positive indicators. This reflects once again the orientation of American social scientists as well as the difficulty in objectively measuring joyful experience. Another problem with objective social indicators is that they are composed by experts who feel competent to tell us how society is doing. This reminds us of the difficulty of objective definitions of social problems considered in Chapter 6: The opinion of the experts on how we ought to feel may bear little resemblance to the way most of us actually do feel. We can avoid this problem regarding social indicators the same way we circumvented it in defining a social problem. We can adopt a subjective definition.

A subjective approach to the quality of life would simply ask people how they feel about life in America. This is easy to do and has a commonsense validity to it. It also generates some perplexing results. For one thing, there is no simple relationship between the subjective estimate of the quality of life and common objective measures. In Chapter 5 it was noted that in spite of substantial gains in the objective indicators between 1950 and 1970, there was no increase in the percentage of people claiming to be very happy.[8] In addition, more people in recent opinion polls could name ways in which life in the United States was getting worse than could name ways it was getting better.[9] William Watts and Lloyd Free, in evaluating the results of one national poll, concluded:

> The people's assessment of the state of the nation in 1971 was unquestionably the most pessimistic recorded since the introduction of public opinion polling almost four decades ago in the midst of the great depression of the 1930s. In fact, the public mood recorded in the 1971 survey might well be designated the "great mental depression" of the early 1970s. . . .[10]

Other subjective measures have not been so bleak, but most recent surveys agree that Americans are neither very happy about the present nor terribly optimistic about the future.[11]

Finer statistical analyses of subjective well-being are also perplexing. For example, comparing across geographical regions, there is little correlation between the objective measures of well-being for the region and the reported life satisfaction of its inhabitants.[12] Poorer areas of the country are just as happy as more affluent ones. Family income is correlated with subjective well-being, but even here there are complications. College graduates do not increase in reported well-being as their income increases.[13] Another interesting fact is that those sixty-five and older report the greatest well-being even though they are relatively low on objective measures, such as income and health.[14]

COMPARING OBJECTIVE AND SUBJECTIVE MEASURES Several possible explanations for the difference between objective and subjective measures can be offered. First, it should be noted that in spite of the air of pessimism, about 90 percent of the people describe themselves as at least "pretty happy." [15] It is possible that people feel rather satisfied with their lives but give themselves all the credit. Meanwhile, the government and other large institutions are blamed for the failures in life. Thus, a sense of national gloom and a feeling of personal satisfaction are not necessarily contradictory. Many people may also feel that the government is more likely to lend them a hand if they complain about the way things are going, and an opinion pollster knocking at the door presents a grand opportunity for energetic griping.

Second, it is likely that happiness itself is a multifaceted concept. For example, those over sixty-five were high on total feelings of well-being because of a high score on satisfaction with their lives as a whole, but they did not report feeling particularly "happy." [16] A feeling of happiness in the "guts" might be quite a different thing from a more intellectual recognition of well-being, and these are just two of the many kinds of subjective satisfaction we can delineate. Man does not live by bread alone, nor apparently by happiness alone.

Third, it might be that those objective measures of the quality of life that show improvement are not all that important in generating well-being. Maybe the crime rate, divorce rate, and other measures that are deteriorating are more relevant than income, housing, education, and those measures that are improving. It is also possible that the social disorganization caused by the introduction of objective improvements is causing a great deal of subjective dissatisfaction.

Lastly, success in objective terms may be negated by changes in comparison level and aspiration level. The leaders of America may have delivered a lot of benefits, but they have promised even more. Perhaps those who are doing well objectively are just the ones who expected to be doing even better, and now they feel all the more frustrated as a result.

In spite of these qualifications, the subjective measure of well-being contains the suggestion that America is doing something seriously wrong in national decision making. The reports of dissatisfaction indicate that in spite of an increase in material benefits on the one hand and the structural safeguards of democracy on the other, people still feel abused in contemporary American society. We have finished our overview of the measurement of the total success of the nation. We will now turn to consideration of three general sources of abuse as they relate to the structure of national decision making, the quality of life, and the maintenance of social problems.

STRUCTURAL ABUSES IN AMERICAN SOCIETY

THE MAJORITY ABUSING A MINORITY

Perhaps the most often noted defect in democratic decision making is the tyranny of the majority over a minority. If we are willing to assume some meaningful comparison of interpersonal utilities for the sake of exposition, the situation can be depicted in terms of arbitrary utilities in Table 9.3. The table shows a slight gain from a proposed action for four members of the community and an excessive loss to the minority of one. In terms of the utility for the total community, the proposed action would have a detrimental effect. But if the society were a democracy, the proposed action might well be chosen because it is in the interest of the majority. Slavery provides an obvious case of this social structure. As long as slavery is in the economic interest of the majority, representative government is no impediment to its development.*

---

* Typically, slaves are also denied their rights of citizenship, but this is not necessary for the majority to abuse them.

One way out of this situation is to appeal to the conscience or religious principles of the majority. Such principles are often expressed in laws that prohibit the abuse of a minority regardless of the will of the majority. This expression is found in the Bill of Rights of the American Constitution and similar documents in other countries. The fact that Thomas Jefferson, the man who inspired the Bill of Rights, also owned slaves demonstrates the limited effectiveness of such documents. Even after the liberation of the slaves in America, blacks were systematically denied voting rights and other constitutional rights by those who prided themselves on their high moral principles. Tens of thousands of law-abiding Japanese-Americans were imprisoned during World War II in clear violation of the Bill of Rights without the majority becoming concerned. The extent to which dominant religious groups have persecuted religious minorities further attests to the fallibility of approaches based on religious teaching. We would have to conclude that appeals to principle have not been terribly successful in combating the tyranny of the majority.

If the utilities in Table 9.3 represented dollars or some other tradable commodity, the use of *side payments* is possible to limit the abuse of the majority. If citizen 5 could give a little more than one utility unit to citizens 3 and 4 to vote against the proposal, it would create a majority against the proposed action and limit citizen 5's loss to about 2. This exemplifies the use of side payments to overcome an abusive utility structure by creating a new, more preferable structure. Side payments can be expensive in themselves, but they have the advantage of not relying on something as transient and uncertain as human kindness and adherence to principle.

TABLE 9.3 THE MAJORITY ABUSING A MINORITY

Citizen	Utility of Proposed Action
1	+1
2	+1
3	+1
4	+1
5	−10
Total utility	−6

One limitation on using side payments is that very often the minority is facing a loss in self-respect, human rights, religious freedom, or some other utility that cannot be easily converted to money to buy off the majority. If slaves had the money to buy their rights, they would not be slaves in the first place. Another difficulty with side payments is that they frequently are illegal. If you think of side payments as "bribes," you will see that they are condemned precisely because they frustrate the will of the majority. If a minority social group wishes to increase its "good will" by funding scholarships for poor students, this is a legal form of side payment. The more effective and inexpensive use of side payments to bribe legislators and government bureaucrats is considered illegal.

Slavery and other more egregious forms of majority tyranny have largely vanished, but because of the difficulties in relying on principle or side payments, a great deal of abuse still continues. You may have perceived that we have circled back to the problem of interest groups and value conflict. From the present perspective, the difficulty presents itself as a logical restriction in democracy. With one vote per person, democracy is structured to represent the *proportion* of preferences among the citizens. It does not represent the *intensity* of preferences.

Curfew laws present a handy illustration of a continuing abuse of a minority. Because many people find some displeasure in seeing juveniles at large at night, and many parents prefer to create a norm rather than use their personal power in keeping their children at home, curfew laws have often been established. Juveniles cannot vote and have little economic power to create side payments.* As a result, their rights have been limited by curfew and other youth-status laws without serious consideration of the negative utility for the youngsters themselves.

Another interesting example is provided by laws against a lifestyle of poverty. Because of welfare, unemployment compensation, Medicaid, food stamp programs and similar welfare benefits, the burden of poverty has been eased in many respects. In other ways, poverty has been rendered more unbearable by the abuse of the poor by the middle-class majority. In bygone days, a poor family could live in a

---

*This does not prevent juveniles from having substantial economic power in some limited segments of the economy. The American recording industry presents an example of an industry dominated by the economic power of teenagers.

shack without plumbing and raise vegetables in the front of the house and a hog in the back. It wasn't much, but one could make a go of it. Many middle-class couples are actually choosing to return to this simple life today, but they have to move out of populated areas to do it. As the suburbs engulfed grandpa's log cabin, so did suburban values and life-style engulf grandpa's way of life. Outhouses were made illegal because they are "disgusting," hogs because they are "unhygienic," and vegetable gardens in front of the house because they "lower property values." It is doubtful if there has been any serious appreciation of the negative utilities created for the poor by enforcing a middle-class lifestyle on those who cannot afford it.

A MINORITY ABUSING THE MAJORITY

By means of the concepts of salience, threshold of concern, and the accumulation of small utilities, we can see how a utility structure very similar to the one shown in Table 9.3 can result in the reverse effect of a minority abusing the majority. If a personal action will hurt almost everyone too little to be noticed and meanwhile help a single individual a great deal, the proposal might well carry even though the total effect on society is very negative. Because most members of society do not recognize their loss, they do not know how to vote or instruct their representatives. The one person whose interest is above threshold, of course, does exert influence, and the majority are hurt to help the "special interest." It is also wise for the special interest to complicate and obscure the situation so that the salience of the loss to the majority is reduced even further. When the complicating and obscuring are done successfully, as in the case of income tax regulations, it is exceedingly difficult for the average person to feel anything but confusion and a vague feeling that someone is getting something he or she isn't.[17]

A similar problem occurs when the loss to the majority is above the threshold of awareness but beneath the threshold of concern. This means that people have a general idea they are being abused, but it is not worth their trouble to do anything about it. This circles back to the paradox of bargaining in which only "irrational" persons would choose to lose utility in order to stop an opponent from winning. As long as it costs more to protect your interest than the slight loss incurred by letting the special interest get its way, only an irrational person (or one pretending to be irrational) would fight the special interest.

In theory this predicament can be overcome by means of organization. If enough members of the majority can band together to share the cost, the loss in utility for any individual may be less than the cost of doing nothing. Unfortunately, this is harder to accomplish in fact than to state in theory. If the loss is beneath the threshold of awareness, the organization will never form in the first place. Even if there is some awareness of the problem, it is difficult to provide the organization, communication, and feedback necessary for effective action. The very fact that there are so many millions of people involved makes it difficult for them to be brought into active participation. The few who do actively fight the special interest must either incur substantial loss for their efforts or be paid for them. If they are paid for them, they are in danger of becoming another special interest themselves. These difficulties can be seen in the most important majority organization in America, the government of the United States, which often fails to protect or inform its constituents, frequently serves special interests at the expense of the majority, and usually acts like a special interest itself.

GUILD LEGISLATION The government often sets aside a certain group as having a special legal status. In the case of curfew and other juvenile-status laws, it is a minority that is denied the rights and privileges maintained by the majority. It is more common, however, for status legislation to deny to the majority the rights maintained by a special interest group. This is accomplished by means of licensing or certification laws that create privileged professional groups known as guilds.[18] As a result of guild legislation the medical guild is granted the power to cure your illnesses, the barber guild to cut your hair, the real estate guild to sell you a house, and the undertakers' guild to bury you when the rest of the guilds are through with you.

Guild legislation must be distinguished from regulations regarding the quality of products. A law that says that any medicine sold must be pure is concerned with the product itself. A law that says that only certain persons (i.e., registered pharmacists) can sell the medicine is guild legislation. Laws of this sort sometimes maintain the quality of the product indirectly. But these legal monopolies also very often abuse the majority by increasing costs, limiting supplies, and decreasing competition.[19]

In the name of protecting the public, guild legislation turns an occupation into a profession, and by means of a "grandfather's clause," entrance into the profession is assured to those who had been in the occupation. Since these people are usually the very ones who supposedly inspired the need for high-quality performance in the first place, it is doubtful that protection of the public was ever the major motive. Furthermore, the profession is usually given a strong hand in policing itself and rarely exercises this power to expel incompetent members.[20] It is also informative that guild legislation, which prevents the average citizen from competing with the guild, rarely compels service from the members of the guild. Those who practice medicine without a license can be imprisoned, but those who hold the license are not imprisoned when they fail to practice their profession, as in the case of a doctors' strike. For these reasons, guild legislation often abuses the majority while favoring the special interests of the guild.

There are other kinds of governmental action similar in structure and effect to guild legislation. Tariffs and import quotas, which limit competition from foreign countries, yield substantial benefits to a select group while increasing the costs of various goods a little for everyone. Creating ways of getting in trouble with the law is a kind of guild legislation for lawyers which increases the business over which they hold a monopoly. In this case, many members of society do not incur a slight loss; rather, they face the slight probability of a large loss. If the average marijuana smoker subjectively expects to be arrested for possession of marijuana with a probability of .001 and expects a lawyer's fee of $1,000 if arrested, the expected value is equivalent to a sure loss of $1 ($EV = .001 \times \$1,000 = \$1$). This loss might not be enough to worry about until the person is arrested, and then it is too late. On the other hand, the lawyers, police, and bureaucrats, who routinely profit from marijuana arrests, are well aware of their personal interest in maintaining the law that increases their business.

Job creation programs provide an additional illustration. The government will tax everyone to create jobs for a particular industry building highways or bombers. The loss to the average person is not salient, while the unions and corporations that benefit are well aware of their advantage. Economist Milton Friedman has described the result on subjective feelings of well-being:

> People hired by the government know who is their benefactor. People who lose their jobs or fail to get them because of the government programs do not know that that is the source of their problem. The good effects are visible. The bad effects are invisible. The good effects gen-

erate votes. The bad effects generate discontent, which is as likely to be directed at private business as at the government.[21]

THIRD PARTYING We have already met the third party ploy for removing the salience of the real source of social power and confusing people about the ultimate cause of their frustration. Here we meet it again as a device for distorting a utility structure so that the majority of the members of society cannot understand or protect themselves from abuse by a special interest. If I am paying for your services and you cheat me, I am likely to complain. But if I think some third party is actually paying for the service, I will probably let the third party worry about it. The trick is that the third party spreads the cost around to so many people that no one is likely to get excited. The more the cost of a personal service is shared by everyone through the third party, the less interest each person has in receiving a fair price. Let someone else complain! Overcharging for materials, substandard service, and other forms of cheating can be established as standard practice when there are third parties to distribute the losses.

The medical industry has been among the most successful in using the third party trick. By 1977 fully 90 percent of the population had some type of insurance covering hospital care.[22] Buying insurance is really creating a third party to pay for something. The wisdom of insurance was considered in Chapter 8 with the example of fire insurance. What was not covered in Chapter 8 was the fact that once you are fully covered by insurance, you no longer care if your house burns down or not. With regard to medical insurance, it is no longer of great interest to you if your doctor is overcharging. Each instance of overcharging costs you perhaps 1¢—not enough to worry about.

> Jane Boutwell of *The New Yorker* tells about the time she was bitten on the hand by an irate Siamese cat. She went to the hospital emergency room, where she was told to go home and soak her hand in hot water. On the way out the cashier said: "That will be forty-five dollars." When Ms. Boutwell questioned that fee for the service she had received, the cashier replied in classic fashion: "Why should you worry? Your insurance will take care of it."[23]

From 1965 to 1975 the average life expectancy in the United States rose about 3 percent.[24] Over the same period, total health care costs soared over 300 percent.[25] Why should you worry? Because you're being third partied, that's why!

EVERYONE ABUSING EVERYONE ELSE

In one week in London in December, 1952, 2,800 persons were killed by a deadly smog.[26] If only a hundredth of that total were killed by something quick, dramatic, bloody and political, like a skyjacking or bombing, the people would have had a good idea who the culprits were. They would have felt the will to act and had at least a rough idea of what to do about it. But many of the killers of the modern world do not present such well-defined targets. It is hard to convince a motorist commuting to work or an industrialist going about his daily business that they are killing people miles away.

Because the effects of pollution are widespread, varied, numerous and insidious, we cannot focus our outrage on any particular aspect of the problem. Our lives are haunted by polychlorinated biphenyls (PCB's), diethylstilbestrol (DES), cyclohexylamine (CHA), and other tongue-twisters beyond our powers of detection. It now requires an in-depth analysis by a team of experts to determine if there is an objective social problem. It then requires an extensive public education campaign to make the objective problem a subjective reality. With crime, poverty, unemployment, and other more dramatic, apparent, and easily comprehended social problems pressing in, the average person often feels no enthusiasm for the invisible ones. As a result, the poisoning of our waterways, the existence of toxic chemicals in our food, and the depletion of our natural resources are not yet overwhelming *subjective* social problems.

Our lives are no longer dictated by a king or an emperor. They are influenced instead by a crazy quilt of interacting special interests. In the last section, we saw how one special interest can abuse the majority. The actual social reality is that myriad interrelated interests are all operating at once. Everyone belongs to some combination or other of these interests and tends to appreciate the needs of his or her group while ignoring the needs of others. The end result is that it is next to impossible to find a single precise cause for any one abuse. Everyone is abusing everyone else.

SOCIAL TRAPS When a large number of people are each performing an action which benefits themselves while it hurts everyone else, the whole sorry business is known as a *social trap*. Littering provides a simple illustration of the way these traps operate. You benefit, say, two utility units by not bothering to pick up your trash, and at the same time everyone, including yourself, loses one utility unit due to the eyesore you leave behind. Your personal expected utility indicates that you should litter. The advantage of littering is all yours; the unpleasantness is shared by everyone. But when everyone does the rational, selfish thing, the total utility to the whole society is strongly negative. Being rational, you would be willing to see everyone, including yourself, stop littering, but if they don't, why should you? The result is a social trap in which everyone is making everyone else a little more miserable. The way out of the trap is to get everyone to agree to be unselfish together.

Thomas Schelling has argued convincingly that social traps are indicated not only by major social problems but also by a lot of the little inconveniences of life that do much to decrease our subjective well-being.[27] Schelling provides an insightful story about a mattress that had fallen off a car and blocked one lane of traffic. As each motorist approached the blockade, he had to wait for an opportunity to pass the mattress, and eventually a long waiting line formed. The problem would be quickly solved if one driver were to simply get out and remove the mattress. But you cannot do this until you get up to the mattress, and by then you are late, frustrated, irritated at the other drivers who did not bother to help you, and find it easier to stay in your car and drive around the blockade. The structure of the situation that turns a minor inconvenience into a major hassle is that you cannot help yourself, you can only help others. John Platt has called this structure the *Missing Hero* trap.[28]

The most dangerous traps are those in which the utilities themselves change as the trap slowly engulfs us. The individual trap of drug addiction shows how this can happen. When someone takes a drug such as alcohol, the result is a combination of positive and negative utilities, or in the terminology of learning theory, the person receives both reward and punishment. The rational approach to drug usage would be to weigh the rewards against the punishments and take the drug if, and only if, the rewards were greater. But because the immediate effects of an action are more powerful and salient influences on learning than the delayed effects, the psychology of learning and salience can conflict with the rational expected utility analysis. Many drugs like alcohol, narcotics, and nicotine can yield immediate pleasure and ultimate misery. The temptation is to enjoy the immediate pleasure and bemoan your fate when the sickness, hangover, or withdrawal finally arrives.

The truly insidious nature of addiction shows itself when the re-inforcements or utilities begin to change. Narcotics show this most clearly. The first time heroin is taken, there may be a substantial plea-sure soon after administration and little if any unpleasantness later on. So it is rational to take heroin the *first* time. However, with each ad-ministration there is a tendency for the immediate pleasure to decrease due to habituation and the ultimate unpleasantness to increase due to addiction. The addict finds himself on an accelerating treadmill; at any moment it is painful to jump off, and at each moment's delay, it be-comes even more painful. If the process is allowed to continue, the ad-dict is eventually working not for pleasure but to postpone misery. The total process of heroin usage has a definite negative utility.

Many social situations are similar to narcotics addiction. A sim-ple example, which can be played as a parlor game, is the "Sell-a-Dollar" game. In playing this game, the seller offers to auction off a dollar to the highest bidder. The only catch is that both the highest bidder, who gets the dollar, and the second highest bidder, who gets nothing, must pay their bids. The prospect of getting the dollar for only a nickel or a dime starts people bidding. But eventually they begin to sink into the trap, and the prospect of losing the bid and getting nothing can keep the bidding escalating past the point of reason.[29] The solution to this trap as well as many others is the use of cooperation and side payments. If the bidders agree to hold down the bidding to, say, 5¢, they can all split the 95¢ profit.

One social phenomenon we have frequently met in our study of social problems is comparison level. We can see now that striving for social status and material wealth can be analogous to addiction or the Sell-a-Dollar game. Because of changes in comparison level, the re-wards of social success are brief, and those who are successful require bigger and bigger "fixes" of success to keep their feeling of well-being. And all the time, they may be haunted by the fear of losing their sta-tus. People start the race for success to gain pleasure, but if they are not careful, they will keep on running to avoid failure.[30]

Economic traps provide another common example of a kind of social trap. If you think a company's stock will decrease in value, you will sell your shares. If you are the only one who feels this way, nothing much will happen. But if many people feel this way, the subsequent rush to sell will create the very phenomenon that was feared. Eventually even those who have faith in the company will unload their stock as they are caught in the self-fulfilling prophecy. On a broader scale, if important industries feel a recession is coming and consequently reduce production, they are caught in a trap which can create the very recession they feared.

One important form of social trap in the modern world is what Garrett Hardin has called the "tragedy of the commons."[31] A commons is any activity or means of production open to everyone; it is common property. The classic case is the English tradition of setting aside a certain amount of pasture land open to everyone. Since the use of the commons is free, everyone feels a personal economic interest in placing as many cattle as possible on the land. The tragic result is that the commons eventually becomes overgrazed, eroded, and deteriorated until it is useless to everyone. The tragedy of the commons is not merely of interest in English history. In the 1970s the extent of the world's deserts increased about 15 million acres every year. The spread of the southern Sahara caused by overgrazing resulted in the death by hunger of an estimated 100,000 West Africans between 1968 and 1973.[32] The tragedy of the commons is still very much with us.

The utility structure of the commons trap is the same as that of the littering example considered earlier. Each person gains greatest personal utility by increasing the negative utility for everyone else. Forseeing the trap enclosing and the ultimate ruin of the commons provides no solution. It only encourages the logical person to make as much use of the commons as possible before it is destroyed. As Hardin has pointed out, the air, the oceans, and many of the best things in life are free; that is, they are commons. When they are the responsibility of everyone, they are the responsibility of no one.

The population explosion is a form of commons trap. A peasant gains greater personal utility from having a large family. They provide workers, comfort, and in some cultures increased status. When everyone does the selfish thing and has a large family, the result is a population explosion, which results in the deterioration of the quality of life for everyone. Forseeing mass starvation will only encourage a selfish person to have as many children as possible in the hope that at least some will survive.

The real tragedy of the commons unfolds when the trap creates irreversible consequences. The possibility of irreparable harm differentiates the present traps caused by culture lag and the inability to adapt to changing technology from the classic economic traps of the past. The purely economic trap eventually runs its course and reverses itself. Sooner or later the recession "bottoms out" and a period of growth follows. The scarcity created by a "hoarding trap" is reversed and a free flow of goods returns. The consequent boom and bust of economic change can leave many personal tragedies in its wake, but the system itself is not irreversibly degraded. Economic and business interests, familiar with economic traps, sometimes do not appreciate the fact that the modern technologically magnified social traps create virtually irreversible results.

Once the topsoil is lost, it stays lost. Once a lake is "killed," it says dead for centuries. Once our oil reserves are gone, they will not be renewed. Many threatened lakes, rivers, and plant and animal species can theoretically replenish themselves forever. But if they are caught in a social trap and destroyed, they are lost to all future generations. The resulting negative utility can be incalculable.[33] In classic economic theory, when a business is run inefficiently, it is replaced by a more efficient one. In our present social traps, when a business makes a serious mistake in the process of destroying itself, it can destroy the potential for all other businesses to take its place. If the Japanese and Russian whaling industries carelessly reduce the whale population past the point of no return, no efficient whaling industry will arise to take their place. This characteristic of some social traps makes it very difficult for businessmen to deal with them successfully.

TOWARD SOLUTIONS

The abuses considered in this chapter create social problems which differ from many other problems in three important respects: (a) They cannot be solved by traditional democratic procedures. (b) The people involved are acting rationally. Removing these abuses will involve something besides teaching a collection of individuals to be good decision makers. (c) These problems cannot be solved by technological innovation. The technology of effective birth control has been available for some time without halting the population explosion. Discovering a technique that makes whales breed faster may only postpone their extermination. Americans who are used to solving problems with new machines and techniques will find it particularly difficult to face these problems of abuse. Nonetheless, certain solutions have been mentioned throughout the chapter, and it would be helpful to draw them together and summarize two general avenues to stopping abuse.

RESTRUCTURING AND ORGANIZATION

There is much the government has done and much more it could do to change the organization and payoffs of American society to overcome the deficiencies of democracy that give rise to abuse. In the case of the paradox of bargaining in which it is irrational to spend a large amount to avoid the loss of a small amount, one obvious answer is to reduce the cost of fighting the abuse. In some legal matters, this can be accomplished by means of small-claims courts. In these courts a lawyer is not required (sometimes a lawyer is not even allowed), and citizens can attempt to redress wrongs more informally and inexpensively than in other courts. An alternative solution to the same paradox is to increase the utility to be gained by successfully attacking abuse. This is the course taken by the class action suit, in which substantial sums can be obtained if the court finds small individual abuses exist for large numbers of people.

The development of lobbies and their attachment to state and federal governments provides an example of changing the organization of government to avoid the abuse of a minority by the majority. The framers of the Constitution took great effort to ensure adequate representation by geographical area, but in present-day America the special interests of various occupational and business groups are national in character and do not coincide with geographical boundaries. The development of the largely informal lobby system now allows special interests to represent themselves to governmental authorities regardless of geographical district.

Many laws can be thought of as creating side payments which reduce various abuses. Increasing the tax on gasoline and reducing taxes for those who insulate their homes are examples of the government manipulating benefits to reduce the consumption of irreplaceable fossil fuels. Increasing taxes on large families could provide side payments to limit the population in the same way that present tax deductions encourage a larger population.

So far, these techniques have yielded quite limited success. Simply passing a law or creating a service does not in itself remove the imbalance in the utility structure that produced the abuse in the first place. These devices must be understood and used by the general public if they are to be effective. All too often, it is the people most in need of governmental services who lack the proper interest, knowledge, or attitudes to make use of them. For example, the small-claims courts are not usually used *by* the average person. They are used instead by a small number of businesses collecting *from* the average person. In one year in the District of Columbia, 11 retailers were responsible for a total of 2,690 small-claims court judgments.[34] What was supposed to be a refuge for the "little man" became a more efficient means to collect from him for those few interests that knew about it.

The misuse of lobbies provides another example. Lobbies can deter the majority from abusing the minority, but at the same time they provide a more effective means for the minority to abuse the majority. An illuminating example of the limitations of lobbies is provided by the enactment of the Marijuana Tax Act of 1937, which outlawed the use of marijuana throughout the country. At the Congressional hearing on the act, representatives of the hempseed oil manufacturers and the birdseed manufacturers, who used marijuana seed in their products, appeared to defend their interests. By showing an unsuspecting Congress that their industries were in danger of unfair restriction, they persuaded the lawmakers to rephrase the law to protect their legitimate interests.[35]*

On the other hand, the one group that was most seriously injured by the legislation, the marijuana smokers themselves, never presented their case to Congress.[37] Being unorganized, spread throughout the country, and ignorant of what was about to befall them, marijuana users were incapable of presenting an organized defense of their rights. Lobbies, like small-claims courts, best serve those groups that are already organized and knowledgeable of the ways of government. More recently, consumer lobbies and other organizations claiming to represent the common man have arisen to overcome these difficulties. With greater public support and participation, they may well be able to compete effectively with the lobbies of special interests. But due to the inherent differences in the utility structures of the diffuse majority and the focused special interest of the few, developing a powerful consumer lobby is a formidable task indeed.

LOVE

Some social traps, especially those which threaten irreversible harm for future generations, may necessitate nothing less than love for

---

*One of the few light moments in the hearings occurred when the birdseed representative was asked if marijuana seed had the same effect on pigeons as the plant had on people. The representative observed no behavioral similarities but admitted that the seed does tend to "bring back the feathers."[36]

their solution. The love required would be a form of empathy and not the heart-throbbing, romantic love more often trumpeted in our society. If we loved others in the sense that we found grief in their pain and joy in their happiness, many of the abuses we have discussed could be eliminated. It would have the effect of altering the utilities so that it would be rational to avoid taking advantage of others.

Without love for our great-great-grandchildren, there is nothing irrational about using up our nonrenewable resources today and letting future generations worry about the consequences. Future generations cannot picket, boycott products, lobby, or vote. They have no way of influencing our actions but through our empathic concern for their well-being. Empathic love for those yet unborn would create a *higher* rationality, to use Tibor Scitovsky's phrase, than the individually oriented rationality of the economic and political marketplace.[38] As George Will has argued:

> The state is more than a device for serving the immediate preferences of its citizens. Its purpose is to achieve collective objectives, and the collectivity—the nation—includes a constituency of generations not yet born. That is why the state, unlike an economic market, has *responsibilities*, and must look down the road farther than citizens generally look in their private pursuits. . . . A conservatism that cannot comfortably accommodate these elementary truths is unserious, and irrelevant to the *political* economy of our nation.[39]

Love, empathy, and a feeling of responsibility for others were often considered unnecessary by past generations of social thinkers. One of the major justifications for fundamental Western social institutions was that they did not require love. It was once thought that as long as they had the vote and a free press, citizens did not have to care for each other to develop stable social well-being. In the same way, the free enterprise system was supposed to work for the betterment of all members of society even if businessmen cared not in the least for the welfare of others. These institutions have worked up to a point, but in some areas, especially those in which technology has greatly magnified our interdependence we have passed that point.

Our discussion of social traps indicates that it is insufficient for only a part of society to feel concern for others. If only a handful refrain from polluting, creating narrow-minded guilds, or abusing the commons, the ensuing problems may be postponed, but they will not be avoided.[40] But if a higher rationality dominates among the majority of citizens, the combination of political and informal pressures they would bring to bear on the shortsighted minority could hold abuse to a minimum.

It will not be easy to incorporate charity and empathy into the basic value system of our society. Love is most easily fostered in small, informal groups and is not easily aroused by abstractions, such as "the common man" or "future generations." But this does not mean that an altruistic, responsible society is impossible. Many social critics, misapplying the principles of Darwinian evolution, encouraged the notion that animals, in general, and the human animal, in particular, are inherently competitive and selfish. We know now that this is incorrect. Recent biological research has indicated that altruistic behavior as well as selfish behavior is common among animals. The existence of empathy in the lower animals or in man in no way conflicts with the principles of contemporary biology.[41]

Another difficulty in understanding the need for love is the tendency among some social scientists, particularly psychologists, to overemphasize the individual as the cause of social problems and underestimate the contribution of social structure and collective values.[42] In terms of the approaches considered in Chapter 6, this reflects an overemphasis on the deviance approach to the neglect of the social disorganization and value conflict perspectives. This fallacy concentrates on what Ralph Nader has called the "Adam and Eve" approach to society, which causes social scientists to think of social problems the way Western theologians think of sin—the collective expression of primeval individual vice.[43]

The social problems discussed in this chapter are not easily reduced to the actions of a few deviants. They are the action of large numbers of rational persons acting in accord with their own selfish interests and the value system of the general society. Social problems solvers will have to concentrate more on the collective values of society and less on deviant individual motives. The need is for a loving society, not a society with a lot of lovers.

It may seem ironic that after consideration of Minimax-loss strategies, maximum expected utility, and cost-benefit analysis, we still need love. But as I pointed out in Chapter 1, you do not choose between reason and love; love is just another value that you may wish to express or maximize. The higher rationality does not contradict individual rationality. It merely inserts empathic concern for others into your utility structure. To say that empathy is necessary to remove certain social abuses is only another way of saying that, in the final analysis, if we expect to help others, we have to want to help them. If we expect them to help us, they have to want to help us. We cannot assume it will happen by chance.

SUMMARY

Even when people are acting rationally, we still can have entrenched social problems. The majority can persecute and discriminate against a minority. This would bring a slight advantage to each member of the majority but a total loss to society because of the great disadvantage to the minority. If a change in utility for the majority is too small to notice or to fight about, a minority can abuse the majority. This is observed in various cases of abuses by special interests, such as guilds, big business, and the medical establishment. Lastly, everyone can abuse everyone else when a positive utility occurs to the individual actor and the negative utility is spread around to everyone. Pollution, overpopulation, the waste of our natural resources, and other social traps exemplify this abuse.

These problems are particularly difficult to deal with because they are compatible with traditional democratic institutions, they cannot be solved by technological innovations, and everyone involved is acting rationally. Two general approaches to a solution can be pursued. First, the government can restructure the utilities by providing side payments which more adequately reflect the cost of an action to the total society. For example, it can provide access to small-claims courts and encourage consumer lobbies to discourage the abuse of the majority by well-organized special interests. Second, some social problems will be solved only when we care for each other and future generations. The necessary empathy or love is not contrary to our natures, but it would represent a change in the traditional collective values of our society.

References

CHAPTER 1. THINK OF IT!

1. Sources: *Washington, D.C., telephone directory;* FBI, *Uniform crime reports, 1976* (Washington, D.C.: U.S. Government Printing Office, 1977), p. 15; U.S. Bureau of the Census, *Statistical abstract of the United States: 1976* (Washington, D.C.: U.S. Government Printing Office, 1976), p. 65.

2. J. Herbert Fill, *The mental breakdown of a nation* (New York: New Viewpoints, 1974), p. 12. (Emphasis in the original)

3. For a description of the characteristics that make a group an easy target for prejudice, see Gordon W. Allport, *The nature of prejudice* (rev. ed., New York: Doubleday Anchor, 1958).

4. Hannes Alfvén and Kerstein Alfvén, *Living on the third planet,* trans. by Eric Johnson (San Francisco: Freeman, 1972), pp. 101–102.

5. Steven Muller, "Colleges in trouble: Expand them, don't fold them," *Psychology Today,* May, 1975, p. 81.

6. Ivan Khorol, cited in "Strain overloading the human brain?" *Chicago Sun-Times,* Nov. 8, 1974.

7. Bergan Evans, *The natural history of nonsense* (New York: Knopf, 1946), p. 187.

8. Carl Rogers, *On becoming a person* (Boston: Houghton Mifflin, 1961), p. 193. (Emphasis added)

REFERENCES

CHAPTER 2. KEEPING UP WITH THE NEWS

1. For a general introduction to human memory and thought, see Peter Lindsay and Donald Norman, *Human information processing* (New York: Academic, 1972).

2. Amos Tversky and Daniel Kahneman, "Availability: A heuristic for judging frequency and probability," *Cognitive Psychology*, 1973, *5*, 207–232.

3. George E. Delury, ed., *The world almanac and book of facts, 1977* (New York: Newspaper Enterprise Association, 1976), *passim*.

4. Laurence Urdang, ed., *The official associated press almanac, 1975* (Maplewood, N.J.: Hammond Almanac, 1974), p. 225.

5. U.S Bureau of the Census, *Statistical abstract of the United States: 1976* (Washington, D.C.: U.S. Government Printing Office, 1976), p. 18.

6. Ibid. See also Edward C. Banfield, *The unheavenly city revisited* (Boston: Little Brown, 1974).

7. *The world almanac and book of facts, 1974*, p. 315.

8. *Associated press almanac, 1975*, p. 221.

9. For a discussion of the effects of the passage of time on retention of a message aimed at changing attitudes, see William J. McGuire, "The nature of attitudes and attitude change," in *The handbook of social psychology*, ed. by Gardner Lindzey and Elliot Aronson (2nd ed.; Reading, Mass.: Addison-Wesley, 1969), vol. 3, pp. 136–314. See especially pp. 254–258.

10. For a discussion of the dangerousness of mental patients, see Henry J. Steadman and Joseph J. Cocozza, "We can't predict who is dangerous," *Psychology Today*, January, 1975, pp. 32 *et seq.*

11. Nahum Z. Medalis and Otto N. Larsen, "Diffusion and belief in a collective delusion: The Seattle windshield pitting epidemic," *American Sociological Review*, 1958, *23*, 180–186.

12. David P. Phillips, "The influence of suggestion on suicide: Substantive and theoretical implications of the Werther effect," *American Sociological Review*, 1974, *39*, 340–354.

13. David P. Phillips, "Motor vehicle fatalities increase just after publicized suicide stories," *Science*, 1977, *196*, 1464–1465.

14. Leonard Berkowitz and Jacqueline Macaulay, "The contagion of criminal violence," *Sociometry*, 1971, *34*, 238–260.

15. Ibid., p. 250.

16. FBI, *Uniform crime reports, 1975* (Washington, D.C.: U.S. Government Printing Office, 1976), p. 19.

17. *Uniform crime reports, 1976*, p. 11.

18. Regarding plea bargaining, see Abraham S. Blumberg, *Criminal justice* (Chicago: Quadrangle, 1967).

19. "Prisoners in U.S. top 249,000, a record, with most under 30," *New York Times*, Apr. 19, 1976, p. 12.

20. U.S. Department of Justice, Michael J. Hindelang et al., eds. *Sourcebook of criminal justice statistics–1976* (Washington, D.C.: U.S. Government Printing Office, 1977), pp. 634–635.

REFERENCES

21. *Statistical abstract, 1976*, pp. 600, 615.
22. Paul A. Samuelson, *Economics* (8th ed.; New York: McGraw-Hill, 1970), p. 388.
23. See, for example, "City's post-storm statistics show a decrease in deaths," *Chicago Sun-Times*, Apr. 10, 1975.
24. "Royal blitz in a troubled realm," *Time*, Aug. 22, 1977, p. 39.
25. *Uniform crime reports, 1974*, p. 109; *1975*, p. 103; *1976*, p. 94.
26. *Uniform crime reports, 1976*, passim.
27. "16 killed in Chicago area's weekend of violence," *Chicago Sun-Times*, Nov. 18, 1974.
28. "Slaughter of the Hutus," *Newsweek*, June 26, 1972, pp. 39–40.
29. FBI, *Uniform crime reports: Bomb summary–1976* (Washington, D.C.: U.S. Government Printing Office, 1977), p. 11.
30. Ibid. For comparison, see *Uniform crime reports, 1975*, p. 19.
31. *Uniform crime reports: Bomb summary–1976*, p. 18; *1975*, p. 16; *1974*, p. 9.
32. "Torches for sale," *Newsweek*, Sept. 12, 1977, pp. 89–90. See also "Arson for hate and profit," *Time*, Oct. 31, 1977, pp. 22–25.
33. "Torches for sale."
34. *Statistical abstract, 1976*, p. 67.
35. W. C. Eller and R. K. Haugen, "Food asphyxiation—restaurant rescue," *New England Journal of Medicine*, 1973, *289*, 81–82, p. 81 quoted.
36. For a discussion of historians' neglect of the private life in the area of the family and the treatment of children, see Lloyd deMause, "The evolution of childhood," in *The history of childhood*, ed. by Lloyd deMause (New York: Psychohistory, 1974), pp. 1–74.
37. See the issues of *Newsweek* for Jan. 11, 1971, p. 50; Jan. 10, 1972, p. 37; Jan. 8, 1973, p. 39; Jan. 7, 1974, p. 40, and *Chicago Sun-Times*, Jan. 2, 1972, and Dec. 28, 1972.
38. Russell Baker, "Poll-ish joke," *New York Times Magazine*, Jan. 26, 1975, p. 6.
39. For an example, see George Gallup, "Mrs. Nixon voted most admired," *Chicago Sun-Times*, Jan. 1, 1973.
40. John B. Williamson, "Beliefs about the welfare poor," *Sociology and Social Research*, 1974, *58*, 163–175.
41. "TV actress tops list of students' heroes," *Senior Scholastic*, Feb. 10, 1977, p. 15.
42. "Who are the kids' heroes and heroines?" *Ladies' Home Journal*, August, 1976, pp. 108–109.
43. Irene Reichbach, "The 15 women you admire most," *Seventeen*, January, 1975, pp. 96–97.
44. Wayland F. Vaughan, *Social psychology* (New York: Odyssey, 1948), p. 154.
45. George F. Will, syndicated column, *Chicago Sun-Times*, Dec. 23, 1975.
46. Staffan Linder, *The harried leisure class* (New York: Columbia University Press, 1970). See also Sebastian deGrazia, *Of time, work, and leisure* (New York: Twentieth Century Fund, 1962).
47. American Council on Education, *A fact book on higher education: Institutions, faculty, and staff* (Washington, D.C.: American Council on Education, 1974, Issue

no. 3), p. 74.127. For comparison, see Charles H. Judd, "Education," in *Recent social trends in the United States*, ed. by President's Research Committee on Social Trends (New York: McGraw-Hill, 1933), pp. 325–381.

48. Oakley S. Ray, *Drugs, society and human behavior* (Saint Louis: Mosby, 1972), pp. 141–143.

49. Victor Cohn, "Mental hospital treatment landmark," *Chicago Sun-Times*, June 9, 1975.

50. *Statistical abstract, 1976*, p. 65. See also Stewart M. Brooks, *The V.D. story* (Totowa, N.J.: Littlefield, Adams, 1972), pp. 13–14.

51. *Statistical abstract, 1976*, p. 65.

52. *Uniform crime reports, 1974*, p. 3.

53. *Statistical abstract, 1976*, p. 158.

54. Ibid.; *Uniform crime reports, 1976*, p. 10.

55. For a discussion of why America is more violent than other cultures, see Ramsey Clark, *Crime in America* (New York: Pocket Books, 1970).

56. Howard S. Becker, *Outsiders: Studies in the sociology of deviance* (New York: Free Press, 1963), p. 157.

57. Kurt Weis and Michael E. Milakovich, "Political misuses of crime rates," *Society*, July/August, 1974, pp. 27–33, p. 27 quoted. (Emphasis added)

58. It should be noted that after the experiment, the hoax was thoroughly explained. Harvey A. Hornstein et al., "Effects of knowledge about remote social events on prosocial behavior, social conception and mood," *Journal of Personality and Social Psychology*, 1975, *32*, 1038–1046; Stephen Holloway, Lyle Tucker, and Harvey A. Hornstein, "The effects of social and nonsocial information on interpersonal behavior of males: The news makes news," *Journal of Personality and Social Psychology*, 1977, *35*, 514–522.

59. Cited in Stephen Holloway and Harvey A. Hornstein, "How good news makes us good," *Psychology Today*, December, 1976, pp. 76–78, 106–108.

60. Ibid., p. 78.

61. See Lawrence S. Wrightsman and Frank C. Noble, "Reactions to the President's assassination and changes in philosophies of human nature," *Psychological Reports*, 1965, *16*, 159–162.

62. Holloway and Hornstein, "How good news makes us good," p. 78. (Emphasis in the original)

CHAPTER 3. CREATING AND USING STATISTICS

1. "More bucks for the bang," *Newsweek*, Apr. 12, 1976, pp. 81–82.

2. "Social–welfare spending up," *Chicago Sun-Times*, Dec. 16, 1976.

3. James M. Henslin and Larry T. Reynolds, "Militarization and war," in *Social problems in American society*, ed. by James M. Henslin and Larry T. Reynolds (Boston: Holbrook, 1973), pp. 309–311.

4. U.S. Bureau of the Census, *Statistical abstract of the United States: 1976* (Washington, D.C.: U.S. Government Printing Office, 1976), p. 396.

5. Ibid.

6. *Statistical abstract, 1975*, p. 571.

REFERENCES

7. U.S. Bureau of the Census, "Household and family characteristics, March 1975" (*Current Population Reports*, Series P-20, No. 291) (Washington, D.C.: U.S. Government Printing Office, 1976), p. 1.

8. Ibid.

9. For more up-to-date and precise figures, see the latest edition of the annual *Statistical abstract of the United States.*

10. *Statistical abstract, 1976*, p. xvii.

11. FBI, *Uniform crime reports, 1976* (Washington, D.C.: U.S. Government Printing Office, 1977), p. 37.

12. *Encyclopaedia Britannica* (Chicago: Encyclopaedia Britannica, Inc., 1972), vol. 14, p. 782.

13. United Nations, *United Nations demographic yearbook, 1974* (New York: United Nations Publishing Service, 1975), p. 105.

14. See, for example, Christopher Jencks et al., *Inequality* (New York: Basic Books, 1972); David Levine and Mary Jo Bane, eds., *The "inequality" controversy* (New York: Basic Books, 1975); Lewis C. Soloman and Paul Taubman, eds., *Does college matter?* (New York: Academic, 1973). For a popular treatment, see Caroline Bird, *The case against college* (New York: David McKay, 1975).

15. Another consideration is whether the payoff that might come from going to college is actually due to whatever is learned in school. It could be due to a bias on the part of employers to hire or promote those with more education, even if they are not better workers. See Soloman and Taubman, *Does college matter?*; Paul Taubman and Terence Wales, *Higher education and earnings* (New York: McGraw-Hill, 1974); and Ivar Berg, *Education and jobs: The great training robbery* (New York: Praeger, 1970).

16. For a discussion of the costs of going to college, see Caroline Bird, *The case against college.*

17. See, for example, Samuel S. Bowles, "Towards equality?" *Harvard Educational Review*, 1968, *38*, 89–99; Fred Hines, Luther Tweeten, and Martin Redfern, "Social and private rates of return to investment in schooling," in *Women in a man-made world*, ed. by Nona Glazer-Malbin and Helen Youngelson Waehrer (Chicago: Rand McNally, 1972), pp. 228–234; and Larry E. Suter and Herman P. Miller, "Income differences between men and career women," in *Changing women in a changing society*, ed. by Joan Huber (Chicago: University of Chicago Press, 1973), pp. 200–212.

18. Rudolf Flesch, *The art of clear thinking* (New York: Barnes and Noble, 1973), p. 134. (Originally published, 1951)

19. See Jencks, *Inequality.*

20. U.S. Bureau of the Census, "A statistical portrait of women in the U.S." (*Current Population Reports: Special Studies*, Series P-23, No. 58) (Washington, D.C.: U.S. Government Printing Office, 1976), p. 56.

21. Ibid., p. 48.

22. William Ryan, *Blaming the victim* (New York: Vintage, 1971), pp. 38–39. (Emphasis in the original)

23. Robert S. Reichard, *The figure finaglers* (New York: McGraw-Hill, 1974), p. 47. This book provides a handy introduction to interpreting common statis-

tics. For statistics in management and business, see Robert S. Reichard, *The numbers game* (New York: McGraw-Hill, 1972).

24. *Statistical abstract, 1976*, pp. xv, 396.

25. George Gallup, "Opinion polling in a democracy," in *Statistics: A guide to the unknown*, ed. by Judith M. Tanur et al. (San Francisco: Holden-Day, 1972), pp. 146–152; and George Gallup, "The influence of polling on politics and the press," in *Politics and the press*, ed. by Richard W. Lee (Washington, D.C.: Acropolis Books, 1970), pp. 129–143.

26. George Gallup, "Opinion polling in a democracy," p. 147.

27. For a brief discussion of common survey techniques, see Charles W. Roll and Albert H. Cantril, *Polls: Their use and misuse in politics* (New York: Basic Books, 1972). See especially pp. 65–116.

28. Louis Harris, *The anguish of change* (New York: Norton, 1973), pp. x–xi.

29. Hobart Rowen, "Unemployment by the numbers," *Chicago Sun-Times*, Feb. 24, 1976.

30. "Cold hit jobless rate only slightly," *Chicago Sun-Times*, Mar. 5, 1977.

31. For a description of how the number of employed and unemployed are obtained, see U.S. Department of Labor, Bureau of Labor Statistics, *How the government measures unemployment* (Washington, D.C.: U.S. Government Printing Office, 1967). For information on recent alterations, see the latest edition of the monthly *Employment and earnings* (Washington, D.C.: U.S. Government Printing Office). For arguments on why the official procedures underestimate the number of unemployed, see John C. Leggett and Claudette Cervinka, "Countdown: How to lie with statistics," in *Social problems in American society*, ed. by Henslin and Reynolds, pp. 234–257.

32. Milton Friedman, "Where has the 'hot' summer gone?" *Newsweek*, Aug. 4, 1975, p. 63.

33. It has been argued that actual unemployment may be twice the official rate. See Thomas A. Johnson, "Jobless figure is called wrong," *New York Times*, Nov. 20, 1975, p. 44.

34. U.S. Bureau of the Census, "Characteristics of the population below the poverty level" (*Current Population Reports*, Series P-60, No. 102) (Washington, D.C.: U.S. Government Printing Office, 1976), p. 4.

35. Art Petacque, "$100 relief payment costs $4,005!" *Chicago Sun-Times*, Jan. 18, 1970.

36. Ibid.

37. Arnold W. Green, *Social problems: Arena of conflict* (New York: McGraw-Hill, 1975), p. 267.

38. Milton Friedman, "The poor man's welfare payment to the middle class," *The Washington Monthly*, May, 1972, pp. 11–16.

39. "Women's work," *Newsweek*, May 10, 1976, p. 97.

40. Donald T. Campbell, "Measuring the effects of social innovations by means of time series," in Tanur, *Statistics: A guide to the unknown*, pp. 120–129; and Marvin E. Wolfgang, "Crime in urban America," in *Police and law enforcement 1972*, ed. by James T. Curran et al. (New York: AMS Press, 1973), pp. 132–148.

41. "A healthy rise in rape," *Newsweek*, July 31, 1972, p. 72.

42. Phillips Cutright, "Illegitimacy and income supplements," in *Studies in public*

welfare; Paper No. 12 (Part I); The family, poverty and welfare programs: Factors influencing family instability, issued by The Joint Economic Committee, Congress of the United States (Washington, D.C.: U.S. Government Printing Office, 1973), pp. 90–138.

CHAPTER 4. WHY OFFICIAL STATISTICS ARE MISLEADING

1. Charles Horton Cooley, *Social organization* (New York: Scribners, 1909).
2. Roger Brown, *Social psychology* (New York: Free Press, 1965), p. 66. Chapter 2 of this book provides a nice introduction to the linguistic aspects of informal and formal relations.
3. Peter M. Blau, *Bureaucracy in modern society* (New York: Random House, 1956), p. 53.
4. Edward A. Shils and Morris Janowitz, "Cohesion and disintegration in the Wehrmacht in World War II," *Public Opinion Quarterly*, 1948, *12*, 280–315.
5. Don G. Campbell, *Understanding stocks* (Garden City, N.Y.: Doubleday, 1965), p. 171. (Emphasis in the original)
6. "Little Teddy pulls vote levers for dad," *Chicago Tribune*, July 2, 1973, Sec. 1, p. 1; Sec. 3, p. 12.
7. "Legislators yell, laugh at photos," *Chicago Tribune*, July 3, 1973, Sec. 1, p. 4.
8. Blau, *Bureaucracy in modern society*, p. 56.
9. For an insightful discussion of one of the major functions of informal rules— protecting the incompetent—see William J. Goode, "The protection of the inept," *American Sociological Review*, 1967, *32*, 5–19.
10. "Britain into a new dark age," *Newsweek*, Jan. 14, 1974, pp. 28–30.
11. Ibid.
12. "The doctors' slowdown," *Newsweek*, Jan. 20, 1975, p. 67.
13. Jerome H. Skolnick, *Justice without trial* (New York: Wiley, 1966); David M. Petersen, "Informal norms and police practice: The traffic quota system," *Sociology and Social Research*, 1971, *55*, 354–362.
14. Petersen, "Informal norms and police practice," p. 358.
15. William Braden and Jim Casey, "Ticket blitz," *Chicago Sun-Times*, Sept. 27, 1972.
16. Paul Molloy and Jim Casey, "Police ticketing campaign slowed," *Chicago Sun-Times*, Sept. 29, 1972.
17. Patricia O'Brien Koval, "Police continue ticket blitz," *Chicago Sun-Times*, Sept. 28, 1972.
18. Ibid.
19. John O'Brien and Frank Haramija, "I'll punish ticket writers: Conlisk," *Chicago Tribune*, Sept. 29, 1972, p. 1.
20. "Policemen and their rights," *Chicago Sun-Times*, Nov. 8, 1972.
21. Tom Fitzpatrick, "The little guy gets it in the neck," *Chicago Sun-Times*, Sept. 29, 1972.
22. O'Brien and Haramija, "I'll punish ticket writers: Conlisk."
23. Ibid.
24. Ibid.
25. Paul Molloy, "Police ticket blitz ending," *Chicago Sun-Times*, Sept. 30, 1972.

REFERENCES

26. Eugene J. Webb et al., *Unobtrusive measures: Nonreactive research in the social sciences* (Chicago: Rand McNally, 1966), p. 77.

27. *Submission of recorded Presidential conversations to the Committee on the Judiciary of the House of Representatives by President Richard Nixon, April 30, 1974* (Washington, D.C.: U.S. Government Printing Office, 1974).

28. Nicolas Wade, "NIH budget: Senate committee holds history's quietest inquiry," *Science*, 1976, *193*, 1100–1101.

29. "Court upsets ban on term–paper sale," *Chicago Sun-Times*, Aug. 13, 1975.

30. Cleveland Amory, "Booze, broads and politicians," *Chicago Sun-Times*, Mar. 11, 1976.

31. "State audit finds city job policies waste millions," *New York Times*, May 30, 1972, p. 1 *et seq.*

32. Ibid.

33. "City employees: On the job vacations," *New York Times*, June 4, 1972, Sec. 4, p. 5.

34. Ibid.

35. For a discussion, see Robin M. Williams, *American society: A sociological interpretation* (rev. ed.; New York: Knopf, 1960). See especially pp. 372–396.

36. Pam Moore, "Nader chides researchers, scores testing," *APA Monitor*, November, 1976, pp. 1 *et seq.*

37. Jack D. Douglas, *American social order: Social rules in a pluralistic society* (New York: Free Press, 1971). See especially pp. 42–78. See also Allan Silver, "The demand for order in civil society," in *The police: Six sociological essays*, ed. by David J. Bordua (New York: Wiley, 1967), pp. 1–24.

38. Douglas, *American social order*, p. 47. (Emphasis in the original)

39. For one approach to a critical analysis of technology, see Jacques Ellul, *The technological society*, trans. by John Wilkinson (New York: Knopf, 1964). For a discussion of America's love-hate relationship with technology, see Leo Marx, *The machine in the garden: Technology and the pastoral ideal in America* (New York: Oxford University Press, 1964).

40. For a discussion, see Douglas, *American social order*, pp. 224–226.

41. "The Paris peace talks resume this week," *Newsweek*, July 17, 1972, p. 25.

42. For a discussion of the development of legalism, see Paul Diesing, *Reason in society* (Urbana, Ill.: University of Illinois Press, 1962), especially chap. 4.

43. Robert S. Reichard, *The figure finaglers* (New York: McGraw-Hill, 1974), p. 211.

44. Robert K. Merton, *Social theory and social structure* (rev. ed.; New York: Free Press, 1957), pp. 71–82. See also Eric L. McKitrick, "The study of corruption," in *Sociology and history: Methods*, ed. by Seymour Martin Lipset and Richard Hofstadter (New York: Basic Books, 1968), pp. 358–370.

45. For a summary of the political and professional process that generated the academic ability test, see Murray Levine, "The academic achievement test: Its historical context and social functions," *American Psychologist*, 1976, *31*, 228–238.

46. For an introduction to this literature, see H. J. Eysenck, *The I.Q. argument: Race, intelligence and education* (New York: Library Press, 1971); H. J. Eysenck, ed., *The measurement of intelligence* (Baltimore: Williams and Wilkins, 1973);

REFERENCES

Arthur R. Jensen, *Genetics and education* (New York: Harper, 1972); John C. Loehlin, Gardner Lindzey, and J. N. Spuhler, *Race differences in intelligence* (San Francisco: Freeman, 1975); and N. J. Block and Gerald Dworkin, eds., *The IQ controversy* (New York: Pantheon, 1976).

47. Raymond M. Hughes, *A manual for trustees of colleges and universities* (Ames, Iowa: Iowa State College Press, 1945), p. 6.

48. Philippe Ariès, *Centuries of childhood: A social history of family life*, trans. by Robert Baldick (New York: Knopf, 1962).

49. For a discussion of why age rather than objectively measured competence is a preferred selection criterion, see Goode, "The protection of the inept."

50. For an introduction to the computer's capability to alter the social fabric, see Fred Gruenberger, ed., *Computers and communications* (Englewood Cliffs, N.J.: Prentice-Hall, 1968); C. C. Gotlieb and A. Borodin, *Social issues in computing* (New York: Academic, 1973); and Abbe Mowshowitz, *The conquest of will: Information processing in human affairs* (Reading, Mass.: Addison-Wesley, 1976).

51. Walter Mischel, *Personality and assessment* (New York: Wiley, 1968), especially pp. 129–135; Richard I. Lanyon and Leonard D. Goodstein, *Personality assessment* (New York: Wiley, 1971), especially pp. 158–168; A. S. Elstein, "Clinical judgment: Psychological research and medical practice," *Science*, 1976, *194*, 696–700.

52. J. F. Gibbons, W. R. Kincheloe, and K. S. Down, "Tutored videotape instruction," *Science*, 1977, *195*, 1139–1146, p. 1139 quoted.

CHAPTER 5. PITFALLS AND PARADOXES IN UNDERSTANDING SOCIAL PROBLEMS

1. Larry Ingrassia, "Let us now braise famous men," *Chicago Sun-Times*, Nov. 29, 1975.

2. "Defense spending still going up," *Chicago Sun-Times*, Feb. 8, 1971.

3. "That old missile gap," *Newsweek*, May 1, 1972, p. 38.

4. "The money machine," *Newsweek*, Apr. 10, 1972, p. 55.

5. Cited by Spiro Agnew, "Agnew reprimands AAAS," *Science*, 1972, *176*, 263.

6. D. O. Hebb, *Textbook of psychology* (3rd ed.; Philadelphia: Saunders, 1972), pp. 239–242.

7. See, for example, Dorothy Hubbard Gampel, "Temporal factors in verbal satiation," *Journal of Experimental Psychology*, 1966, *72*, 201–206.

8. John W. Thibaut and Harold H. Kelley, *The social psychology of groups* (New York: Wiley, 1959), especially p. 251.

9. Ibid., pp. 126–135.

10. For a discussion of a variety of third party ploys, see David Hapgood, *The screwing of the average man* (New York: Bantam Books, 1975).

11. For versions of this technique in interrogation, see Fred E. Inbau and John E. Reid, *Criminal interrogations and confessions* (Baltimore: Williams and Wilkins, 1962), pp. 58–60; and "War crimes," *Ramparts*, February, 1971, p. 12.

12. Crane Brinton, *The anatomy of revolution* (rev. ed.; New York: Vintage Books, 1965); and Richard Hofstadter and Michael Wallace, eds., *American violence* (New York: Vintage Books, 1970), p. 64.

REFERENCES

13. For a discussion, see Harry Kaufmann, *Aggression and altruism* (New York: Holt, 1970).

14. See, for example, B. F. Skinner, *Beyond freedom and dignity* (New York: Knopf, 1971); and Harvey Wheeler, ed., *Beyond the punitive society: Operant conditioning: Social and political aspects* (San Francisco: Freeman, 1973).

15. As of 1975, George E. Delury, ed., *The world almanac and book of facts, 1976* (New York: Newspaper Enterprise Association, 1975), p. 334.

16. Ibid., p. 41.

17. For a discussion of the need for stimulation, see D. E. Berlyne, *Conflict, arousal and curiosity* (New York: McGraw-Hill, 1960); Donald W. Fiske and Salvatore R. Maddi, eds., *Functions of varied experience* (Homewood, Ill.: Dorsey, 1961); G. B. Kish, "Studies of sensory reinforcement," in *Operant behavior: Areas of research and application*, ed. by Werner K. Honig (New York: Appleton-Century-Crofts, 1966), pp. 109–159.

18. Berlyne, *Conflict, arousal and curiosity*, pp. 122–127, 197–201.

19. John Lofland, *Deviance and identity* (Englewood Cliffs, N.J.: Prentice-Hall, 1969), especially pp. 104–117.

20. For a discussion of some ways to create a happy society in spite of the tendency to increase expectations, see Philip Brickman and Donald T. Campbell, "Hedonic relativism and planning the good society," in *Adaptation-level theory*, ed. by M. H. Appley (New York: Academic, 1971), pp. 287–302.

21. For an introduction to this literature on comparison level, see John W. Thibaut and Harold H. Kelley, *The social psychology of groups* (New York: Wiley, 1959); George C. Homans, *Social behavior: Its elementary forms* (New York: Harcourt, 1961); Thomas F. Pettigrew, "Social evaluation theory," in *Nebraska symposium on motivation, 1967*, ed. by David Levine (Lincoln, Neb.: University of Nebraska Press, 1967), pp. 241–311; and Faye Crosby, "A model of egoistical relative deprivation," *Psychological Review*, 1976, *83*, 85–113.

22. This is not to say that it is easy to specify exactly which groups will form the comparison group; see Pettigrew, "Social evaluation theory."

23. Angus Campbell, Philip E. Converse, and Willard L. Rodgers, *The quality of American life* (New York: Russell Sage Foundation, 1976), pp. 26–27.

24. Nathan Glazer, "The Negro's stake in America's future," *New York Times Magazine*, Sept. 22, 1968, pp. 30 *et. seq.*; and Richard Ashmore and John B. McConahay, *Psychology and America's urban dilemmas* (New York: McGraw-Hill, 1975), pp. 113–120.

25. Brinton, *The anatomy of revolution.*

26. James C. Davies, "Toward a theory of revolution," *American Sociological Review*, 1962, *27*, 5–19.

27. Pettigrew, "Social evaluation theory," especially pp. 293–302; and Glazer, "The Negro's stake in America's future."

28. Leon Festinger, *A theory of cognitive dissonance* (Evanston, Ill: Row, Peterson, 1957).

29. Approaching attitude change from the perspective of self-perception provides an additional reason to expect that greater rewards will be associated with the least attitude change. See Daryl J. Bem, "Self-perception: An alternative interpretation of cognitive dissonance phenomena," *Psychological Review*, 1967, *74*, 183–200; and Daryl J. Bem, "Self-perception theory," in *Advances in experi-*

mental social psychology, ed. by Leonard Berkowitz (New York: Academic, 1972), vol. 6, pp. 1–62.

30. For a summary of this research, see Festinger, *A theory of cognitive dissonance;* Jack W. Brehm and Arthur R. Cohen, *Explorations in cognitive dissonance* (New York: Wiley, 1962); and Elliot Aronson, "The theory of cognitive dissonance: A current perspective," in *Advances in experimental social psychology*, ed. by Leonard Berkowitz (New York: Academic, 1969), vol. 4, pp. 1–34.

31. For a review, see Edward L. Deci, *Intrinsic motivation* (New York: Plenum, 1975); and John Condry, "Enemies of exploration," *Journal of Personality and Social Psychology*, 1977, *35*, 459–477.

32. Mark R. Lepper, David Greene, and Richard E. Nisbett, "Undermining children's intrinsic interest with extrinsic reward," *Journal of Personality and Social Psychology*, 1973, *28*, 129–137; David Greene and Mark R. Lepper, "Effects of extrinsic rewards on children's subsequent intrinsic interest," *Child Development*, 1974, *45*, 1141–1145; and Mark R. Lepper and David Greene, "Turning play into work," *Journal of Personality and Social Psychology*, 1975, *31*, 479–486.

33. Bobby J. Calder and Barry M. Staw, "Self-perception of intrinsic and extrinsic motivation," *Journal of Personality and Social Psychology*, 1975, *31*, 599–605.

34. Skinner, *Beyond freedom and dignity;* Wheeler, *Beyond the punitive society;* and Jacobo Varela, *Psychological solutions to social problems* (New York: Academic, 1971).

35. Alan C. Filley, *Interpersonal conflict resolution* (Glenview, Ill.: Scott, Foresman, 1975), pp. 23–24.

36. Isidor Chein, "The concept of power," in *Psychology and the problems of society*, ed. by Frances F. Korten, Stuart W. Cook, and John I. Lacey (Washington, D.C.: American Psychological Association, 1970), pp. 327–343, p. 343 quoted.

37. John von Neumann and Oskar Morgenstern, *Theory of games and economic behavior* (Princeton, N.J.: Princeton University Press, 1944).

38. Thomas C. Schelling, *The strategy of conflict* (Cambridge, Mass.: Harvard University Press, 1960).

39. Quoted in Stanley Milgram and Hans Toch, "Collective behavior: Crowds and social movements," in *The handbook of social psychology*, ed. by Gardner Lindzey and Elliot Aronson (2nd ed.; Reading, Mass.: Addison-Wesley, 1969) vol. 4, pp. 507–610, p. 576.

40. Schelling, *The strategy of conflict*, p. 22.

41. "Now everyone is really scared," *Time*, Oct. 13, 1975, p. 20.

42. "How to save New York," *Time*, Oct. 20, 1975, pp. 9 *et seq.*, p. 9 quoted.

43. "Last chance for the big apple," *Time*, Sept. 15, 1976, pp. 20 *et seq.*, p. 20 quoted.

44. "Fighting the unthinkable," *Time*, Sept. 8, 1975, pp. 8 *et seq.*, p. 9 quoted.

45. Arthur L. Stinchcombe, *Constructing social theories* (New York: Harcourt, 1968), pp. 164–165.

46. Paul Swingle, "Dangerous games," in *The structure of conflict*, ed. by Paul Swingle (New York: Academic, 1970), pp. 235–276.

47. Elliot P. Currie, "Crimes without criminals: Witchcraft and its control in Renaissance Europe," *Law and Society Review*, 1968, *3*, 7–32.

48. The President's Commission on Law Enforcement and the Administration of

REFERENCES

Justice, *Task force report: The courts* (Washington, D.C.: U.S. Government Printing Office, 1967), p. 9.

49. U.S. Department of Justice, Michael J. Hindelang et al., eds., *Sourcebook of criminal justice statistics–1976* (Washington, D.C.: U.S. Government Printing Office, 1977), pp. 603–604.

50. Ibid.

51. Abraham S. Blumberg, *Criminal Justice* (Chicago: Quadrangle, 1967); Abraham S. Blumberg, "The practice of law as confidence game," *Law and Society Review*, 1967, *1*, 15–39; and Jonathan D. Casper, *American criminal justice: The defendant's perspective* (Englewood Cliffs, N.J.: Prentice-Hall, 1972).

52. Jerome H. Skolnick, *Justice without trial: Law enforcement in democratic society* (New York: Wiley, 1966), p. 13. See also Gordon Tullock, *The logic of the law* (New York: Basic Books, 1971), pp. 174–186.

53. *Task force report: The courts*, p. 38.

54. Cited in James Mills, "I have nothing to do with justice," *Life*, Mar. 12, 1971, pp. 56 et seq., p. 62. (Emphasis in the original)

55. Regarding the copout ceremony, see Blumberg, *Criminal justice*, pp. 88–91, 131–136; Blumberg, "The practice of law as confidence game"; and Casper, *American criminal justice*, pp. 81–86.

56. Blumberg, *Criminal justice*, pp. 88–92.

57. *Task force report: The courts*, p. 9.

CHAPTER 6. APPROACHES TO UNDERSTANDING SOCIAL PROBLEMS

1. For a discussion of the problem of defining a social problem, see Irving Tallman and Reece McGee, "Definition of a social problem," in *Handbook on the study of social problems*, ed. by Erwin O. Smigel (Chicago: Rand McNally, 1971), pp. 19–58.

2. James M. Henslin and Larry T. Reynolds, eds., *Social problems in American society* (Boston: Holbrook, 1973), p. 3.

3. Edward C. McDonagh and Jon E. Simpson, eds., *Social problems: Persistent challenges* (New York: Holt, 1969), p. v.

4. Robert A. Dentler, ed., *Major American social problems* (Chicago: Rand McNally, 1967), p. 15.

5. Earl Rubington and Martin S. Weinberg, eds., *The study of social problems* (New York: Oxford University Press, 1971), pp. 5–6.

6. Paul B. Horton and Gerald R. Leslie, *The sociology of social problems* (4th ed.; New York: Appleton-Century-Crofts, 1970), p. 4.

7. Michael McKee and Ian Robertson, *Social problems* (New York: Random House, 1975), p. 4.

8. For a discussion of this difficulty, see Howard S. Becker, "Introduction," in *Social problems: A modern approach*, ed. by Howard S. Becker (New York: Wiley, 1966), pp. 1–31.

9. For a discussion of the problems of a subjective approach to social problems, see Jerome G. Manis, "The concept of social problems," *Social Problems*, 1974, *21*, 305–315; and Jerome G. Manis, "Assessing the seriousness of social problems," *Social Problems*, 1974, *22*, 1–15.

REFERENCES

10. See Arnold W. Green, *Social problems: Arena of conflict* (New York: McGraw-Hill, 1975), pp. 31–66.

11. Stephen A. Richardson et al., "Cultural uniformity in reaction to physical disabilities," *American Sociological Review*, 1961, *26*, 241–247; and Norman Goodman et al., "Variant reactions to physical disabilities," *American Sociological Review*, 1963, *28*, 429–435.

12. D. O. Hebb and W. R. Thompson, "The social significance of animal studies," in *Handbook of social psychology* ed. by Gardner Lindzey and Elliot Aronson (2nd ed.,; Reading, Mass.: Addison-Wesley, 1968), vol. 2, pp. 729–774. See especially p. 766.

13. Erving Goffman, *Stigma: Notes on the management of spoiled identity* (Englewood Cliffs, N.J.: Prentice-Hall, 1963).

14. Frances Cooke Macgregor, *Transformation and identity: The face and plastic surgery* (New York: Quadrangle, 1974), pp. 39, 160.

15. Ava Leach James, *Little talks to boys and girls* (Grand Rapids, Mich.: Zondervan, 1949), p. 23.

16. Macgregor, *Transformation and identity*, p. 73.

17. There is a fair amount of evidence that people do need to think this is a just world and blame the victim. See Elaine Walster, "Assignment of responsibility for an accident," *Journal of Personality and Social Psychology*, 1966, *3*, 73–79; Melvin J. Lerner and Gail Matthews, "Reactions to suffering of others under conditions of indirect responsibility," *Journal of Personality and Social Psychology*, 1967, *5*, 319–325; and Alan L. Chaikin and John M. Darley, "Victim or perpetrator?" *Journal of Personality and Social Psychology*, 1973, *25*, 268–275.

18. Regarding the psychological advantages of blaming the victims of poverty, see John E. Tropman, "The image of public welfare: Reality or projection?" *Public Welfare*, Winter 1977, 17–23.

19. For one view of the implications of blaming the victim for the general understanding of social problems, see William Ryan, *Blaming the victim* (New York: Vintage Books, 1971).

20. See "Council unit votes repeal of 'disgusting' ordinance," *Chicago Sun-Times*, Oct. 18, 1973.

21. Harry Golden, Jr., "Pigeons and uglies get the code shoulder," *Chicago Sun-Times*, July 2, 1972.

22. T. George Harris, "Affluence: The fifth horseman of the Apocalypse: A conversation with Jean Mayer," *Psychology Today*, January, 1970, pp. 43 *et seq.*, p. 43 quoted.

23. Ibid.

24. Werner J. Cahnman, "The stigma of obesity," *The Sociological Quarterly*, 1968, *9*, 283–299; and Natalie Allon, "Group dieting rituals," *Society*, January/February, 1973, 36–42.

25. Barbara Ford, "Prejudice: Society shuns the short, fat, and ugly," *Science Digest*, May, 1974, 18–23; and Janet Chase, "Obese in the land of milk and honey," *Human Behavior*, June, 1975, 56–63.

26. Ford, "Prejudice," p. 20.

27. "F is for fat," *Newsweek*, Oct. 24, 1977, p. 112.

28. For a review of the research on prejudice against the unattractive, see Ellen

REFERENCES

Berscheid and Elaine Walster, "Physical attractiveness," in *Advances in experimental social psychology*, ed. By Leonard Berkowitz (New York: Academic, 1974), vol. 7, pp. 158–215.

29. Ibid., pp. 191–192.
30. Ibid., pp. 193–194.
31. "Short workers of the world, unite!" *Psychology Today*, August, 1971, p. 102; and Saul D. Feldman, "The presentation of shortness in everyday life—height and heightism in American society: Toward a sociology of stature," In *Life styles: Diversity in American society*, ed. by Saul D. Feldman and Gerald W. Thielbar (Boston: Little Brown, 1975), pp. 437–442.
32. "Heightism," *Time*, Oct. 4, 1971, p. 64.
33. Paul R. Wilson, "Perceptual distortion of height as a function of ascribed academic status," *The Journal of Social Psychology*, 1968, *74*, 97–102.
34. Mary Shelley, *Frankenstein: Or the modern Prometheus* (New York: Dell, 1965). (Originally published, 1818)
35. Chase, "Obese in the land of milk and honey," p. 62.
36. Robert K. Merton, *Social theory and social structure* (rev. ed.; New York: Free Press, 1957), pp. 131–160.
37. Ira L. Reiss, "Premarital sex as deviant behavior," *American Sociological Review*, 1970, *35*, 78–87.
38. Edwin H. Sutherland, *Principles of criminology* (Philadelphia: Lippincott, 1939).
39. Ibid., p. 5.
40. Philip G. Zimbardo, "The human choice," in *Nebraska symposium on Motivation, 1969*, ed. by William J. Arnold and David Levine (Lincoln, Neb.: University of Nebraska Press, 1969), pp. 237–307, pp. 287–290, quoted.
41. Ibid., p. 290.
42. For discussion of some of these meanings, see Merton, *Social theory and social structure*, pp. 19–25.
43. Ryan, *Blaming the victim*, p. 115.
44. Herbert J. Gans, "The positive functions of poverty," *American Journal of Sociology*, 1972, *78*, 275–289.
45. John Lofland, *Deviance and identity* (Englewood Cliffs, N.J.: Prentice-Hall, 1969), pp. 136–137.
46. Beliefs that are universally accepted can actually be strengthened by presenting weak attacks on them in the same way that an inoculation strengthens resistance to the disease of which the inoculation is a weak form. See William J. McGuire, "Inducing resistance to persuasion," in *Advances in experimental social psychology*, ed. by Leonard Berkowitz (New York: Academic, 1964), vol. 1, pp. 191–229.
47. This metaphor was suggested in Lewis A. Coser, "Some functions of deviant behavior and normative flexibility," *American Journal of Sociology*, 1962, *68*, 172–181. See also Lofland, *Deviance and identity*, pp. 302–307.
48. Kai T. Erikson, "Notes on the sociology of deviance," *Social Problems*, 1962, *9*, 307–314, p. 310 quoted. (Emphasis in the original)
49. Merton, *Social theory and social structure*, pp. 60–66.
50. See Garrett Hardin, "To trouble a star: The cost of intervention in nature, *Bulletin of the Atomic Scientists*, January, 1970, 17–20.

REFERENCES

51. John Platt, "What we must do," *Science*, 1969, *166*, 1115–1121, p. 1115 quoted.
52. William F. Ogburn, *Social change* (rev. ed.; Gloucester, Mass.: Peter Smith, 1964). (Originally published, 1922)
53. William F. Ogburn, "The influence of invention and discovery," in President's Research Committee on Social Trends, *Recent social trends* (New York: McGraw-Hill, 1933), pp. 122–166.
54. Regarding the inappropriateness of modern war, see Kurt Finsterbusch and H. C. Greisman, "The unprofitability of warfare in the twentiety century," *Social Problems*, 1975, 22, 450–463. For the possible adaptive value of violence in premodern times, see Marshall F. Gilula and David N. Daniels, "Violence and man's struggle to adapt," *Science*, 1969, *164*, 396–405.
55. George Herbert Mead, *On social psychology: Selected papers*, ed. by Anselm Strauss (Chicago: University of Chicago Press, 1964).
56. Howard S. Becker, *Outsiders* (New York: Free Press, 1963). See also Edwin M. Lemert, *Human deviance, social problems, and social control* (2nd ed.; Englewood Cliffs, N.J.: Prentice-Hall, 1972), pp. 62–92.
57. Edwin M. Schur, *Labeling deviant behavior: Its sociological implications* (New York: Harper, 1971), p. 24. (Emphasis in the original)
58. Becker, *Outsiders*, p. 9. (Emphasis in the original)
59. Martin Gold and Jay R. Williams, "National study of the aftermath of apprehension," *Prospectus*, December, 1969, pp. 3–12; see also Jay R. Williams and Martin Gold, "From delinquent behavior to official delinquency," *Social Problems*, 1972, *20*, 209–229.
60. Gold and Williams, "National study of the aftermath of apprehension," p. 3.
61. See Robert Rosenthal and L. Jacobson, *Pygmalion in the classroom* (New York: Holt, 1968).
62. Thomas S. Szasz, *Ideology and insanity* (Garden City, N.Y.: Doubleday-Anchor, 1970), pp. 204–206.
63. D. L. Rosenhan, "On being sane in insane places," *Science*, 1973, *179*, 250–258.
64. See, for example, Jane M. Murphy, "Psychiatric labeling in cross-cultural perspective," *Science*, 1976, *191*, 1019–1028.
65. Rosenhan, "On being sane in insane places," 253.
66. Ibid., 252.
67. Erikson, "Notes on the sociology of deviance."
68. Rosenhan, "On being sane in insane places," 253.

CHAPTER 7. DECISIONS, DECISIONS

1. Erich Fromm, *Escape from freedom* (New York: Rhinehart, 1941).
2. From a short review of existentialism, see William Barrett, *Irrational Man* (Garden City, N.Y.: Doubleday, 1958); and Robert G. Olson, *An introduction to existentialism* (New York: Dover, 1962).
3. For a discussion of the value of life, see E. J. Mishan, *Cost-benefit analysis* (New York: Praeger, 1971), pp. 153–174. For a discussion of the way juries in different cultures determine the amount to be paid for wrongful death, see Steven

Phillips and Marc Moller, "Putting a price on death," *Psychology Today*, May, 1977, pp. 70–76.

4. Herbert A. Simon, *Models of man: Social and rational* (New York: Wiley, 1957). See especially chaps. 14 and 15.

5. See Charles E. Lindblom, "The science of 'muddling through'," in *The making of decisions*, ed. by William J. Gore and J. W. Dyson (New York: Free Press, 1964), pp. 155–169.

6. Daniel Bernoulli, "Exposition of a new theory on the measurement of risk," trans. by Louise Sommer, *Econometrica*, 1954, *22*, 23–36. (Originally published, 1738)

7. Donald R. Cressey, *The theft of a nation: The structure and operations of organized crime in America* (New York: Harper, 1969), p. 74.

8. For further discussion of the possible rewards of gambling, see Tibor Scitovsky, *The joyless economy* (New York: Oxford University Press, 1976); and D. O. Hebb and W. R. Thompson, "The social significance of animal studies," in *The handbook of social psychology*, ed. by Gardner Lindzey and Elliot Aronson (2nd ed.; Reading, Mass.: Addison-Wesley, 1968), vol. 2, pp. 729–774.

9. For a discussion, see David W. Miller and Martin K. Starr, *The structure of human decisions* (Englewood Cliffs, N.J.: Prentice-Hall, 1967).

CHAPTER 8. MISTAKES IN SOCIAL DECISION MAKING

1. See Ward Edwards and Amos Tversky, eds., *Decision making* (Baltimore: Penguin, 1967); and Lawrence D. Phillips, *Bayesian statistics for social scientists* (New York: Crowell, 1973).

2. For a discussion of the difficulties in comparing utilities across individuals, see Ajik K. Dasgupta and D. W. Pearce, *Cost-benefit analysis* (New York: Harper, 1972).

3. The "classic" work on Jewish mothers is Dan Greenburg, *How to be a Jewish mother* (Los Angeles: Price, Stern, Sloan, 1965).

4. *Books in print* (New York: Bowker, 1975).

5. Donald Zochert, "Chicken, cheese and other PhDs," *Chicago Daily News*, May 24, 1974, Sec. 1, p. 7.

6. *Sociological Abstracts* (San Diego, Cal.: Sociological Abstracts Inc., 1975), vol. 22.

7. *Psychological Abstracts, Index* (Washington, D.C.: American Psychological Association, 1974), vols. 51 and 52.

8. This is not to deny that romantic love is a problem. See Denis de Rougement, *Love in the Western world*, trans. by Montgomery Belgion (rev. ed.; New York: Pantheon, 1956); and Lawrence Casler, "Toward a re-evaluation of love," in *Symposium on love*, ed. by Mary Ellen Curtin (New York: Behavioral Publications, 1973), pp. 1–36.

9. William Warren Bartley, *Wittgenstein* (Philadelphia: Lippincott, 1973), pp. 64–65. (Emphasis in the original)

10. Robert B. Zajonc, "Attitudinal effects of mere exposure," *Journal of Personality and Social Psychology* (June monograph supplement, No. 2, Part 2), 1968, *9*, 1–27.

REFERENCES

11. Marvin M. Kristein, Charles B. Arnold, and Ernst L. Wynder, "Health economics and preventive care," *Science*, 1977, *195*, 457–462.
12. Michael Miner, "Abortion-aid ban—what will it cost government?" *Chicago Sun-Times*, July 4, 1977.
13. Jeff Jones, "Erecting barriers to suicide," *APA Monitor*, September/October, 1977, pp. 18–19.
14. William C. Schutz, *Joy: Expanding human awareness* (New York: Grove, 1967).
15. For an introduction to the study of prosocial behavior, see J. Macaulay and L. Berkowitz, eds., *Altruism and helping behavior* (New York: Academic, 1970); Lauren G. Wispé, issue ed., "Positive forms of social behavior," *The Journal of Social Issues*, 1972, *28* (3); and Dennis L. Krebs, "Altruism—an examination of the concept and a review of the literature," *Psychological Bulletin*, 1970, *73*, 258–302.
16. Louis A. Fliegler, *Curriculum planning for the gifted* (Englewood Cliffs, N.J.: Prentice-Hall, 1961), pp. 7–8.
17. Willard Abraham, *Common sense about gifted students* (New York: Harper, 1958), p. 5. (.Emphasis in the original)
18. For a discussion, see Tibor Scitovsky, *The joyless economy* (New York: Oxford University Press, 1976).
19. Lois Murphy, cited in Maya Pines, "In praise of the 'invulnerables'," *APA Monitor*, December, 1975, p. 7.
20. Ibid.
21. Allen E. Bergin, "Psychotherapy can be dangerous," *Psychology Today*, November, 1975, pp. 96 *et seq.* See also Dianna Hartley, Howard B. Roback, and Stephen I. Abramowitz, "Deterioration effects in encounter groups," *American Psychologist*, 1976, *31*, 247–255.
22. The wager is described in article 233 of the *Pensées*. See *Pascal* (vol. 33 of *Great books of the Western world*), ed. by Robert Maynard Hutchins (Chicago: Encyclopaedia Britannica, 1952), pp. 213–216.
23. For an introduction to Ellis' thought, see Albert Ellis and Robert A. Harper, *A guide to rational living* (North Hollywood, Cal.: Wilshire, 1971).
24. For a discussion of computer crime, see Tom Alexander, "Waiting for the great computer rip-off," *Fortune*, July, 1974, pp. 143 *et seq.*; and W. Thomas Porter, "Computer raped by telephone," *New York Times Magazine*, Sept. 8, 1974, pp. 33 *et seq.*
25. Erwin O. Smigel, "Public attitudes toward stealing as related to the size of the victim organization," *American Sociological Review*, 1956, *21*, 320–327.
26. Christoph Hohenemser, Roger Kasperson, and Robert Kates, "The distrust of nuclear power," *Science*, 1977, *196*, 25–34.
27. R. K. Mark and D. E. Stuart-Alexander, "Disasters as a necessary part of benefit-cost analysis," *Science*, 1977, *197*, 1160–1162.
28. Ibid.
29. See, for example, Alex Thio, "Toward a fuller view of American success ideology," *Pacific Sociological Review*, 1972, *15*, 381–389.
30. Philip M. Stern, *The rape of the taxpayer* (New York: Vintage Books, 1972), p. 9.

REFERENCES

31. Joseph Schumpeter, *Capitalism, socialism, and democracy* (New York: Harper, 1950), pp. 73–74.
32. See Thio, "Toward a fuller view of American success ideology"; William Watts and Lloyd A. Free, *State of the nation* (New York: Universe Books, 1973), pp. 170–172; and John E. Tropman, "The image of public welfare: Reality or projection?" *Public Welfare*, Winter 1977, 17–23.
33. Marvin Karlins, Thomas L. Coffman, and Gary Walters, "On the fading social stereotypes," *Journal of Personality and Social Psychology*, 1969, *13*, 1–16.
34. Roger Brown, *Social psychology* (New York: Free Press, 1965), pp. 172–191.
35. For a discussion of the intimacy between value statements and factual ones, see J. Samuel Bois, *The art of awareness* (Dubuque, Iowa: William C. Brown, 1966), pp. 43–60.
36. Robert K. Merton, *Social theory and social structure* (rev. ed.; New York: Free Press, 1957), pp. 426–430. See also Donald T. Campbell, "Stereotypes and the perception of group differences," *American Psychologist*, 1967, *22*, 817–829.
37. Louis E. Raths, Merrill Harmin, and Sidney B. Simon, *Values and teaching: Working with values in the classroom* (Columbus, Ohio: Charles E. Merrill, 1966).
38. For a collection of value clarification techniques, see Sidney B. Simon, Leland W. Howe, and Howard Kirschenbaum, *Values Clarification* (New York: Hart, 1972).
39. George Goodman, "Welfare clients getting photo I.D.," *New York Times*, April 8, 1972, p. 1.
40. Ibid.
41. Watts and Free, *State of the nation*, p. 175.

CHAPTER 9. INDIVIDUAL INTELLIGENCE AND SOCIAL INTELLIGENCE

1. See Kenneth J. Arrow, *Social choice and individual values* (2nd ed.; New York: Wiley, 1963), p. 3. See also Richard Niemi and William H. Riker, "The choice of voting systems," *Scientific American*, June, 1976, pp. 21–27.
2. See Ward Edwards, Harold Lindman, and Lawrence D. Phillips, "Emerging technologies for making decisions," in *New directions in psychology*, ed. by Theodore M. Newcomb (New York: Holt, 1965), vol. 2, pp. 261–325.
3. Garrett Hardin, "To trouble a star," *Bulletin of the Atomic Scientists*, January, 1970, 17–20.
4. Walter E. Westman, "How much are nature's services worth?" *Science*, 1977, *197*, 960–964.
5. Published by the U.S. Bureau of the Census (Washington, D.C.: U.S. Government Printing Office).
6. Raymond A. Bauer, "Detection and anticipation of impact: The nature of the task," in *Social indicators*, ed. by Raymond A. Bauer (Cambridge, Mass.: Massachusetts Institute of Technology Press, 1966), pp. 1–67, p. 20 quoted.
7. For an introduction to the quality of life concept, see Bauer, *Social indicators*; Environmental Protection Agency, *The quality of life concept: A potential new tool for decision-makers* (Washington, D.C.: U.S. Government Printing Office, 1973); and Karl A. Fox, *Social indicators and social theory*, ed. by Terry N. Clark (New York: Wiley, 1974).

REFERENCES

8. Angus Campbell, Philip E. Converse, and Willard L. Rodgers, *The quality of American life* (New York: Russell Sage Foundation, 1976), p. 26.
9. Ibid., pp. 268–275. See also Environmental Protection Agency, *The quality of life concept*, p. I-13.
10. William Watts and Lloyd A. Free, *State of the nation* (New York: Universe Books, 1973), p. 27.
11. For national opinion data on a variety of topics relevant to the subjective quality of life, see ibid.; Campbell et al., *The quality of American life;* and Louis Harris, *The anguish of change* (New York: Norton, 1973).
12. Cited in Angus Campbell, "Subjective measures of well-being," *American Psychologist*, 1976, *31*, 117–124. See also Mark Schneider, "The quality of life in large American cities: Objective and subjective social indicators," *Social Indicators Research*, 1975, *1*, 495–509.
13. Campbell et al., *The quality of American life*, pp. 56–57.
14. Ibid., p. 52.
15. Ibid., p. 26.
16. See ibid., pp. 36–37.
17. For a discussion of abuses in the income tax system, see Philip M. Stern, *The rape of the taxpayer* (New York: Vintage Books, 1972).
18. Gordon Tullock, *The logic of the law* (New York: Basic Books, 1971), pp. 136–147.
19. For a discussion, see Milton Friedman, *Capitalism and freedom* (Chicago: University of Chicago Press, 1962), especially pp. 137–160; and Jeffrey Pfeffer, "Administrative regulation and licensing," *Social Problems*, 1974, *21*, 468–479.
20. See William J. Goode, "The protection of the inept," *American Sociological Review*, 1967, *32*, 5–19: and David Hapgood, *The screwing of the average man* (New York: Bantam Books, 1975).
21. Milton Friedman, "Humphrey-Hawkins," *Newsweek*, Aug. 2, 1976, p. 55.
22. Marvin M. Kristein, Charles B. Arnold, and Ernst L. Wynder, "Health economics and preventive care," *Science*, 1977, *195*, 457–462.
23. Hapgood, *The screwing of the average man*, p. 120.
24. *The world almanac and book of facts, 1977*, p. 955.
25. Kristein et al., "Health economics and preventive care, p. 458.
26. "London struck again by lung-stinging fog," *New York Times*, Dec. 28, 1952, p. 12; and "Donora report to aid Britain in smog fight," *New York Times*, Dec. 29, 1952, p. 6.
27. Thomas C. Schelling, "On the ecology of micromotives," *The Public Interest*, Fall, 1971, 61–98.
28. John Platt, "Social traps," *American Psychologist*, 1973, *28*, 641–651.
29. Ibid.
30. Tibor Scitovsky, *The joyless economy* (New York: Oxford University Press, 1976), pp. 126–131.
31. Garrett Hardin, "The tragedy of the commons," *Science*, 1968, *162*, 1243–1248. See also Schelling, "On the ecology of micromotives." For a discussion of a mathematical model of the tragedy of the commons, see R. M. Dawes, J. Delay, and W. Chaplin, "The decision to pollute," *Environment and Planning*, 1974, *6*, 3–10.

REFERENCES

32. "Lethal spread of the sands," *Newsweek*, Sept. 19, 1977, p. 80.
33. See Norman Myers, "An expanded approach to the problem of disappearing species," *Science*, 1976, *193*, 198–202.
34. J. Skelly Wright, "The courts have failed the poor," *New York Times Magazine*, Mar. 9, 1969, pp. 26 *et seq.*
35. Howard S. Becker, *Outsiders* (New York: Free Press, 1963), pp. 135–146.
36. Ibid., p. 145.
37. Ibid.
38. Scitovsky, *The joyless economy*, p. 174.
39. George F. Will, "Taking a ride with Ronnie," *Newsweek*, May 31, 1976, p. 76. (Emphasis in the original)
40. For a discussion, see Hardin, "The tragedy of the commons."
41. See Konrad Lorenz, *On aggression*, trans. by Marjorie Kerr Wilson (New York: Harcourt, 1966), especially pp. 109–138; and Edward O. Wilson, *Sociobiology: The new synthesis* (Cambridge, Mass.: Harvard University Press, 1975).
42. See, for example, William Ryan, *Blaming the victim* (New York: Vintage Books, 1971); Nathan Caplan and Stephen D. Nelson, "On being useful," *American Psychologist*, 1973, *28*, 199–211; Donald T. Campbell, "On the conflicts between biological and social evolution and between psychology and moral tradition," *American Psychologist*, 1975, *30*, 1103–1126; and Albert Pepitone, "Toward a normative and comparative biocultural social psychology," *Journal of Personality and Social Psychology*, 1976, *34*, 641–653.
43. Pam Moore, "Nader chides researchers, scores testing," *APA Monitor*, November, 1976, pp. 1 *et seq.*

Name Index

Abraham, Willard, 180, 239
Abramowitz, Stephen I., 239
Addams, Jane, 39, 193
Agnew, Spiro, 231
Alexander, Tom, 239
Alfvén, Hannes, 223
Alfvén, Kerstein, 223
Allon, Natalie, 235
Allport, Gordon W., 223
Amory, Cleveland, 230
Anthony, Susan B., 39
Ariès, Philippe, 88, 231
Arnold, Charles B., 239, 241
Aronson, Elliot, 233
Arrow, Kenneth J., 240
Ashmore, Richard, 232

Baker, Russell, 38, 225
Bane, Mary Jo, 227
Banfield, Edward C., 224
Barrett, William, 237
Barrymore, John, 40
Bartley, William Warren, 178, 238

Bauer, Raymond A., 202, 240
Becker, Howard S., 43, 138, 143, 226, 234, 237, 242
Bem, Daryl J., 232
Berg, Ivar, 227
Bergin, Allen E., 239
Berkowitz, Leonard, 31, 224, 239
Berlyne, D. E., 232
Bernoulli, Daniel, 168, 238
Berscheid, Ellen, 236
Bird, Caroline, 227
Blau, Peter M., 71, 229
Block, N. J., 231
Blumberg, Abraham S., 224, 234
Bois, J. Samuel, 240
Borodin, A., 231
Bowles, Samuel S., 227
Braden, William, 229
Brehm, Jack W., 233
Brickman, Philip, 232
Brinton, Crane, 231, 232
Brooks, Stewart M., 226
Brown, Roger, 69n, 191, 229, 240

Cahnman, Werner J., 235
Calder, Bobby J., 233
Campbell, Angus, 232, 241
Campbell, Don G., 229
Campbell, Donald T., 228, 232, 240, 242
Cantril, Albert H., 228
Caplan, Nathan, 242
Carter, Jimmy, 14n
Casey, Jim, 229
Casler, Lawrence, 238
Casper, Jonathan D., 234
Cervinka, Claudette, 228
Chaikin, Alan L., 235
Chaplin, W., 241
Chase, Janet, 235, 236
Chein, Isidor, 108, 233
Clark, Ramsey, 226
Cocozza, Joseph J., 224
Coffman, Thomas L., 240
Cohen, Arthur R., 233
Cohn, Victor, 226
Condry, John, 233
Converse, Philip E., 232, 241
Cooley, Charles Horton, 69, 229
Coser, Lewis A., 236
Crawford, Joan, 40
Cressey, Donald R., 238
Crosby, Faye, 232
Currie, Elliot P., 233
Cutright, Phillips, 66, 228

Daniels, David N., 237
Darley, John M., 235
Dasgupta, Ajik K., 238
Davies, James C., 232
Dawes, R. M., 241
Day, Dorothy, 39
Deci, Edward L., 233
Delay, J., 241
Dentler, Robert A., 234
Diesing, Paul, 230
Douglas, Jack D., 83, 230
Down, K. S., 231
Dworkin, Gerald, 231

Edwards, Ward, 238, 240
Einstein, Albert, 40
Eisenhower, Dwight D., 40
Eller, W. C., 225
Ellis, Albert, 185, 239
Ellul, Jacques, 230
Elstein, A. S., 231

Erdmann, Martin, 115
Erikson, Kai T., 138, 146, 236, 237
Evans, Bergan, 17, 223
Eysenck, H. J., 230

Fawcett-Majors, Farrah, 40
Feldman, Saul D., 236
Festinger, Leon, 105, 232, 233
Fill, J. Herbert, 223
Filley, Alan C., 233
Finsterbusch, Kurt, 237
Fiske, Donald W., 232
Fitzpatrick, Tom, 229
Flesch, Rudolf, 54, 227
Fliegler, Louis A., 239
Ford, Barbara, 235
Fox, Karl A., 240
Free, Lloyd A., 204, 240, 241
Friedman, Milton, 62, 211, 228, 241
Fromm, Erich, 152, 237

Galileo, 14
Gallup, George, 225, 228
Gampel, Dorothy H., 231
Gandhi, Mahatma, 40
Gans, Herbert J., 137, 236
Garmezy, Norman, 182
Gibbons, J. F., 89, 231
Gilula, Marshall F., 237
Glazer, Nathan, 232
Goffman, Erving, 124, 235
Gold, Martin, 145, 237
Golden, Harry, 235
Goldwater, Barry, 145
Goode, William J., 229, 231, 241
Goodman, George, 240
Goodman, Norman, 235
Goodstein, Leonard D., 231
Gotlieb, C. C., 231
Graham, Billy, 38
Grazia, Sebastian de, 225
Green, Arnold W., 228, 235
Greenburg, Dan, 238
Greene, David, 233
Greisman, H. C., 237
Gruenberger, Fred, 231
Guinan, Texas, 40
Gutenberg, Johann, 89

Hapgood, David, 231, 241
Haramija, Frank, 229
Hardin, Garrett, 201, 216, 236, 240, 241

NAME INDEX

Harding, Warren, 77
Harmin, Merrill, 240
Harper, Robert A., 239
Harris, Louis, 57, 228, 241
Harris, T. George, 235
Hartley, Dianna, 239
Haugen, R. K., 225
Hebb, D. O., 231, 235, 238
Henslin, James M., 226, 234
Hindelang, Michael J., 224, 234
Hines, Fred, 227
Hofstadter, Richard, 231
Hohenemser, Christoph, 239
Holloway, Stephen, 44, 45, 226
Homans, George C., 232
Hoover, Herbert, 14n
Hope, Bob, 38
Hornstein, Harvey A., 44, 45, 226
Horton, Paul B., 234
Howe, Leland W., 240
Hughes, Howard, 76
Hughes, Raymond M., 231
Hutchins, Robert, 89

Inbau, Fred E., 231
Ingrassia, Larry, 231

Jacobson, L., 237
James, Ava Leach, 235
Janowitz, Morris, 71, 229
Jencks, Christopher, 227
Jensen, Arthur R., 231
Johnson, Thomas A., 228
Jones, Jeff, 239
Judd, Charles H., 226

Kahneman, Daniel, 224
Karlins, Marvin, 190, 240
Kasperson, Roger, 239
Kates, Robert, 239
Kaufmann, Harry, 232
Kelley, Harold H., 231, 232
Kennedy, Edward, 77
Kennedy, John F., 31, 77
Khorol, Ivan, 223
Kincheloe, W. R., 231
King, Billy Jean, 40
King, Martin Luther, 193
Kirschenbaum, Howard, 240
Kish, G. B., 232
Kissinger, Henry, 84
Koval, Patricia O'Brien, 229

Krebs, Dennis L., 239
Kristein, Marvin M., 239, 241

Landon, Alfred E., 57
Lanyon, Richard I., 231
Larsen, Otto N., 224
Le Duc Tho, 84
Leggett, John C., 228
Lemert, Edwin M., 237
Lepper, Mark R., 233
Lerner, Melvin J., 235
Leslie, Gerald R., 234
Levine, David, 227
Levine, Murray, 230
Levitt, Arthur, 82
Lindblom, Charles E., 238
Linder, Staffan, 225
Lindman, Harold, 240
Lindsay, John, 79
Lindsay, Peter, 224
Lindzey, Gardner, 231
Loehlin, John C., 231
Lofland, John, 102, 138, 232, 236
Lorenz, Konrad, 242

Macaulay, Jacqueline, 31, 224, 239
Macgregor, Frances Cooke, 235
Maddi, Salvatore R., 232
Manis, Jerome G., 234
Mark, R. K., 239
Marx, Karl, 40
Marx, Leo, 230
Matthews, Gail, 235
Mause, Lloyd de, 225
Mayer, Jean, 126
McConahay, John B., 232
McDonagh, Edward C., 234
McGee, Reece, 234
McGuire, William J., 224, 236
McKee, Michael, 234
McKitrick, Eric L., 230
McPherson, Aimee, 40
Mead, George Herbert, 143–44, 237
Medalis, Nahum Z., 224
Merton, Robert K., 85, 130, 139, 192, 230, 236, 240
Milakovich, Michael, 44, 226
Milgram, Stanley, 233
Miller, David W., 238
Miller, Herman P., 227
Mills, James, 234
Mills, Wilbur, 77

Miner, Michael, 239
Mischel, Walter, 231
Mishan, E. J., 237
Mitchell, John N., 44
Moller, Marc, 238
Molloy, Paul, 229
Monroe, Marilyn, 31
Moore, Pam, 230, 242
Morgenstern, Oskar, 233
Mowshowitz, Abbe, 231
Muller, Steven, 223
Murphy, Jane M., 237
Murphy, Lois, 239
Myers, Norman, 242

Nader, Ralph, 39, 83, 221
Nelson, Stephen D., 242
Neumann, John von, 233
Niemi, Richard, 240
Nisbett, Richard E., 233
Nixon, Richard M., 78, 92
Noble, Frank C., 226
Norman, Donald, 224

O'Brien, John, 229
Ogburn, William F., 141, 237
Olson, Robert G., 237

Paine, Tom, 193
Pascal, Blaise, 183
Paul VI, 38
Pavlov, Ivan, 100n
Pearce, D. W., 238
Pepitone, Albert, 242
Petacque, Art, 228
Petersen, David, 229
Pettigrew, Thomas F., 232
Pfeffer, Jeffrey, 241
Phillips, David P., 31, 224
Phillips, Lawrence D., 238, 240
Phillips, Steven, 238
Pines, Maya, 239
Platt, John, 141, 214, 237, 241
Porter, W. Thomas, 239

Raths, Louis E., 193, 195, 240
Ray, Oakley S., 226
Redfern, Martin, 227
Reichard, Robert S., 227, 228, 230
Reichbach, Irene, 225
Reid, John E., 231

Reiss, Ira L., 236
Reynolds, Larry T., 226, 234
Richardson, Stephen A., 235
Riker, William H., 240
Roback, Howard B., 239
Robertson, Ian, 234
Rockefeller, Nelson, 102
Rodgers, Willard L., 232, 241
Rogers, Carl, 18, 223
Roll, Charles W., 228
Roosevelt, Franklin D., 40, 57, 77, 79
Rosenhan, D. L., 146, 237
Rosenthal, Robert, 237
Rougement, Denis de, 238
Rowen, Hobart, 61, 228
Rubington, Earl, 234
Ryan, William, 227, 235, 236, 242

Samuelson, Paul A., 225
Sanger, Margaret, 39
Schelling, Thomas C., 111, 214, 233, 241
Schneider, Marc, 241
Schumpeter, Joseph, 189, 240
Schur, Edwin M., 143, 237
Schutz, William C., 239
Scitovsky, Tibor, 220, 238, 239, 241, 242
Shelley, Mary, 128n, 236
Shils, Edward A., 71, 229
Silver, Allan, 230
Simon, Herbert A., 159, 238
Simon, Sidney B., 240
Simpson, Jon E., 234
Simpson, O. J., 40
Skinner, B. F., 107, 232, 233
Skolnick, Jerome H., 229, 234
Smigel, Erwin O., 239
Soloman, Lewis C., 227
Speck, Richard, 31
Spock (Mr.), 18
Spuhler, J. N., 231
Stalin, Joseph, 40
Starr, Martin K., 238
Staw, Barry M., 233
Steadman, Henry J., 224
Stern, Philip M., 239, 241
Stinchcombe, Arthur L., 112, 233
Stuart-Alexander, D. E., 239
Suter, Larry E., 227
Sutherland, Edwin H., 131, 236
Swingle, Paul, 233
Szasz, Thomas S., 145, 237

Tallman, Irving, 234
Taubman, Paul, 227
Thibaut, John W., 231, 232
Thio, Alex, 239, 240
Thompson, W. R., 235, 238
Toch, Hans, 233
Tropman, John E., 235, 240
Tucker, Lyle, 226
Tullock, Gordon, 234, 241
Tversky, Amos, 224, 238
Tweeten, Luther, 227

Varela, Jacobo, 233
Vaughan, Wayland F., 225

Wade, Nicholas, 230
Wales, Terence, 227
Wallace, George, 79n
Wallace, Michael, 231
Walster, Elaine, 235, 236
Walters, Gary, 240
Watts, William, 204, 240, 241

Webb, Eugene J., 230
Weinberg, Martin S., 234
Weis, Kurt, 44, 226
West, Mae, 40
Westman, Walter E., 240
Wheeler, Harvey, 232, 233
Whitman, Charles, 143
Will, George F., 40, 220, 225, 242
Williams, Jay R., 145, 237
Williams, Robin M., 230
Williamson, John B., 225
Wilson, Edward O., 242
Wilson, Paul R., 127, 236
Wispé, Lauren G., 239
Wolfgang, Marvin E., 228
Wright, J. Skelly, 242
Wrightsman, Lawrence S., 226
Wynder, Ernst L., 239, 241

Zajonc, Robert B., 238
Zimbardo, Philip G., 133, 236
Zochert, Donald, 238

Subject Index

Abortion, 179
Addiction, 214–15
Admired persons, 38–41
Age, and social classification, 87–88
Aggression, 100, 102
Anomie, 131
Arson, 36–37
Attitudes, 94, 104–7, 121, 191–92. *See also* Prejudice
Automobile
  buying, 85
  and commuting, 15
  deaths, 9n, 31, 34
  population, 50
  repair simile and social problems, 148–50
  stripping, 133
Average, 58–60
  capita cost, 50–51
  mean, 59–60
  median, 59–60
  mode, 60

Bargaining, 99, 107–17, 163
Blaming the victim, 125–26, 128n, 189n

Bombing, 36–37
Bureaucracy, 64–65, 70–74, 76, 84–90

Catastrophizing, 185–86, 200
Change
  as reward, 102
  salience of, 94–96
Choking, 37
Class action suit, 218
Cognitive dissonance, 105–6
Commons, tragedy of, 216–17
Comparison level, 103–4, 158–60, 206, 215
Complexity of modern life, 15–17. *See also* Technology
Compounding, 51–54
Computers, 85, 88–90, 187
Consumers, 85, 219
Copout ceremony, 116, 146
Correlation, 54
Cost
  capita, 50–51
  of social programs, 49–51, 63–65, 196
Cost-benefit analysis, 200–202

SUBJECT INDEX

Crime, 98, 110, 113, 131–33, 144–45, 196. *See also* specific crimes
  and mental illness, 29
  statistics, 65–66, 83–84
  violent, 31–32
  white collar, 187
Culture lag, 141–43, 216–17

Dams, 188, 201–2
Decision making, 94, 151–74
  mistakes in, 175–92
  and problem solving, 9
  with uncertainty, 160–65
Delinquency. *See* Crime; Deviance
Delusion, collective, 30–31
Deviance, 129–34, 138–39, 221
  and labeling, 143–47
Differential association, 131–32
Discrimination, 123–28, 131, 206–8. *See also* Women, status of; Race
Dithering, 182–83
"Doomsday device," 110
Drugs, 101, 120, 133, 147, 211, 214–15, 219

Ecology, 140. *See also* Social disorganization
Education, 16–17, 53–55, 86–87, 89–90, 101, 126–27, 140, 145, 180–82

Freedom, 105, 129–30, 152–53
  and bargaining, 109–12
  and predictability, 18, 56
Functionalism, 136–38
Funnel interview, 94

Gambling, 165, 169–73, 189
Games, 161–65, 170–73, 215
Gifted children, 180–81
"Going by the rules," 74–76
Good guy—bad guy routine, 98–99, 109
Group
  conflict, 95–96, 108, 111, 134–39, 198, 208–12
  primary. *See* Relations
  reference, 135, 138–39
Guilds, 210–12

Happiness, 104, 166–67, 177–78, 180, 204–6, 214–15. *See also* Utility
Health, 74, 179–80
  insurance, 212
  mental, 29, 145–47, 180
Homicide, 31–32, 35–36, 42–43

Illegitimacy, 66, 131, 136
Income, 65, 80–81, 189
  and education, 53–54
  personal disposable, 50
  as reward, 102
Insurance, 169–70, 212
IQ, 85–88, 124n, 125
Irrationality
  as a bargaining strategy, 110–12, 115, 209

"Jewish mother," 176–77
"Just world" phenomenon, 125–26, 128n, 189n

Labeling, 143–47
Learning, 99–107, 214
  of deviant behavior, 130–34, 144
  punishment, 99, 100–102, 112
  reward, 99, 101–7
Legislatures, 72–73, 78, 125–26, 157, 194
Lobbies, 218–19
Love, 178, 219–21

Memory, 9, 25–26
Minimax, 161–64, 176
Money, 156, 187. *See also* Income
Moralizing
  and decision making, 153, 183–86
  about social problems, 129–30, 147–48
Murder. *See* Homicide
Mutt and Jeff routine, 98–99, 109

Negative thinking, 176–83, 185–86, 204
  and education, 180–82
  and game playing, 162–65
  in the news, 41–45
  and norms, 96
  and official records, 91
  and professional problem solvers, 24, 43–45, 122, 137–38, 177–82
Negotiation. *See* Bargaining
News, 61, 78–79, 108
  bias in, 28–45, 178
  scenarios in, 161
Norms, 95–96, 129–34
Numbers
  large, 49–51
  small, 51–56
  and social classification, 87–88

Obesity, 126, 128n
Objective approach
  to defining social problems, 120
  to quality of life, 202–6

Paradoxes, 93
  in bargaining, 107–17, 209, 218–19
  in defining social problems, 121–22
  in gambling, 169–73
  of learning, 99–107
  of salience, 93–99
  statistical, 59, 65–66, 203
  of voting, 199–200
Participant observation, 90–91
Pascal's wager, 183–85
Percentages, 51–56, 160–61
Personal power, 97–98. *See also* Freedom
Plea bargaining, 113–17
Pleasantly fearful, 102, 171
Police, 75–76, 83–84, 97
Politicians, 72–73, 77–79, 85–86, 102, 125–27,
  153, 161
Polls, 56–58, 122, 195, 204–5
Pollution, 83, 213–17
Population
  growth, 52–53, 142–43, 216
  and sample size, 57
Poverty, 62–63, 103, 137, 170–73, 208–9. *See also*
  Welfare
Power. *See* Personal power; Group conflict
Prejudice, 190–92. *See also* Discrimination; Race;
  Women, status of
  against the ugly, 123–28
Principle of least interest, 113
Privacy, 76–79
Probability, 160–61, 164–65, 184, 187–89,
  191–92
Problem
  eureka, 8
  orientation. *See* Negative thinking
  social. *See* Social problems
  solvers, professional, 24, 43–45, 122, 130,
    137–38, 144–47, 221
  solving and decision making, 9
Prohibition, 121, 135
Prostitution, 136–37
Psychological Abstracts, 177–78
Psychotherapy, 182–83

Quality of life, 202–6

Race, 24, 29, 53–55, 65, 86, 104, 120, 124n,
  190–92, 207
Radio, 141–42
Rape, 9n, 51, 66

Reality
  formal and informal, 70–76, 84–85
  social, 123
Relations
  formal and informal, 69–91
  informal and love, 221
  informal in trials, 114–17
Revolution, 99, 104
Riots, 104, 110, 140

Salience, 93–99, 105, 138–39, 209–12, 214
Sampling. *See* Polls
Satisficing, 158–60
Science, 13–14, 16, 192–95. *See also* Technology
Self-concept, 143–47
  and self-respect, 101–2, 106–7, 111, 115n
Sex, 66, 130–31, 179, 181. *See also* Illegitimacy
Side payments, 207–8, 215, 218
Slavery, 206–8
Small claims court, 218–19
Social disorganization, 139–43, 154, 201
Social indicators, 202–6
Social problems
  approaches to, 128
  definition of, 118–23
  experience with, 23–26, 29–30
Social status, 76–81, 86–88, 103–4, 127, 215
Social traps, 213–17
Sociological Abstracts, 177
Statistics, 48–66, 70, 73–74, 79–84, 117, 202–3
Status legislation, 208, 210–12
Stereotypes
  science fiction, 18, 127, 128n
  social, 26–27, 190–92
Subjective approach
  to defining social problems, 120–23
  to quality of life, 204–6
Suicide, 31, 111–12, 179

Technology
  as cause of social problems, 12–14, 141–43,
    216–17
  and informal relations, 85–90
Terrorism, 35–37, 98–99
Tests, 147
  intelligence, 85–88
  personality, 89
Thinking. *See also* Decision making
  definitions of, 6
  and emotions, 17–18, 221–22
  serious, 6–18
Third party tactic, 97–98, 212

SUBJECT INDEX

Threshold, 186–87, 209–212
"Ticket blitz," 75–76
Transitivity, 199–200
Trials, criminal, 33, 113–17, 139, 144–45

Unemployment, 61–63, 65, 83
Utility, 165–73, 183–86, 199–202. *See also* Value
  and social structure, 210, 213–22

Value, 138–39, 148, 190–95. *See also* Attitudes
  clarification, 195–97
  conflict, 134–39, 208–9
  expected, 164–68, 195–97, 200–202
  measurement, 153–58

Venereal disease, 42, 131, 181
Volunteer effect, 65–66, 80

War, 71–72, 92, 98–99, 104, 139, 142, 177
  Vietnam, 32, 61, 84, 112, 185–86
Welfare, 39, 51, 64–65, 81–82, 102, 128, 179,
  195–96
  economics, 200–202
Windshield pitting, 30–31
Win-win strategy, 108, 163
Witches, 113–14, 120, 127
Women, status of, 41, 53, 55, 65, 124n

Zero-sum game, 162–63

47470

Hastings

How to think about social problems

DATE DUE			
NOV 8 '81			
GAYLORD			PRINTED IN U.S.A.